PEANUTS

A Treasury of Happiness

By Charles M. Schulz

This book may be ordered by mail from the publisher. Please include $3.00 for postage and handling.
Please support your local bookseller first!

Books published by Cider Mill Press Book Publishers are available at special discounts for bulk purchases in the United States by corporations, institutions, and other organizations. For more information, please contact the publisher.

Cider Mill Press Book Publishers
"Where good books are ready for press"
12 Port Farm Road
Kennebunkport, Maine 04046

Visit us on the web!
www.cidermillpress.com

Design by: Jason Zamajtuk

Printed in China
4 5 6 7 8 9 0
A PEANUTS CLASSIC Edition

Happiness is a thumb and a blanket.

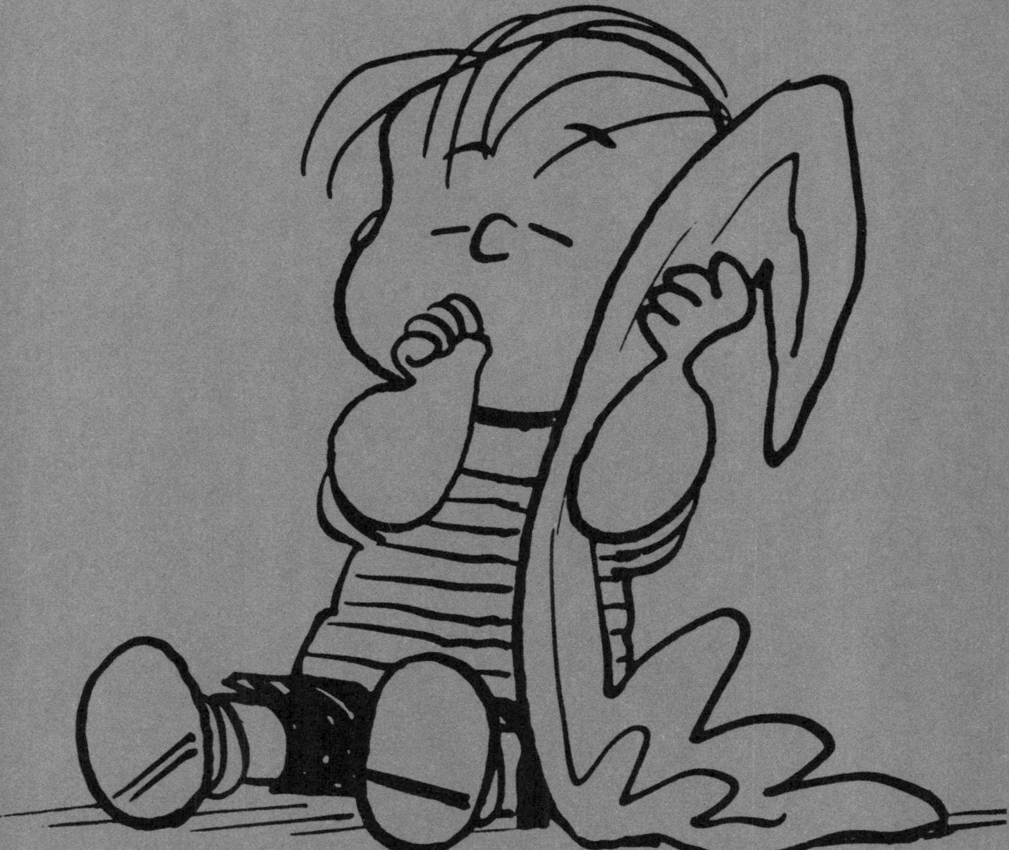

Happiness is an umbrella and a new raincoat.

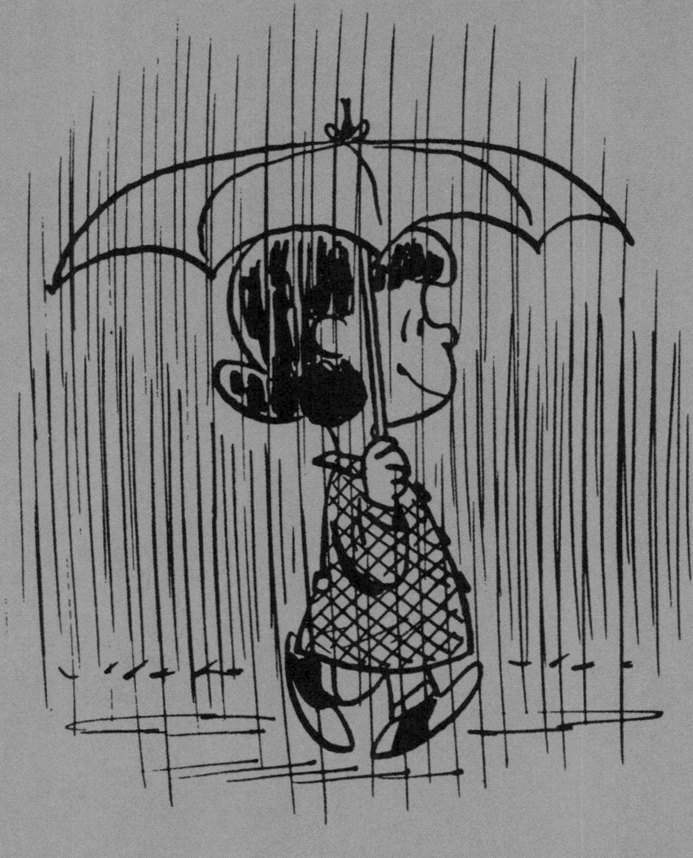

Happiness

is

a

pile

of leaves.

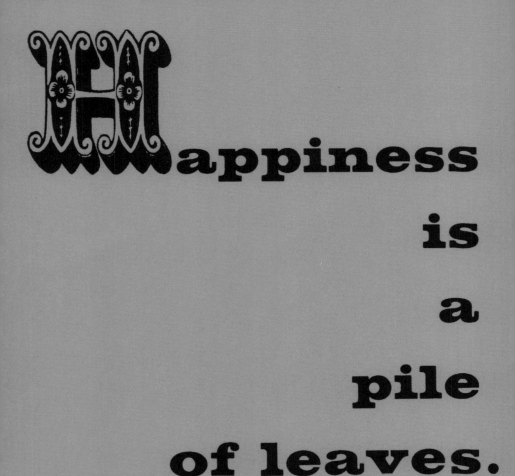

Happiness is a warm puppy.

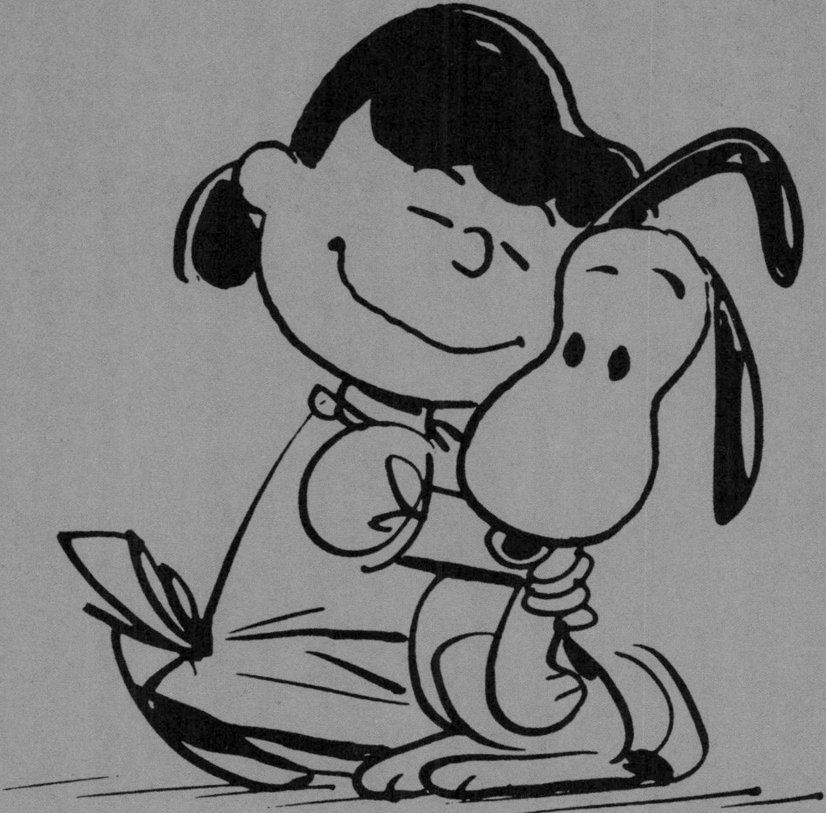

Happiness is an "A" on your spelling test.

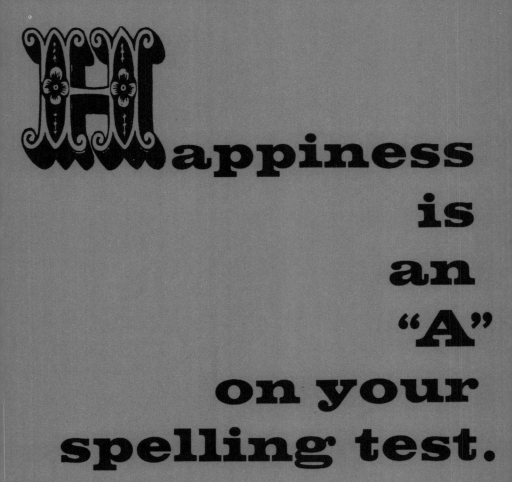

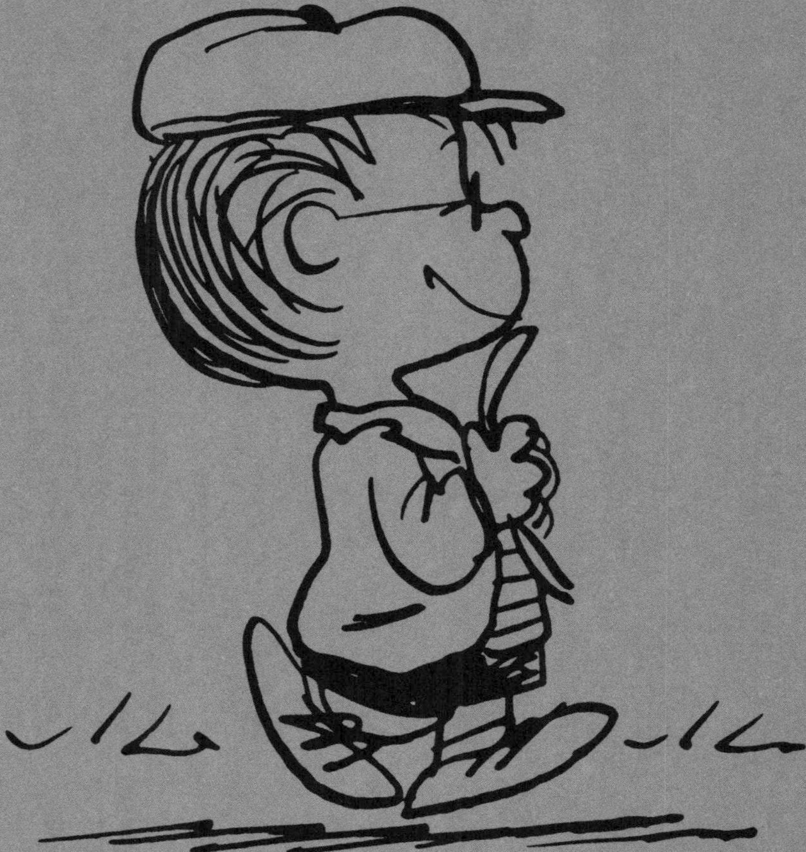

Happiness is finding someone you like at the front door.

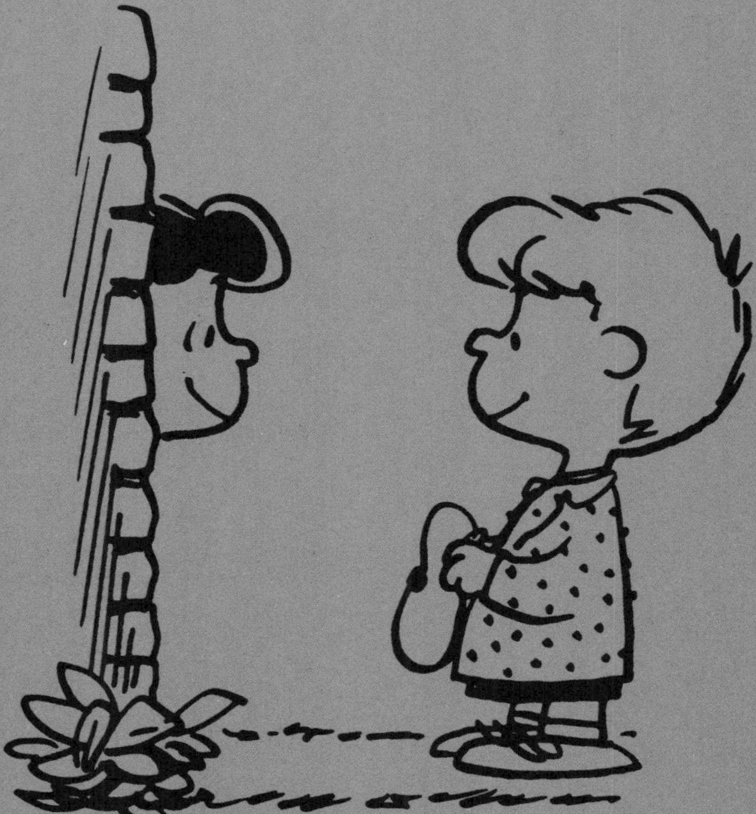

Happiness is three friends in a sandbox ...with no fighting.

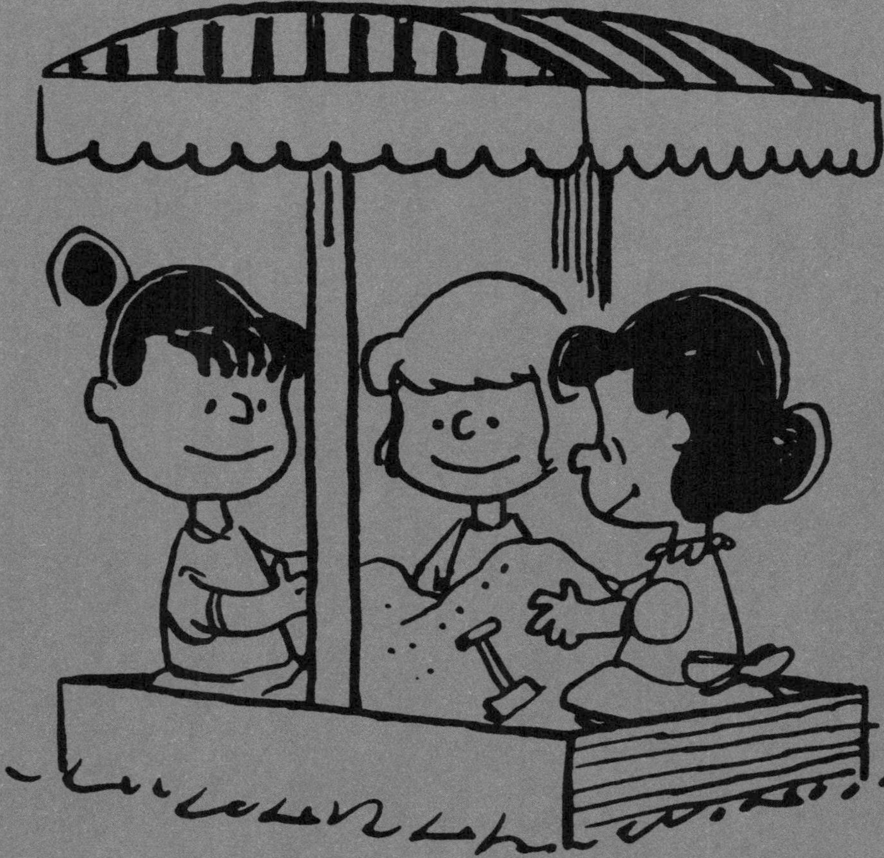

Happiness
is
sleeping
in
your
own bed.

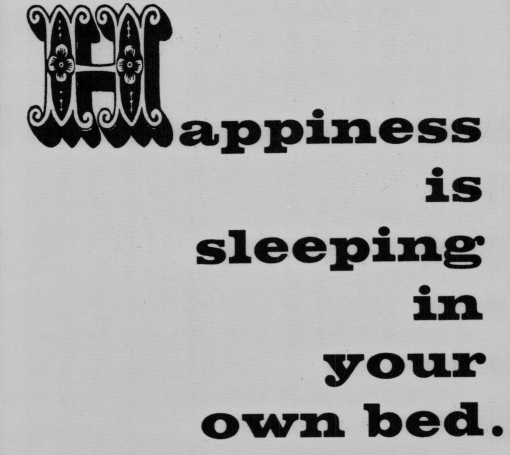

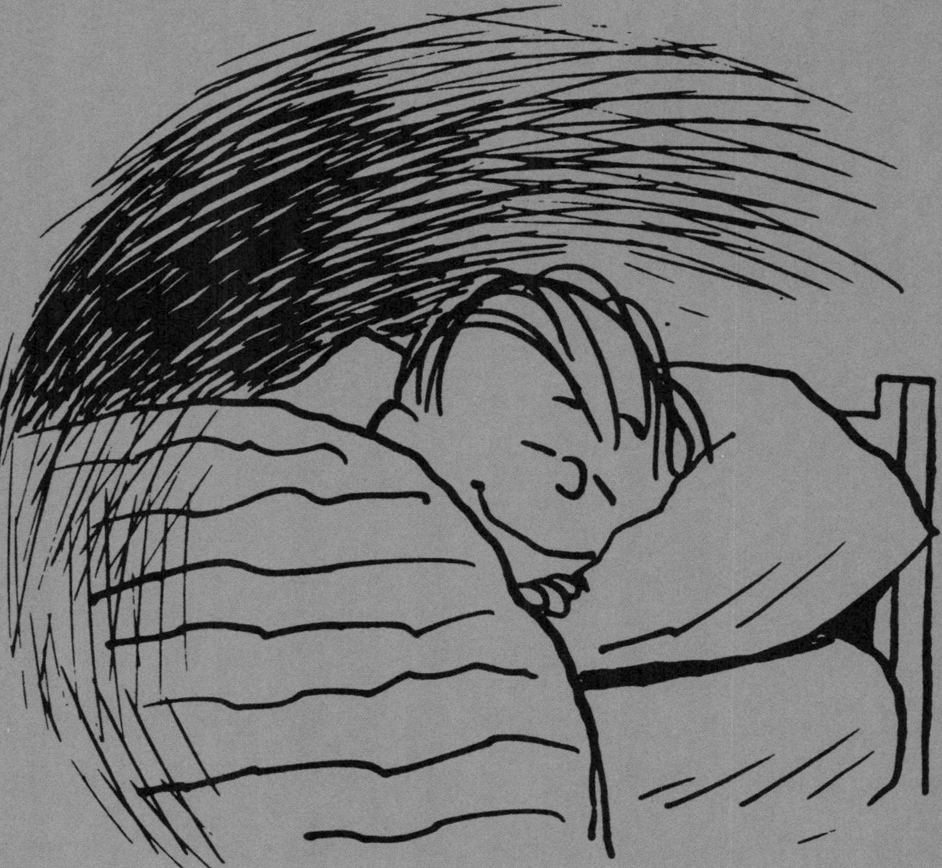

Happiness is a chain of paper clips.

Happiness is getting together with your friends.

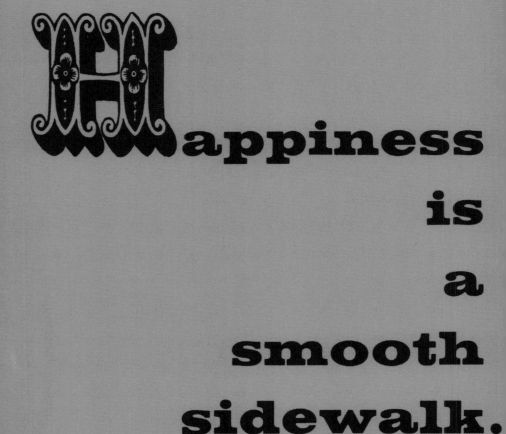

Happiness is a smooth sidewalk.

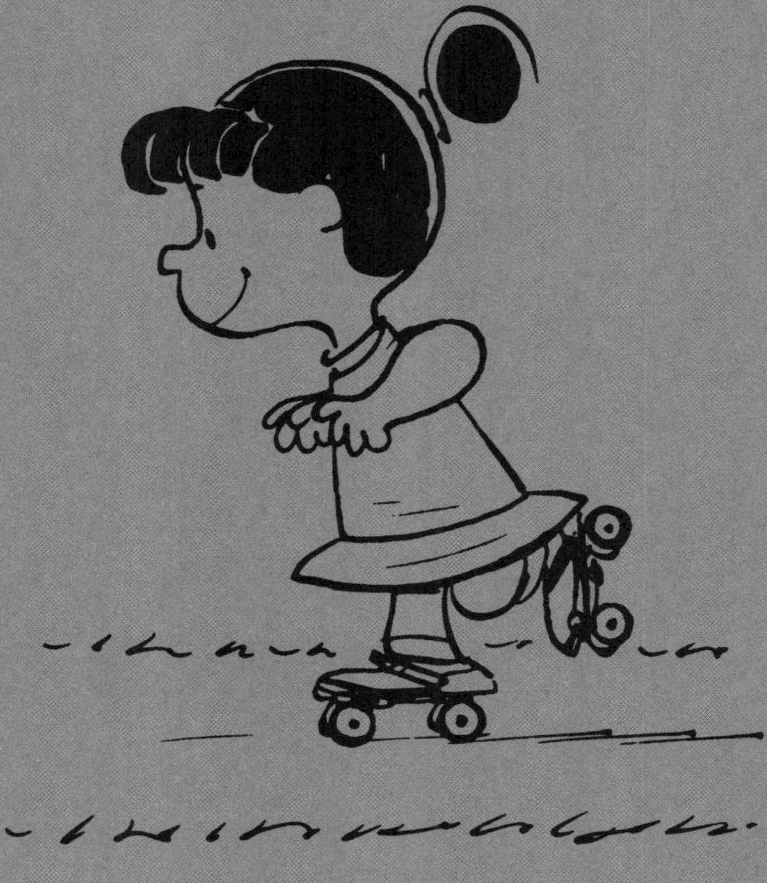

Happiness is finally getting the sliver out.

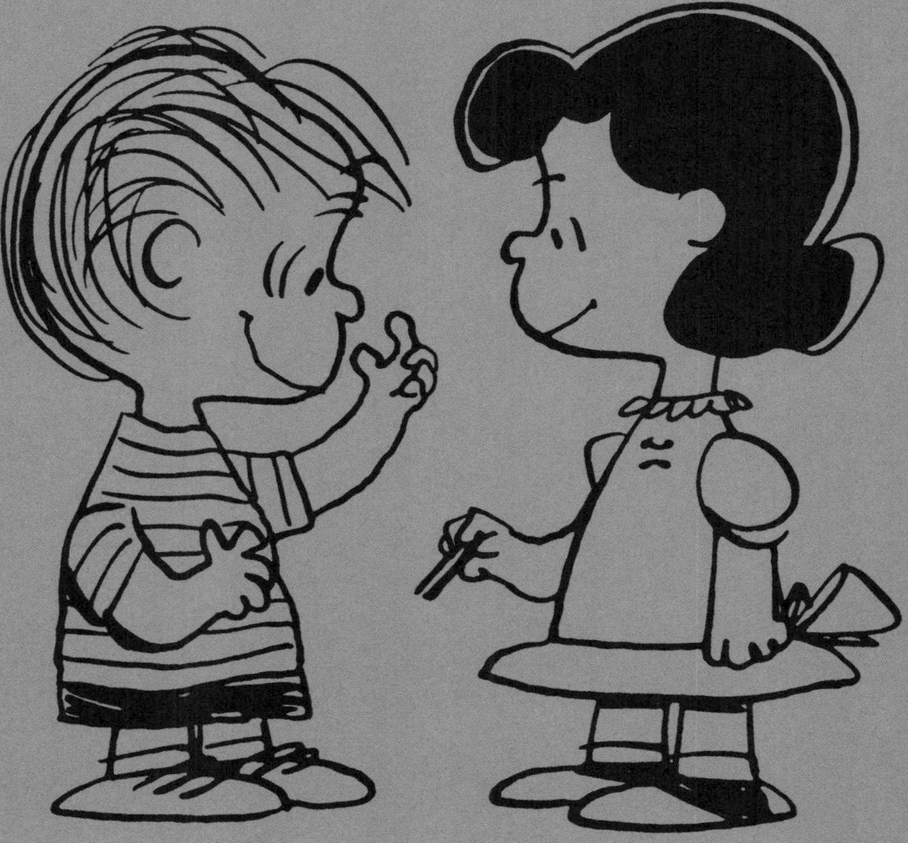

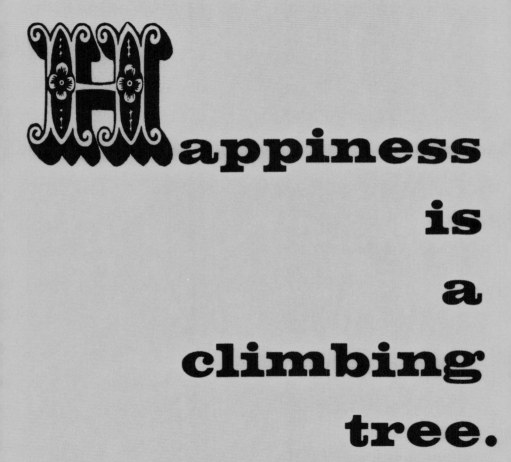

Happiness is a climbing tree.

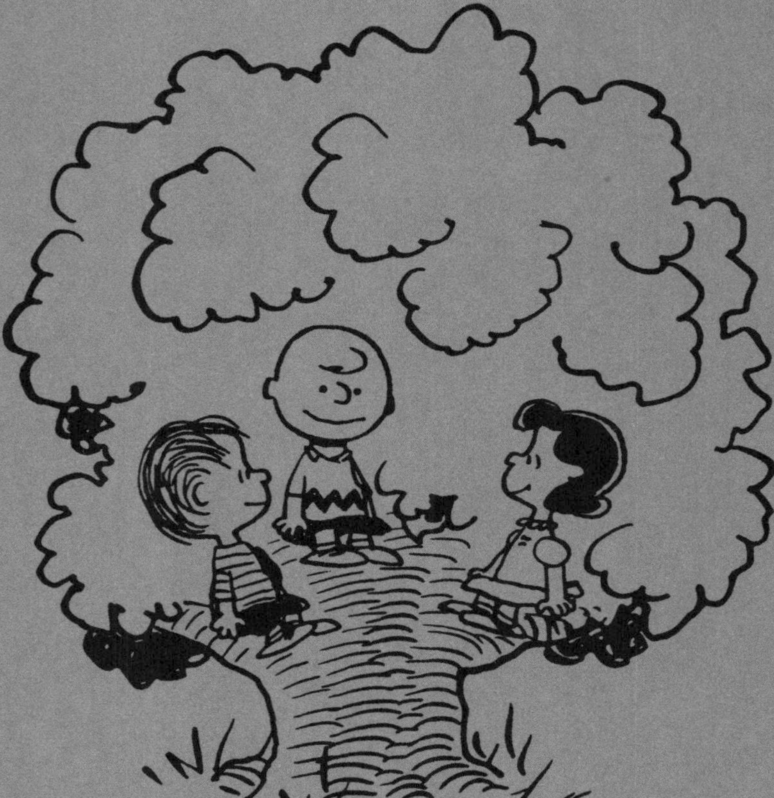

Happiness is lots of candles.

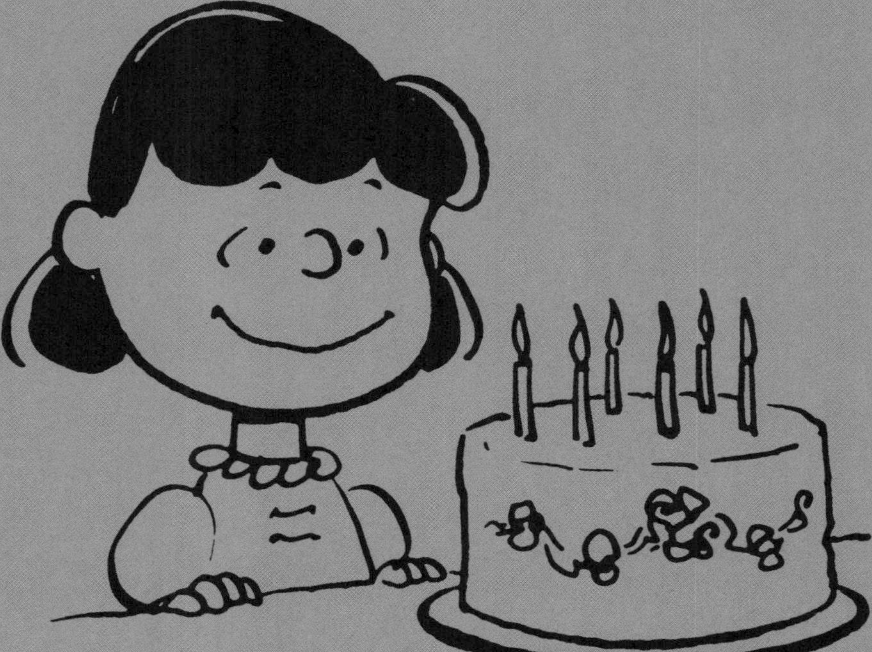

Happiness
is
being
able
to reach the
doorknob.

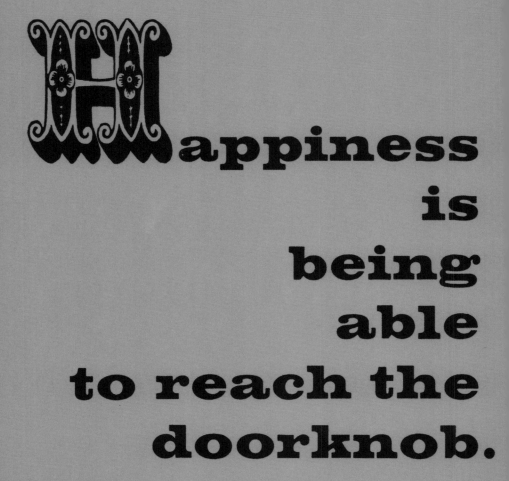

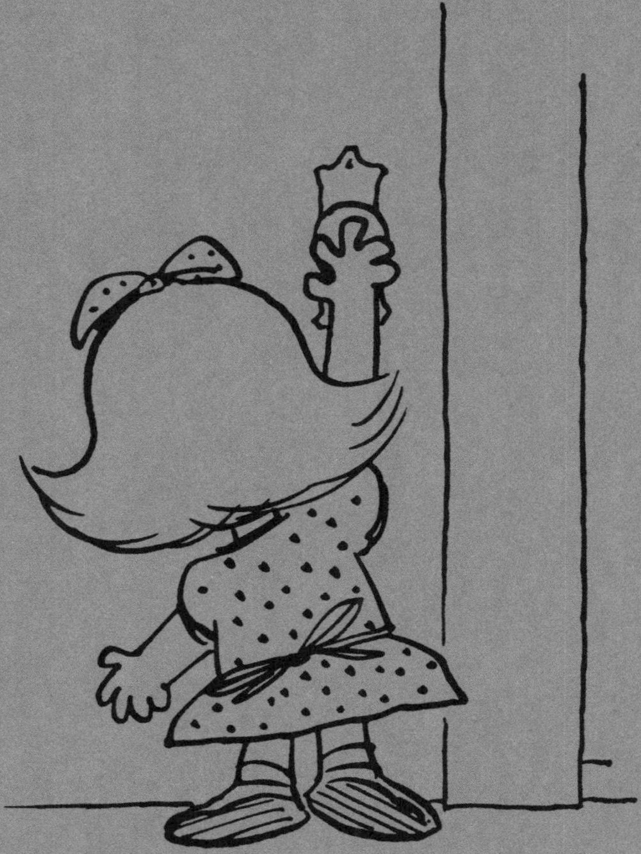

Happiness is knowing all the answers.

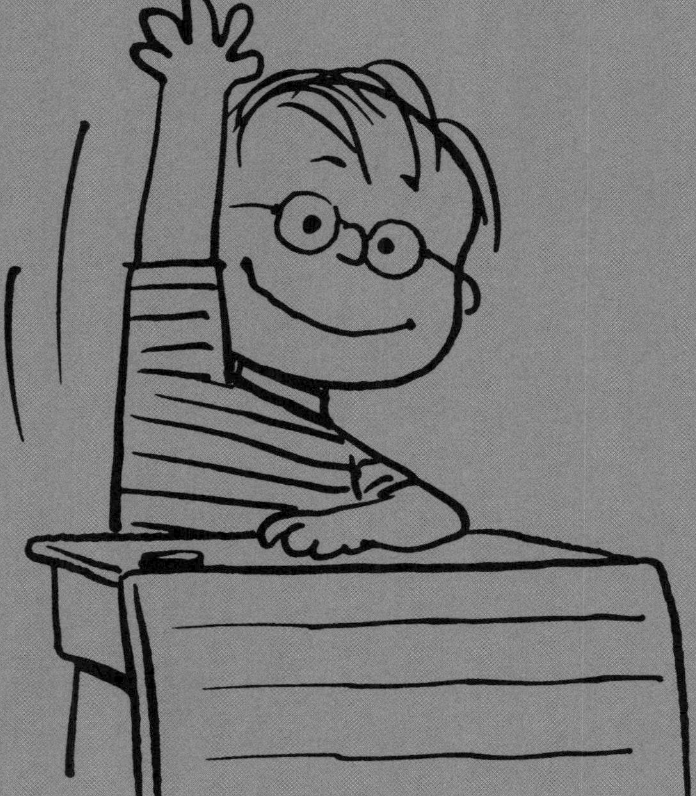

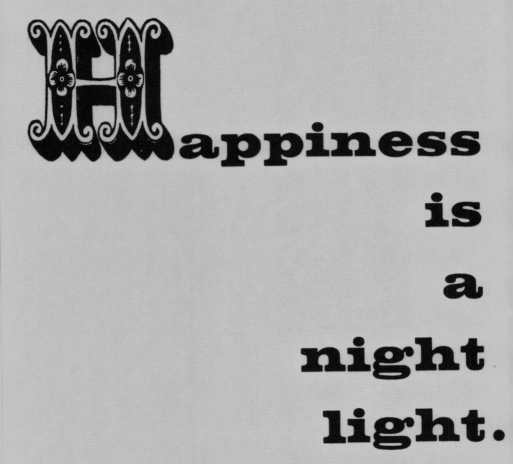

Happiness is a night light.

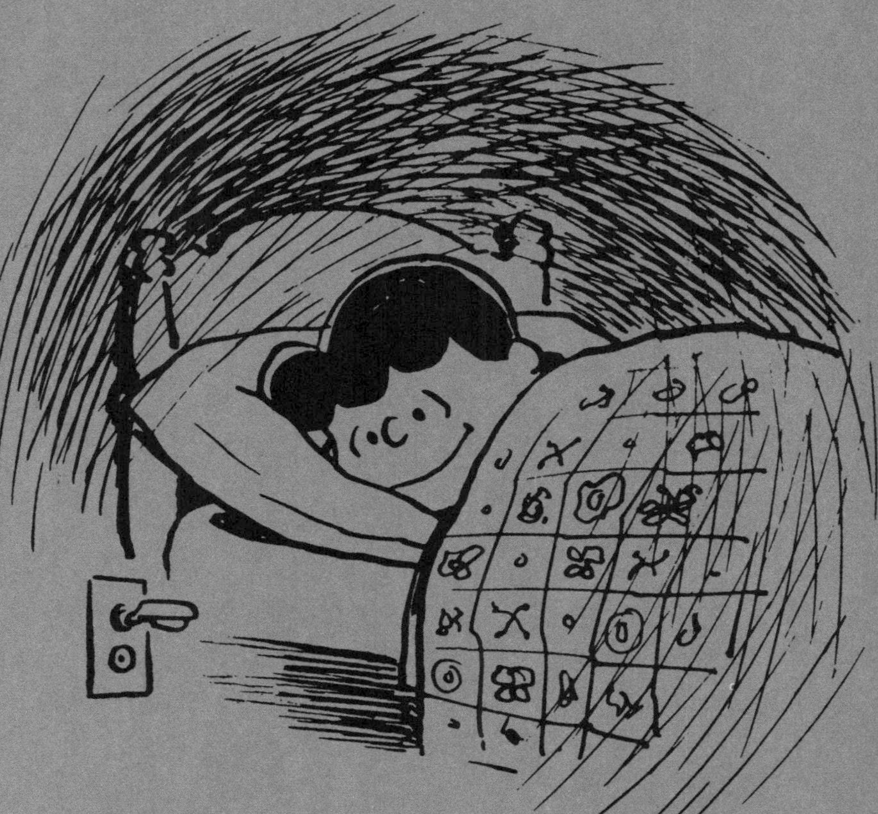

Happiness is some black, orange, yellow, white and pink jelly beans, but no green ones.

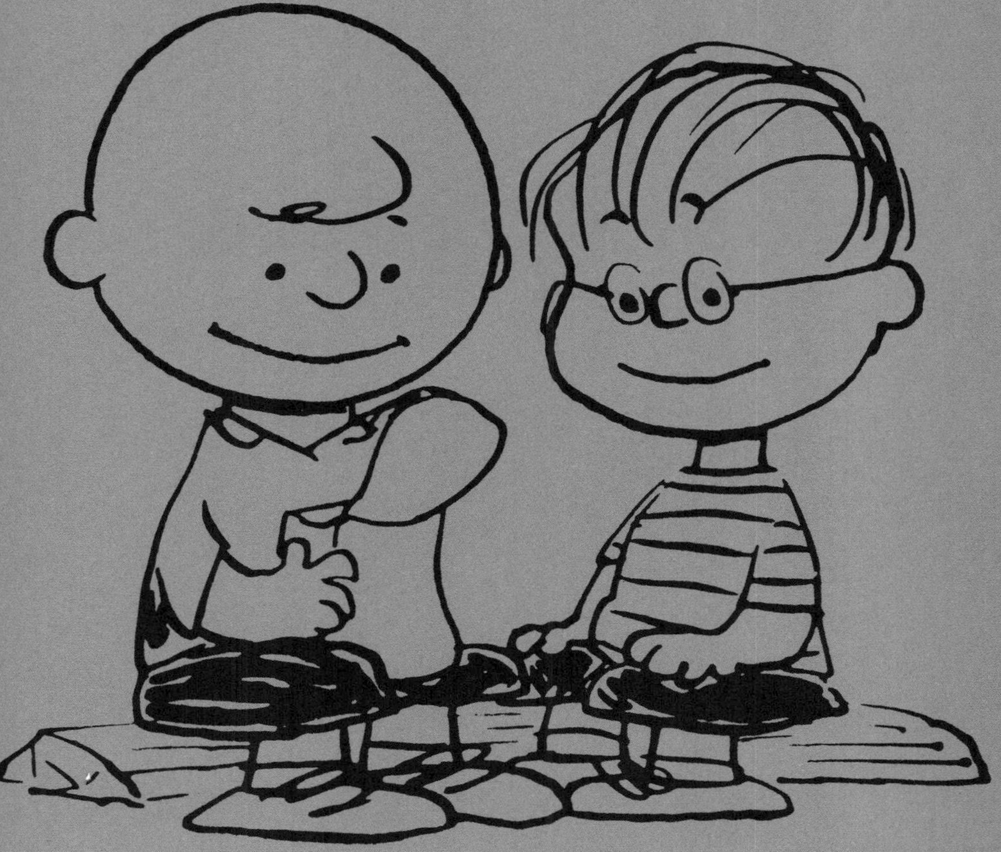

Happiness is the hiccups ...after they've gone away.

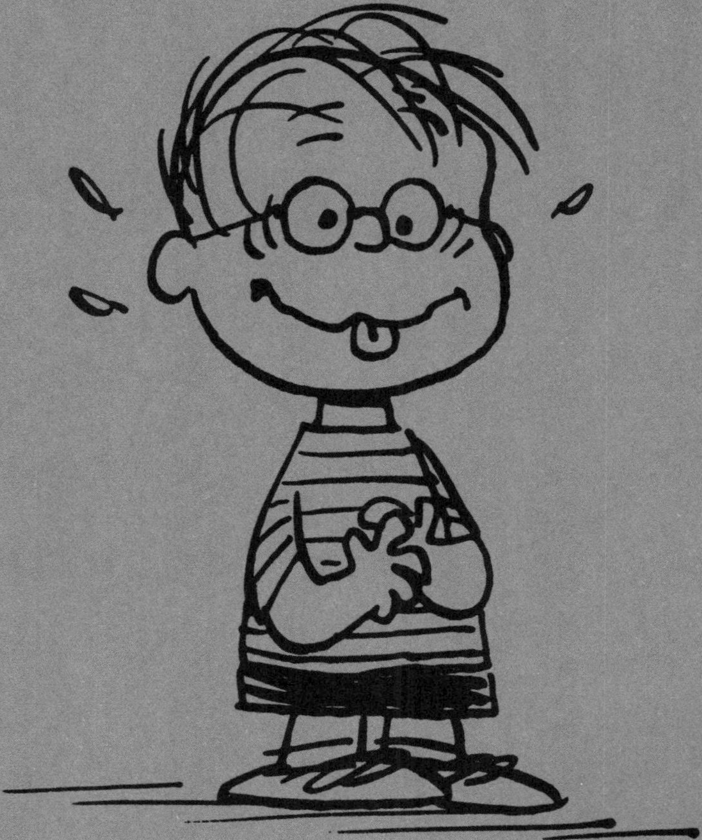

Happiness is a good old fashioned game of hide and seek.

Happiness is a fuzzy sweater.

Happiness
is
a
bread
and butter
sandwich
folded over.

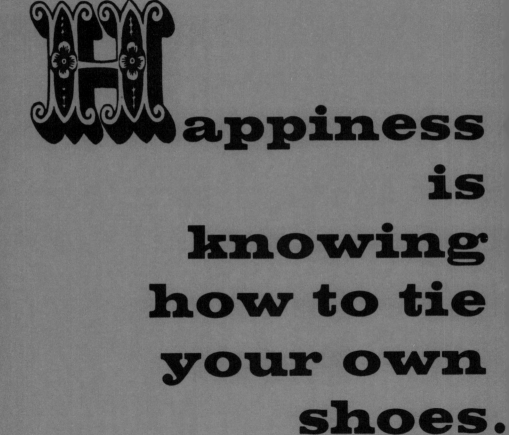

Happiness is knowing how to tie your own shoes.

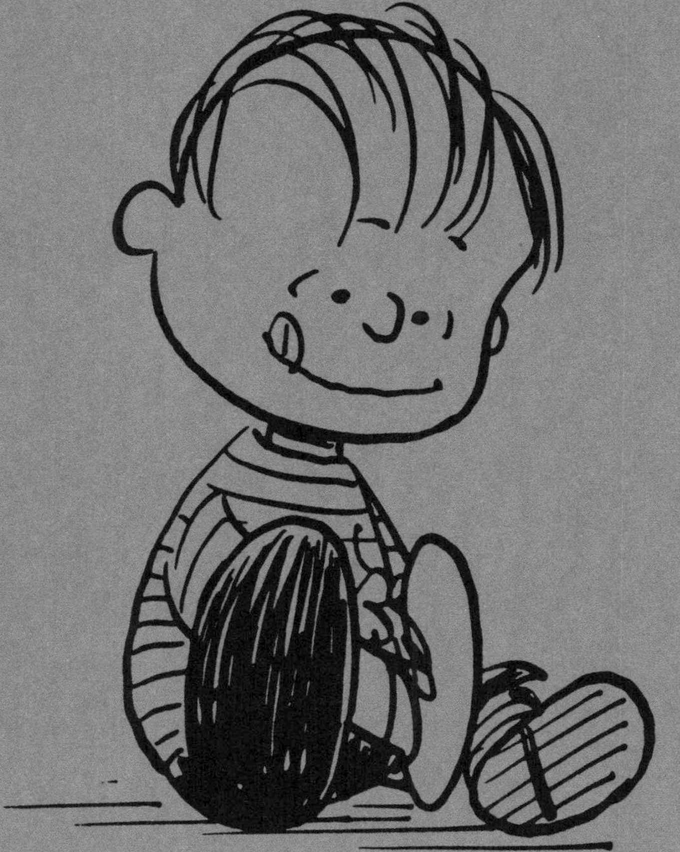

Happiness
is
walking
in the grass
in your
bare feet.

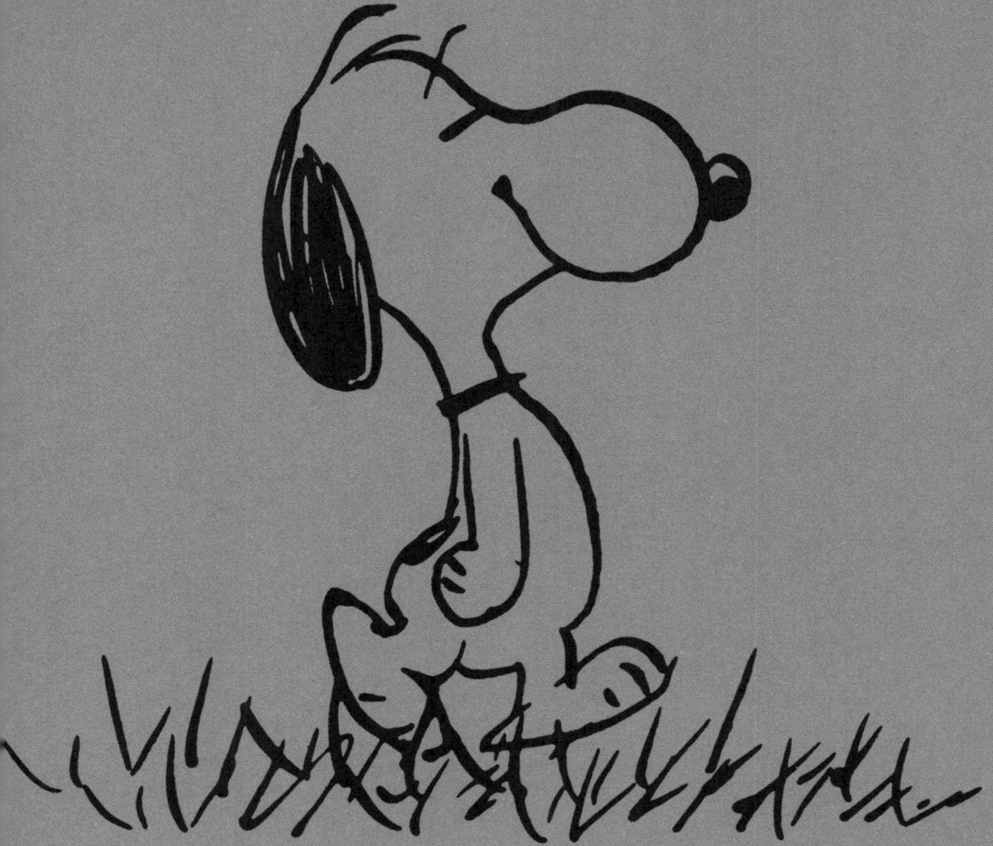

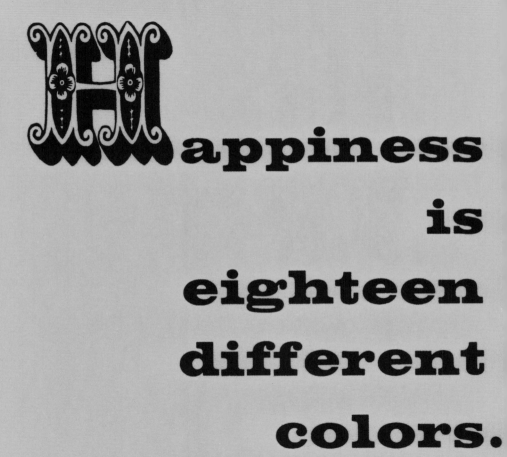

Happiness is eighteen different colors.

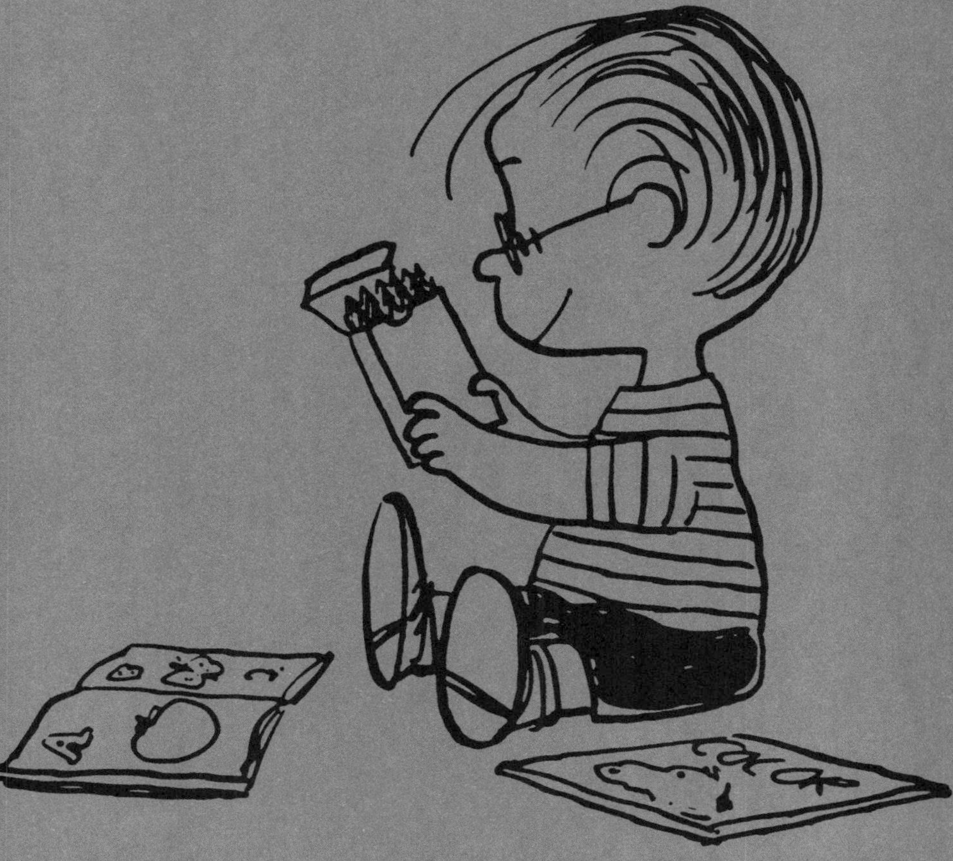

appiness
is
a piece
of fudge
caught
on the
first bounce.

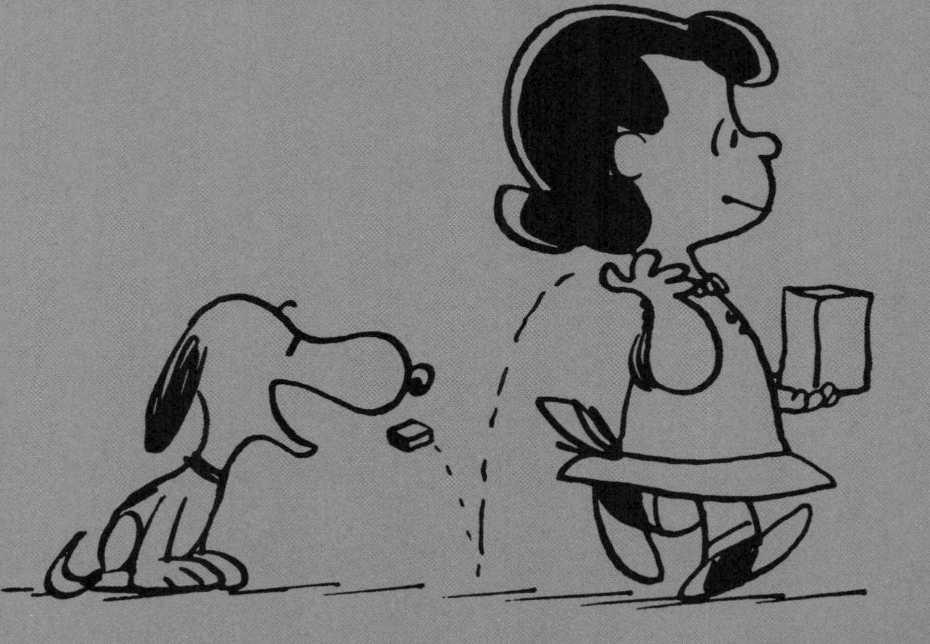

Happiness is finding the little piece with the pink edge and part of the sky and the top of the sailboat.

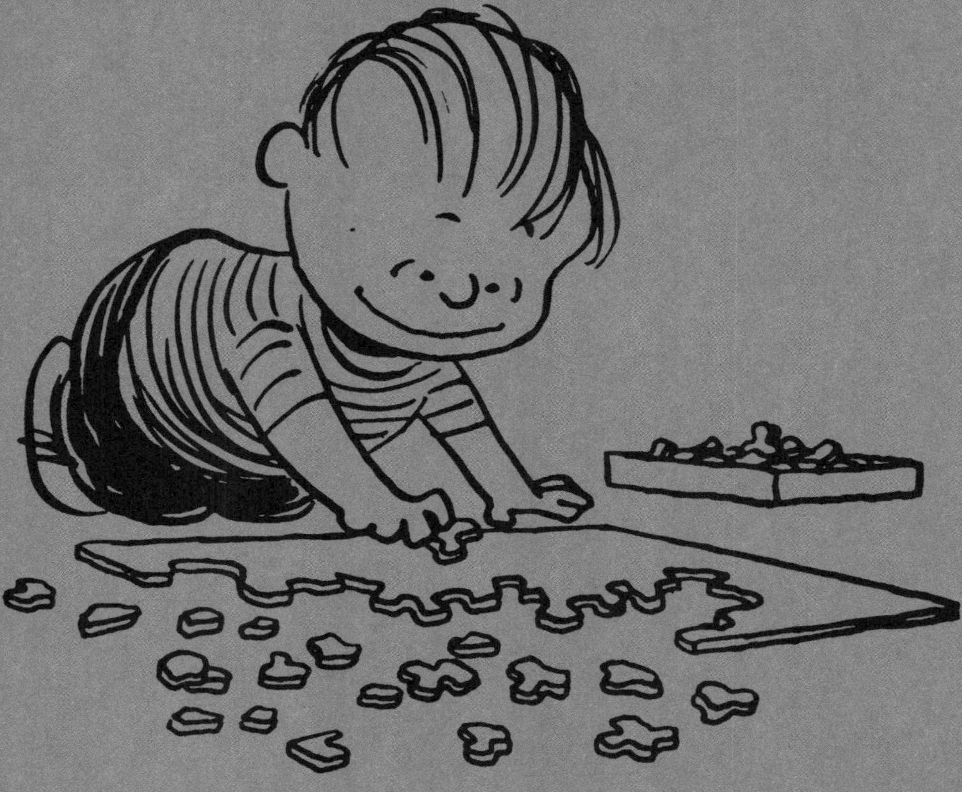

Happiness is finding out you're not so dumb after all.

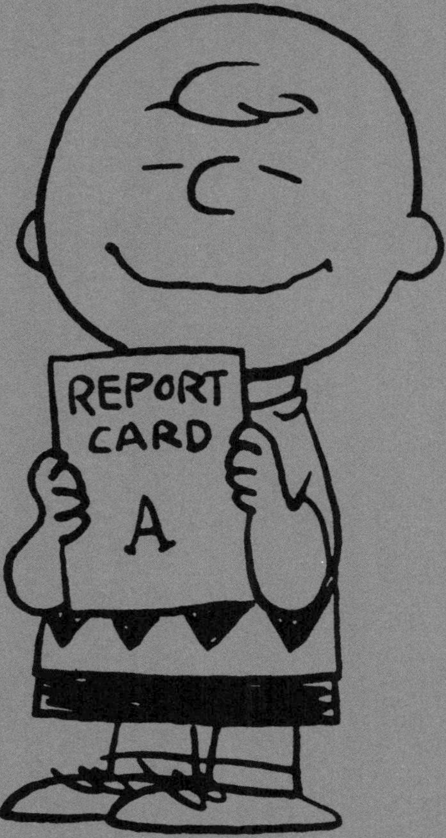
REPORT
CARD
A

Happiness is thirty-five cents for the movie, fifteen cents for popcorn and a nickel for a candy bar.

Happiness is one thing to one person and another thing to another person.

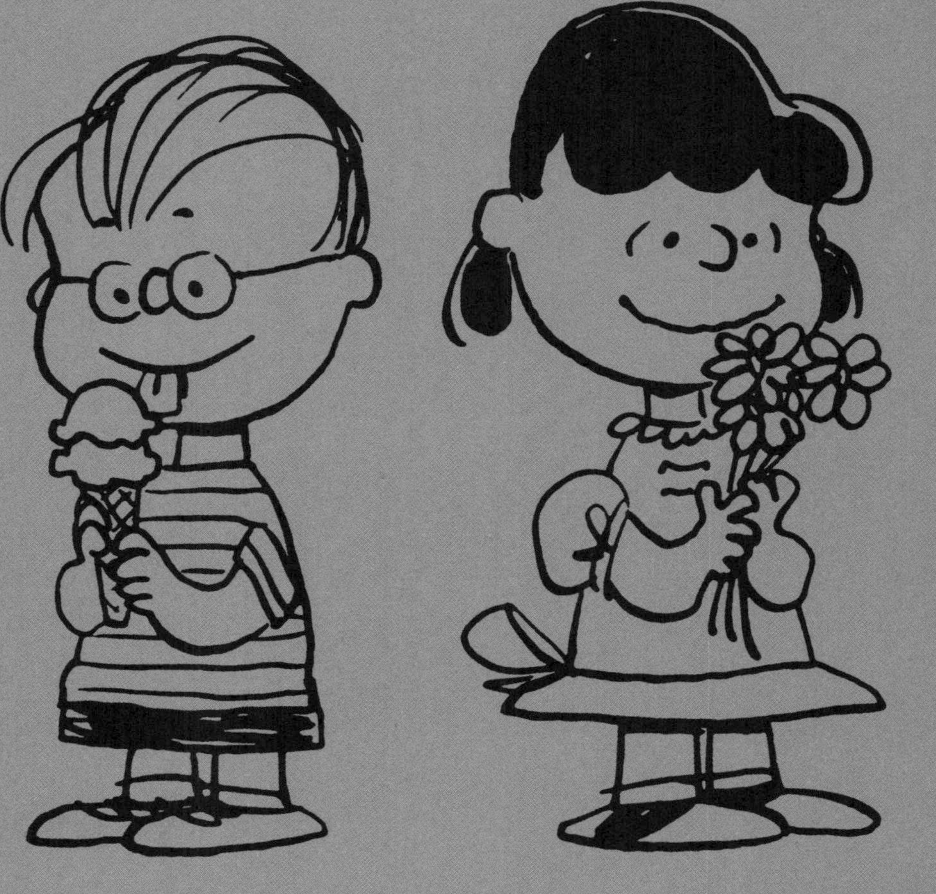

Security
is having
someone
to lean
on.

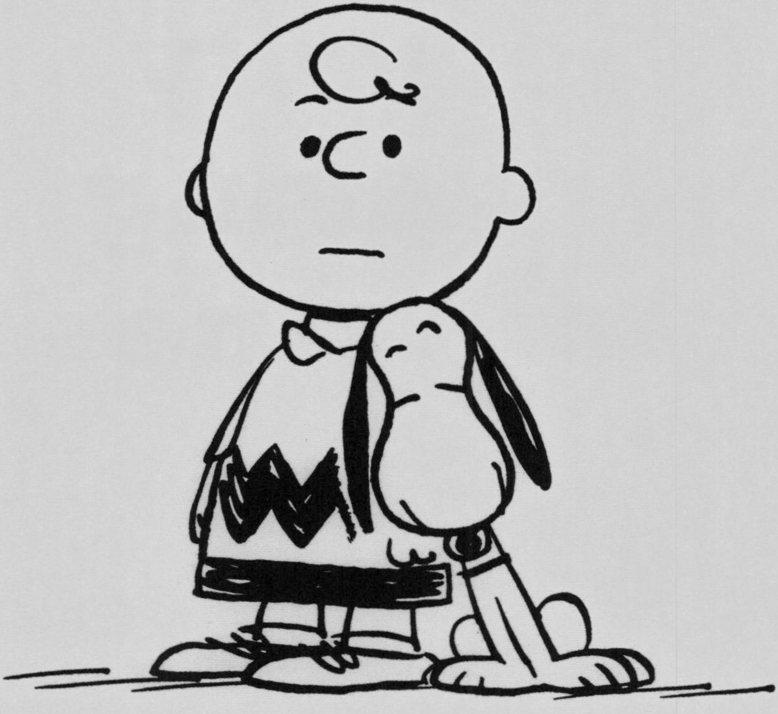

**Security
is knowing
you won't be
called on
to recite.**

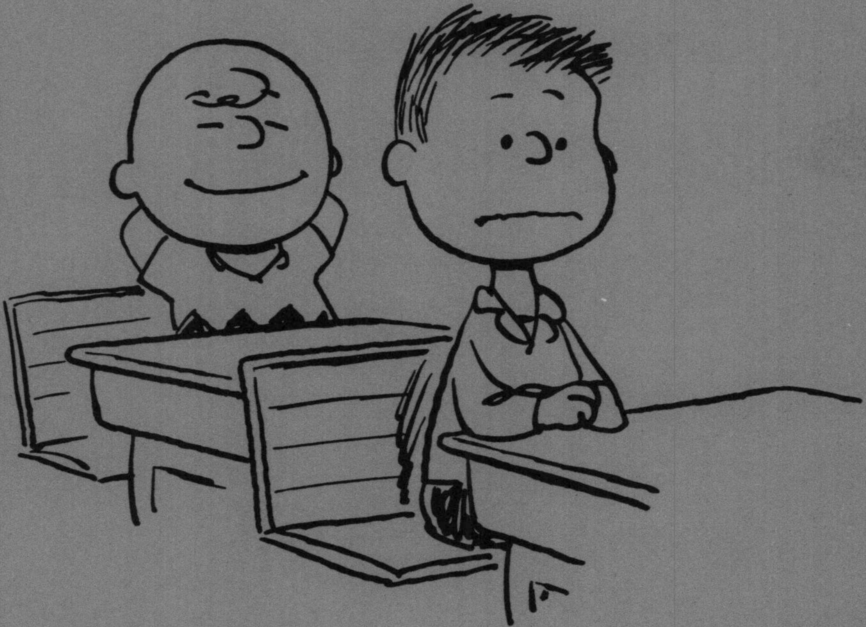

Security is knowing who the baby sitter is.

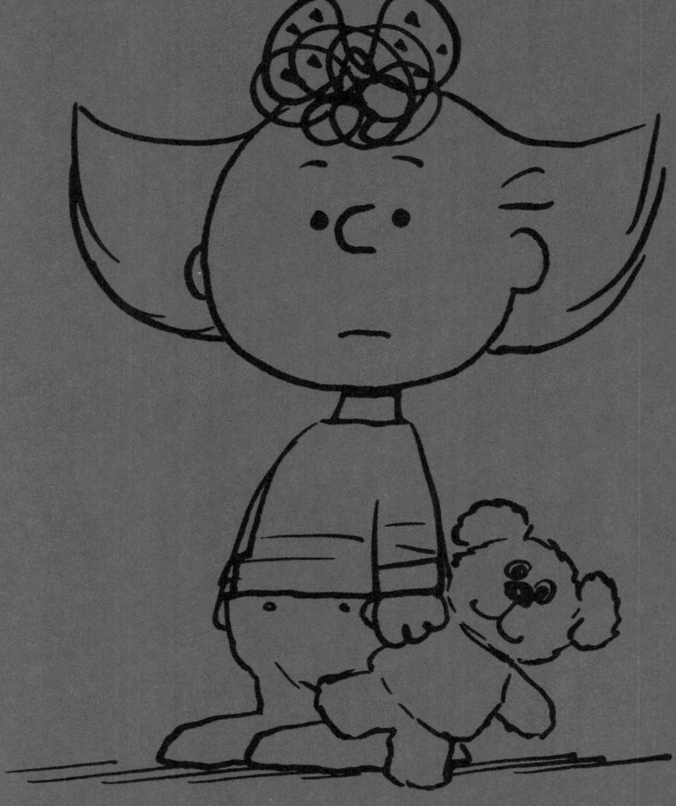

**Security
is having
your socks
match.**

**Security
is knowing
you still have
quite a few
years to go.**

Security
is owning
your own
home.

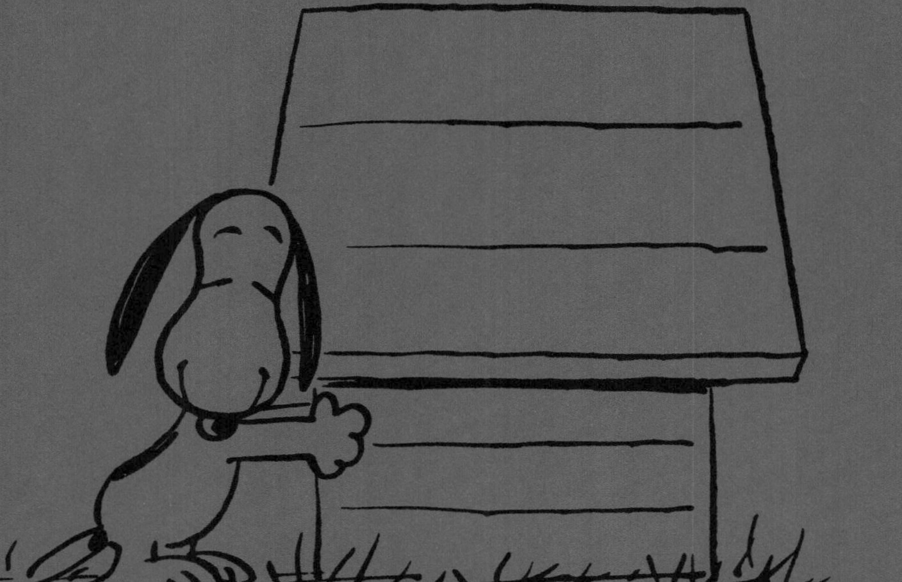

Security is having the music in front of you.

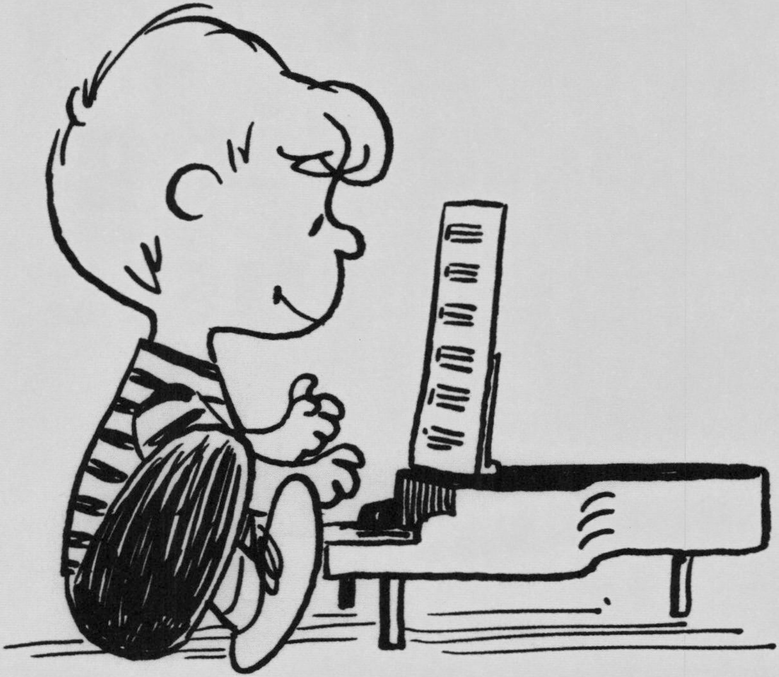

Security is having a big brother.

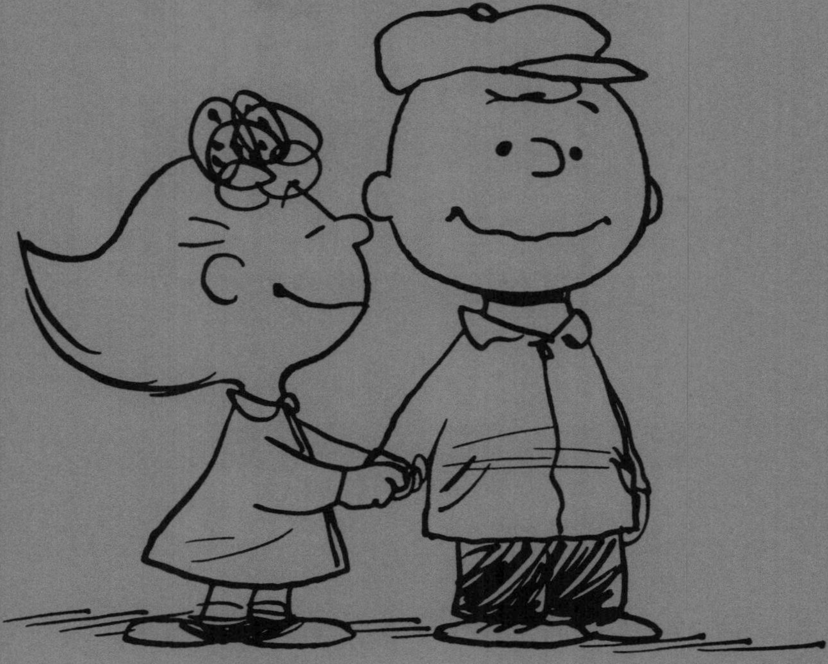

Security
is sitting
in a box.

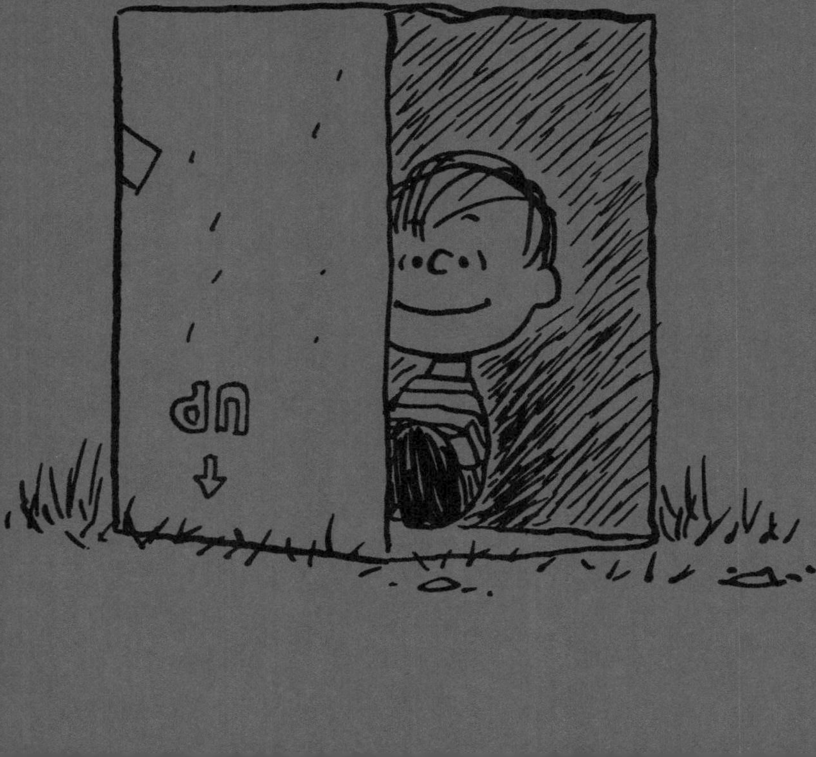
UP

Security
is having a
good infield
behind you.

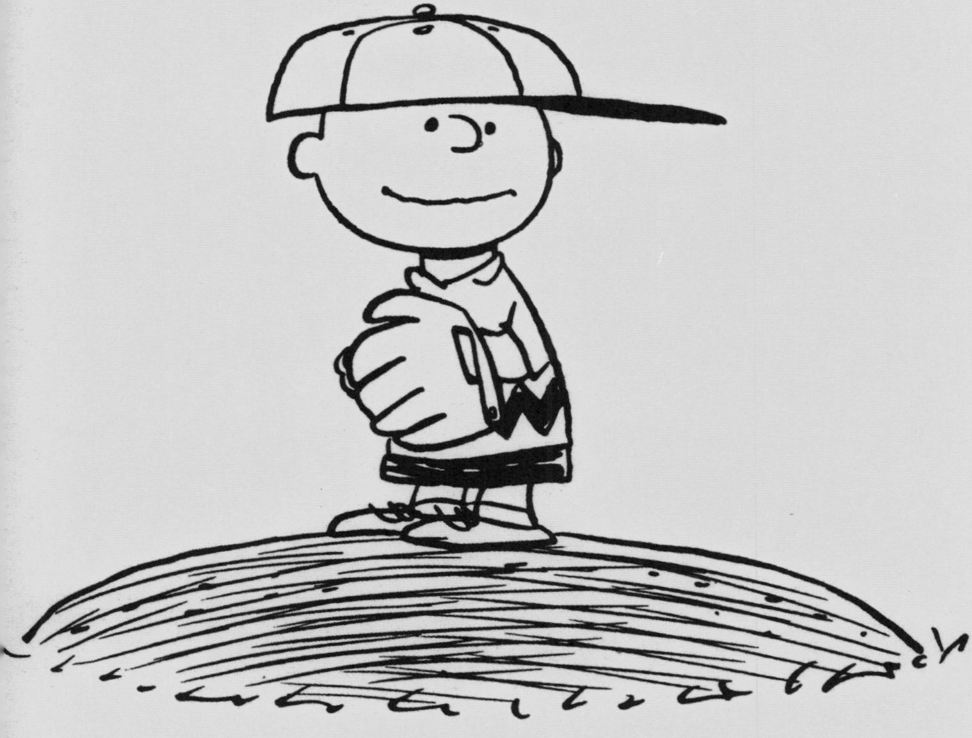

Security
is having
naturally
curly
hair.

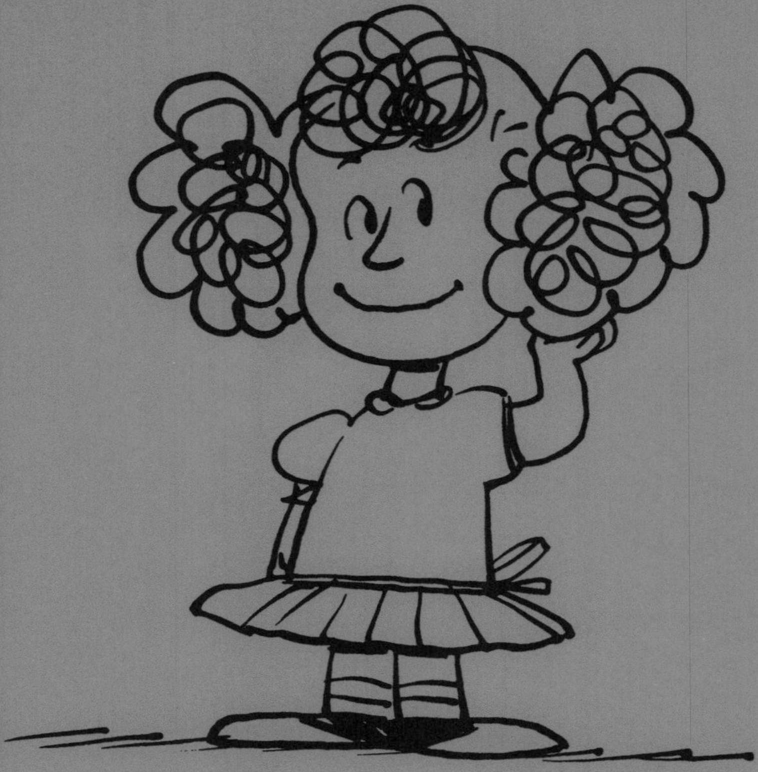

**Security
is knowing
that big dog
can't really
get out.**

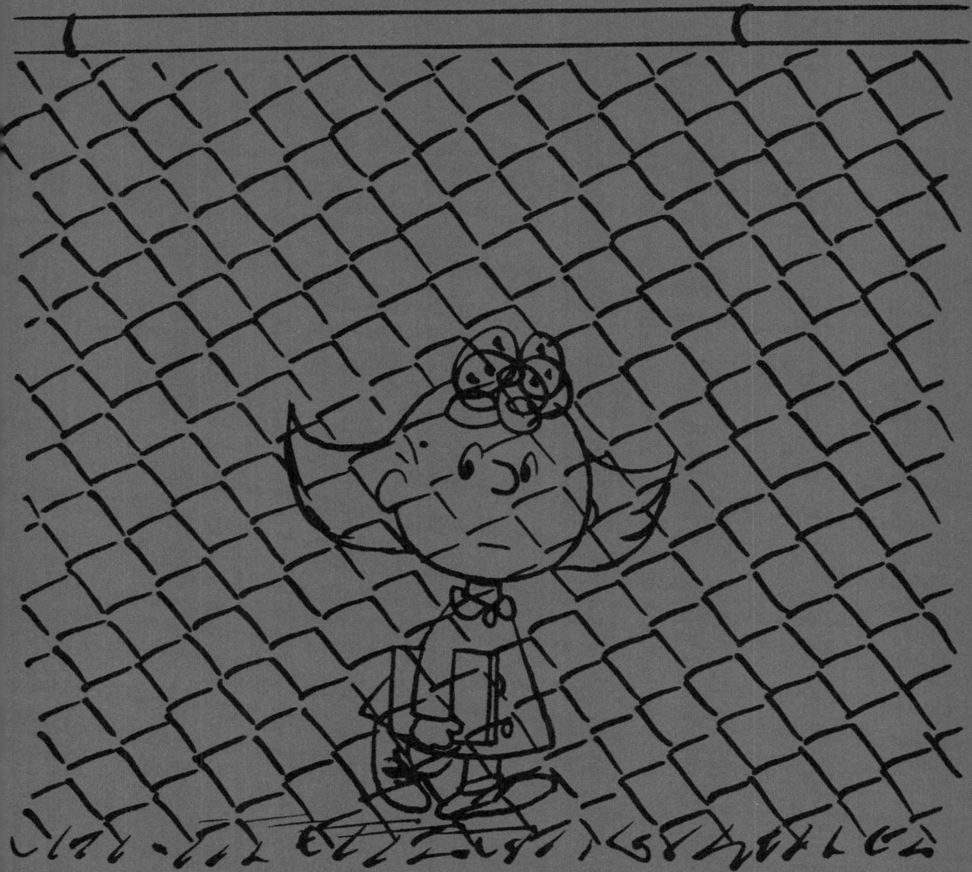

Security is having a few bones stacked away.

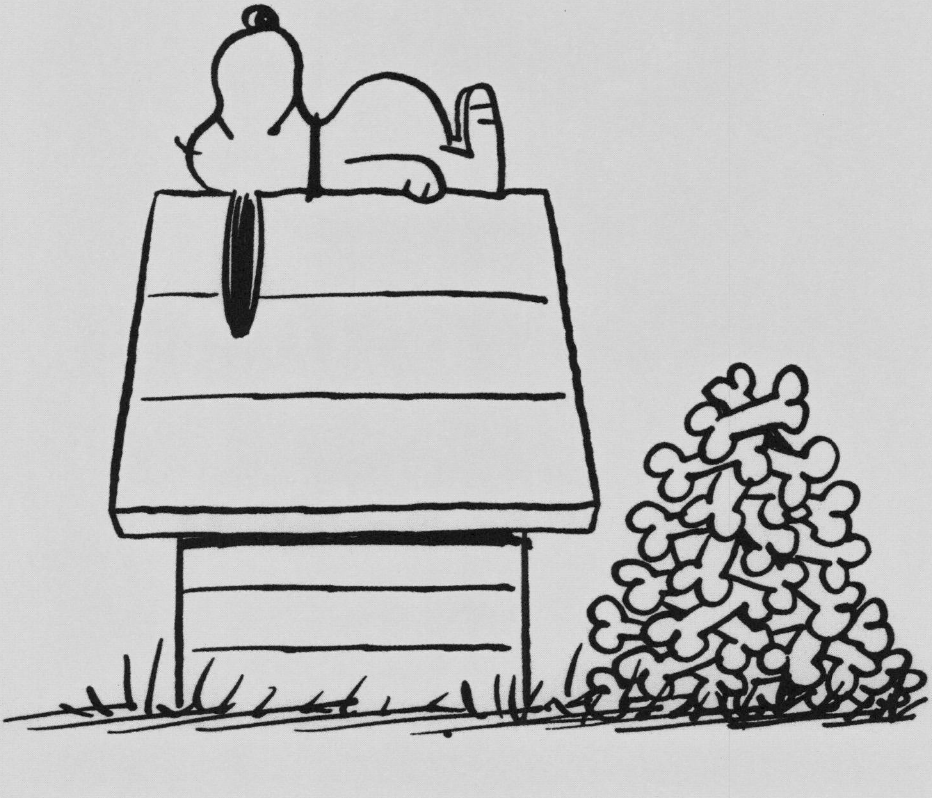

Security
is holding
the tickets
in your
hand.

Security is carrying an extra safety pin in your purse.

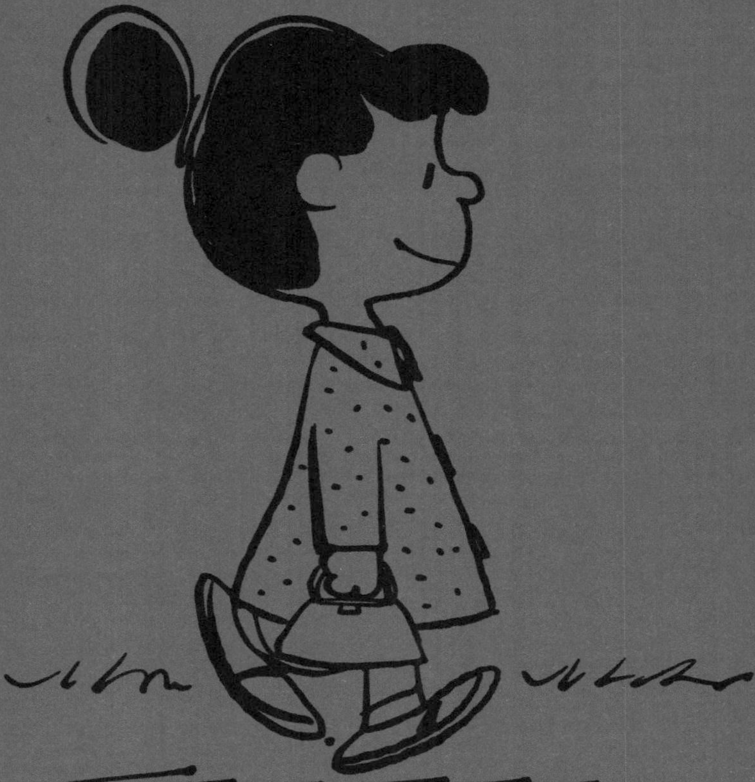

Security is writing down your locker combination.

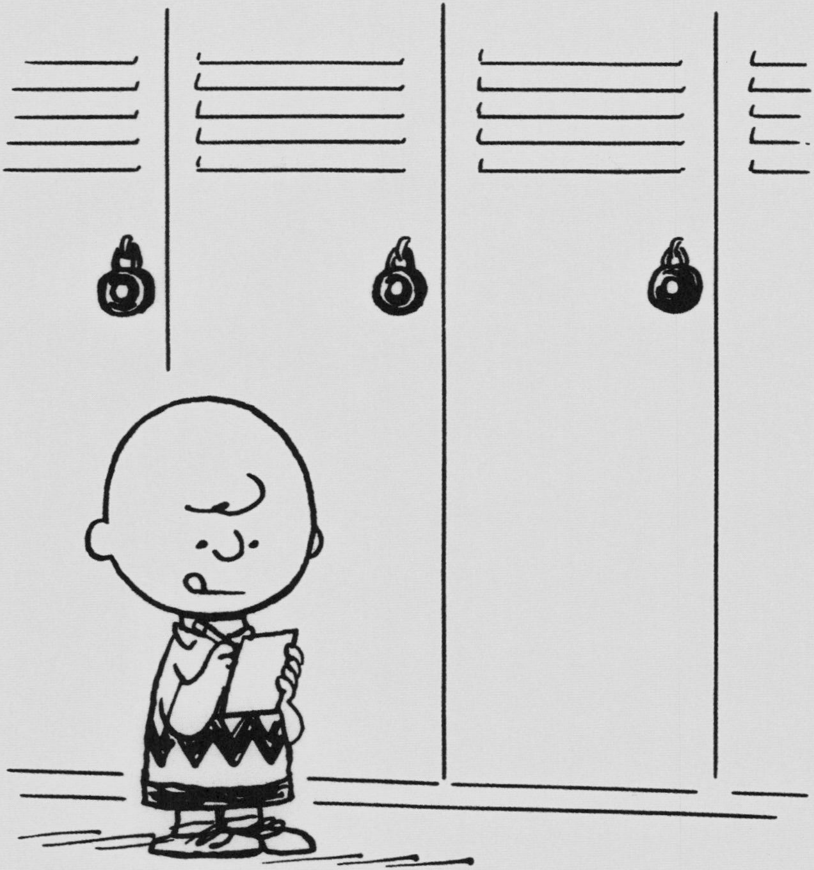

Security is having some friends sleep overnight.

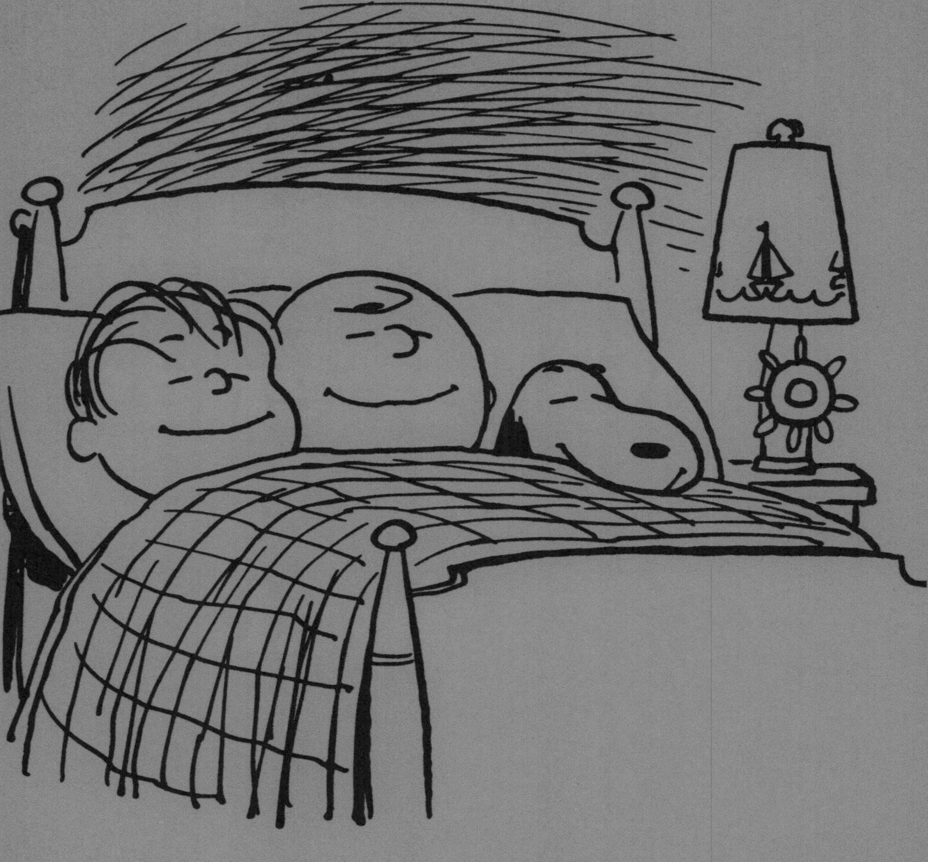

Security is being able to touch bottom.

Security is giving the mailbox lid an extra flip.

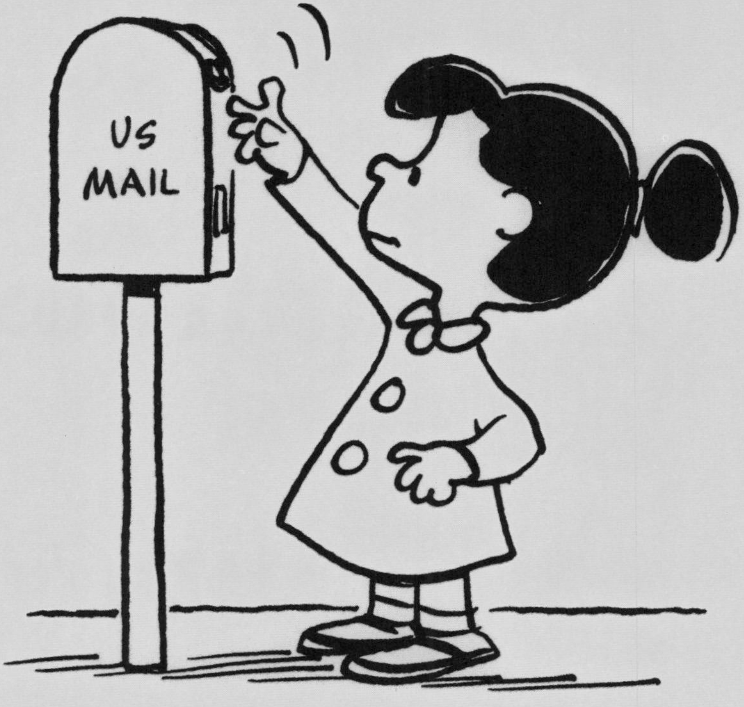
US
MAIL

Security
is being
one of
the gang.

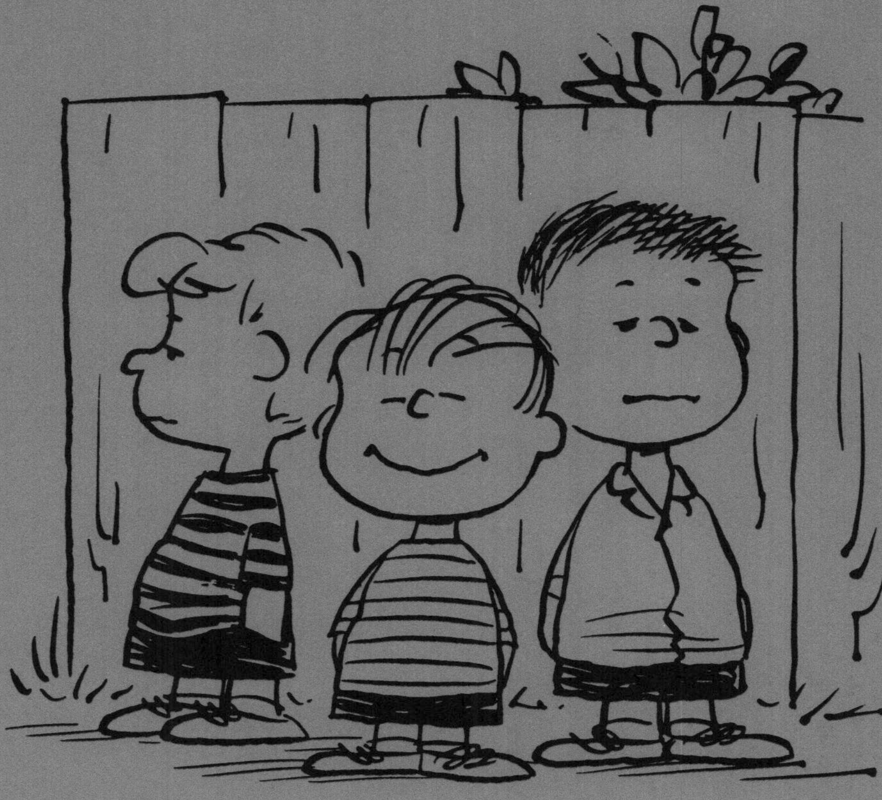

Security
is having
someone
listen
to you.

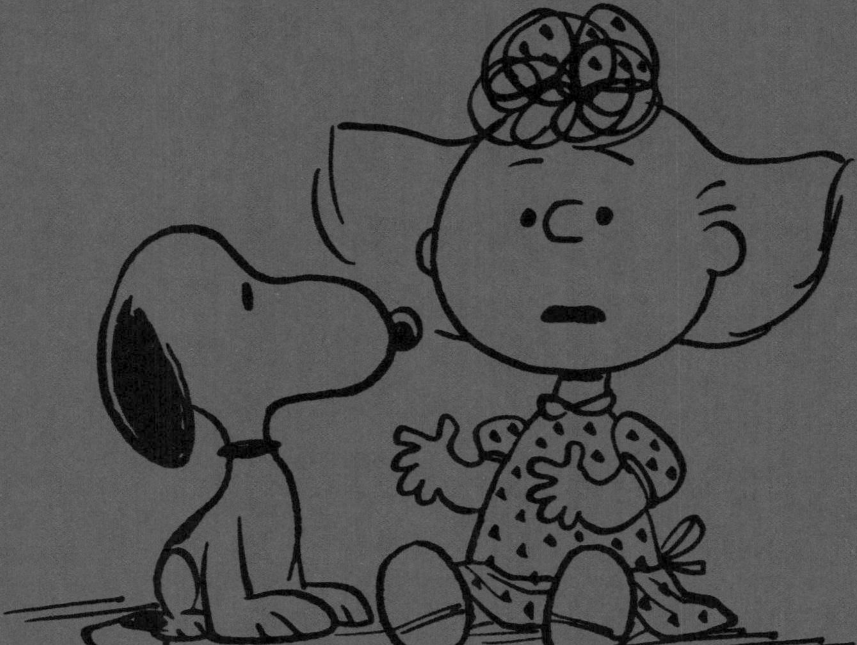

Security is returning home after a vacation.

Security is having a home town.

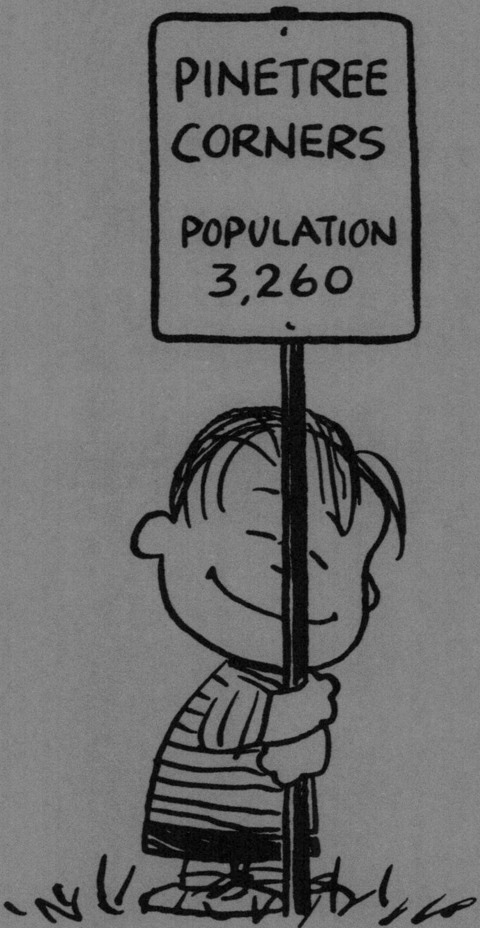
PINETREE CORNERS
POPULATION 3,260

**Security
is getting
to the theater
before the
box office
opens.**

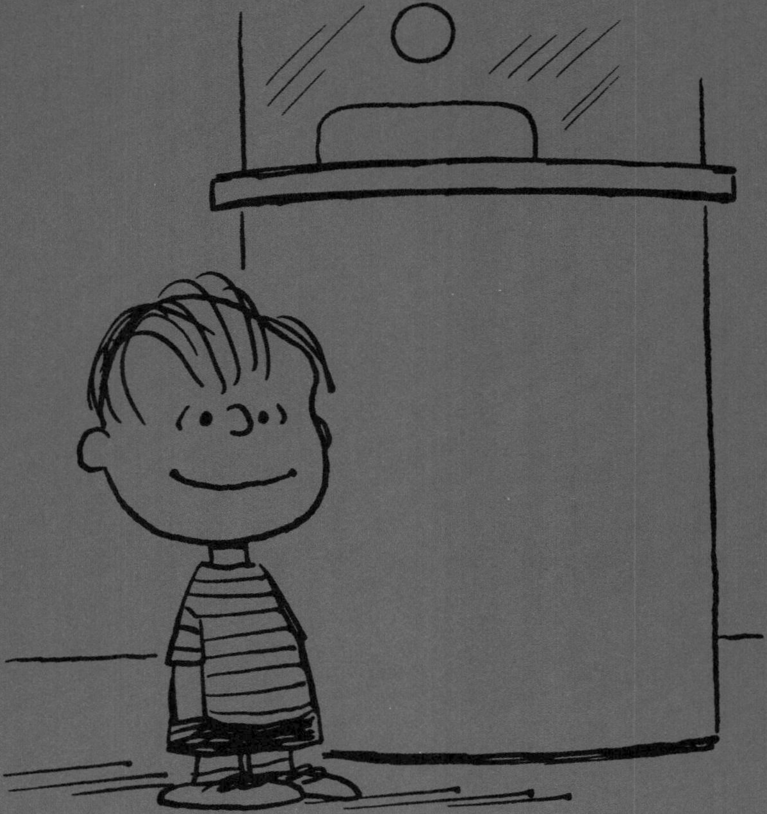

Security is knowing there's some more pie left.

Security
is hiding
an extra key
to the
back door.

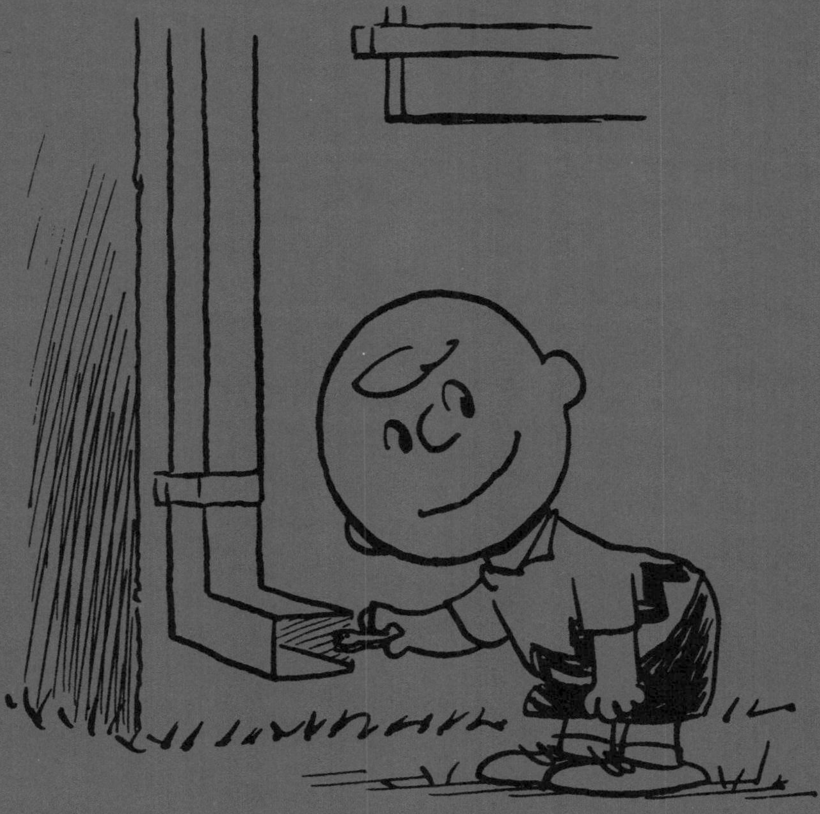

Security is knowing all your lines.

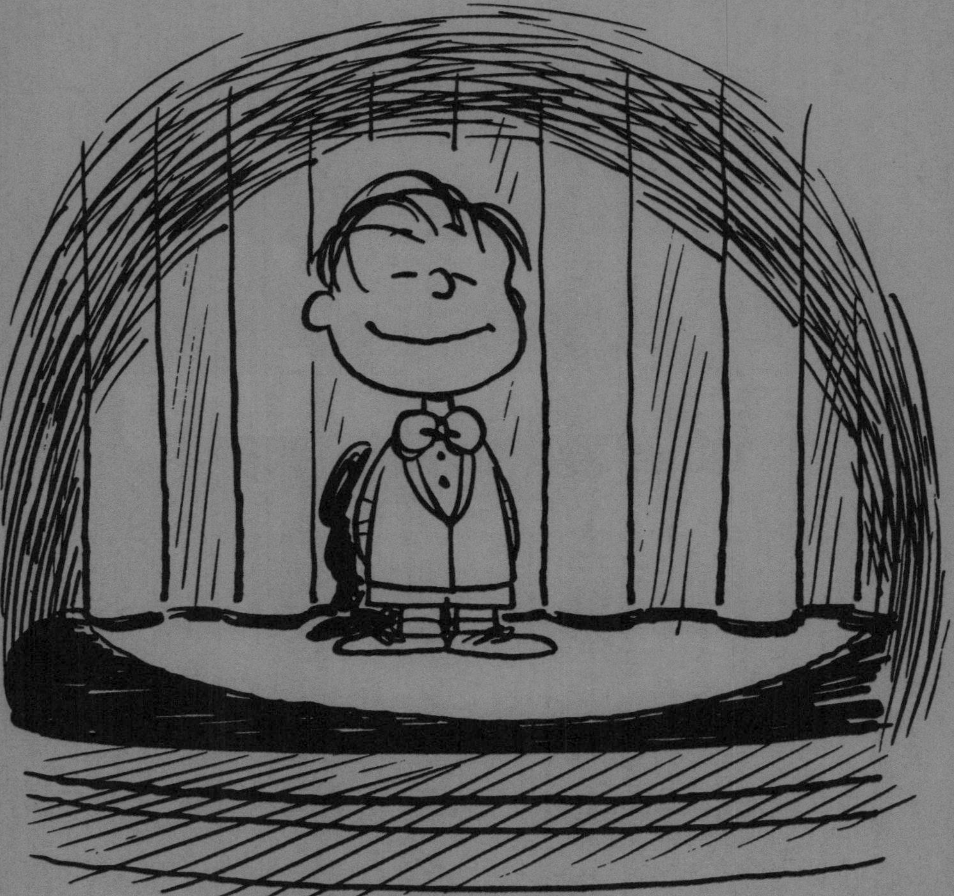

Security is
a candy bar
hidden in
the freezer.

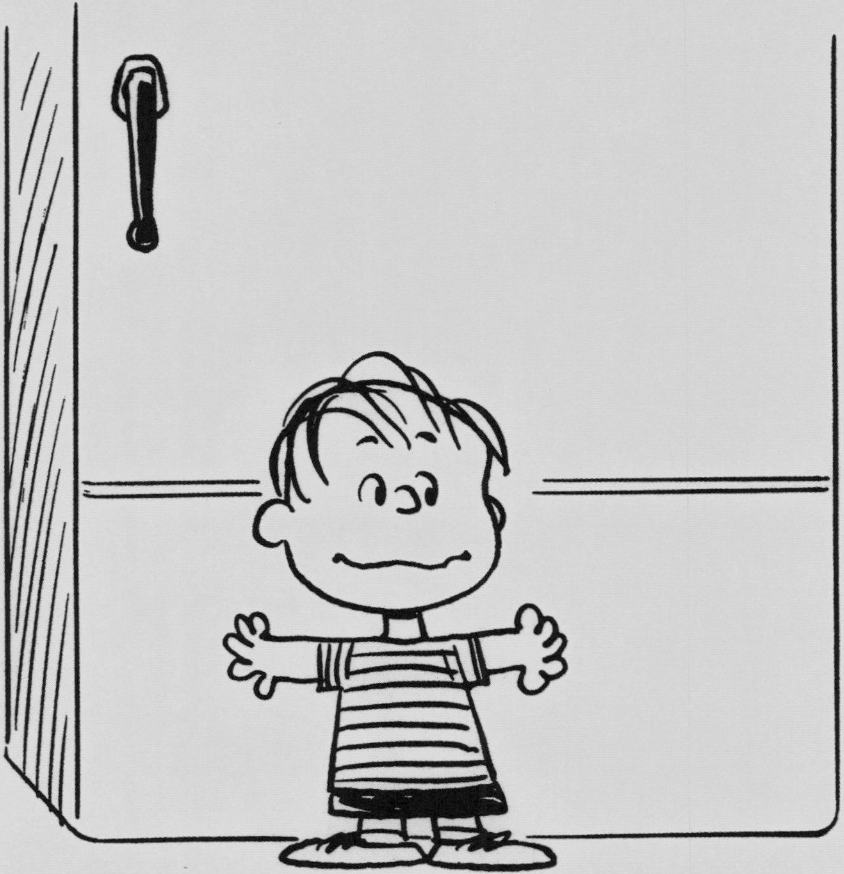

Security is hearing your mother in the kitchen when you come home from school.

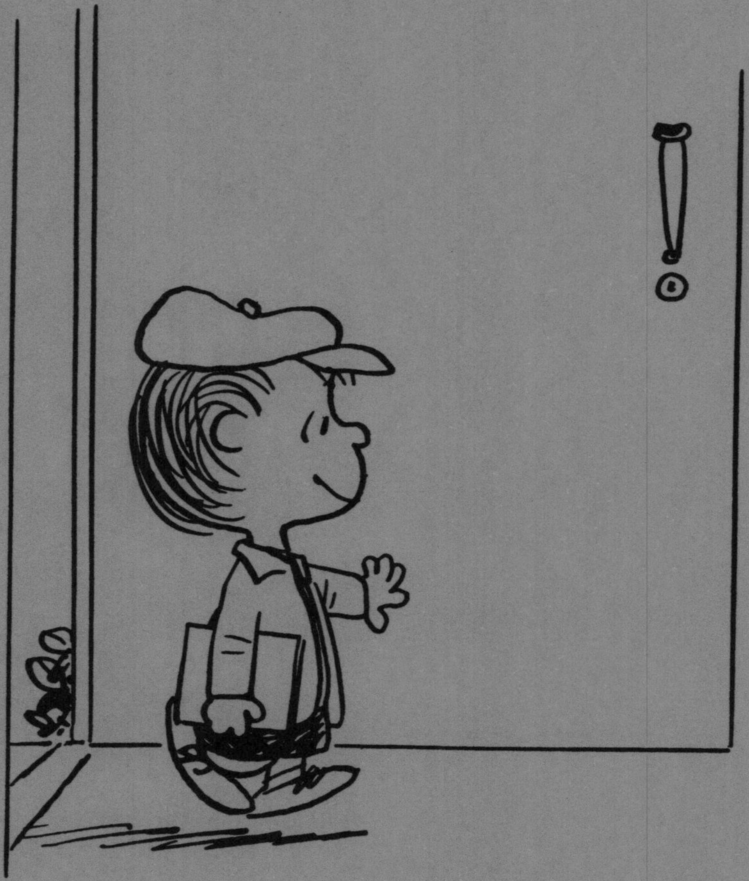

Security
is knowing
you're not
alone.

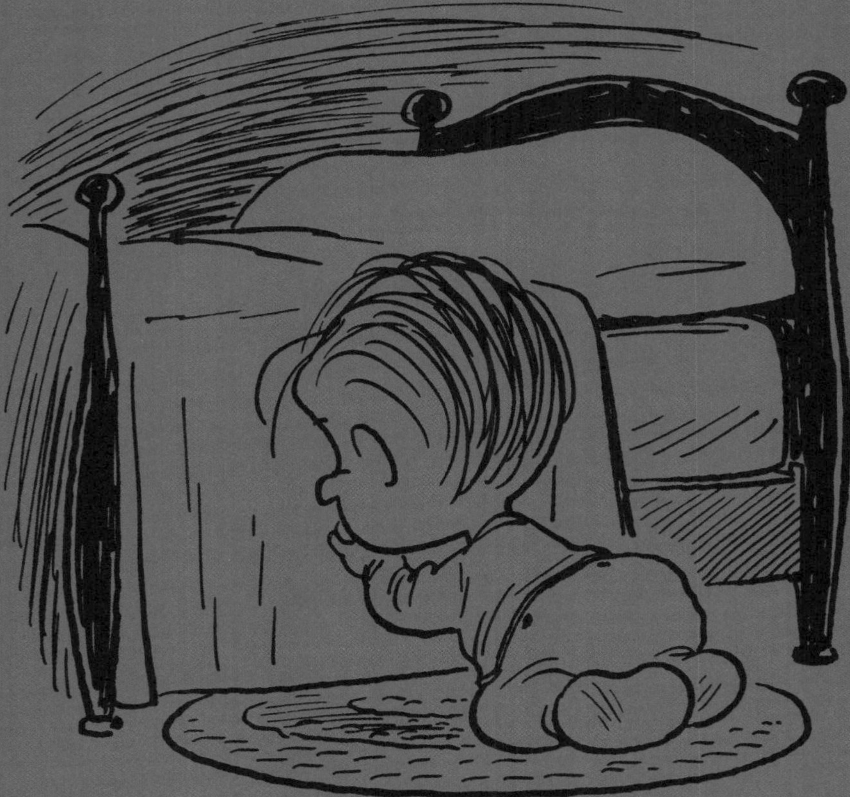

"Well,
I hate
to spoil all
the fun, but I
have to be
going."

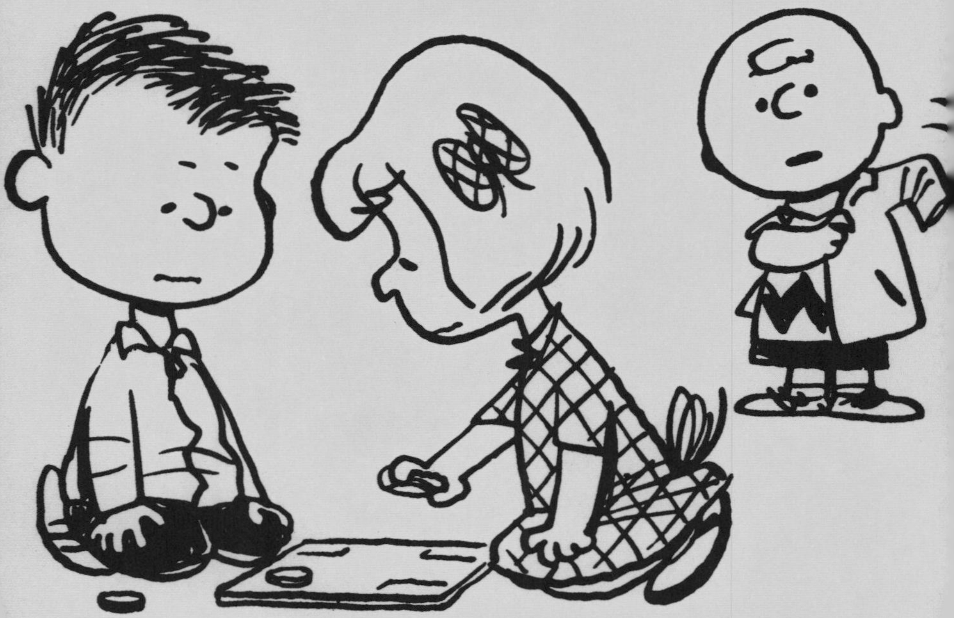

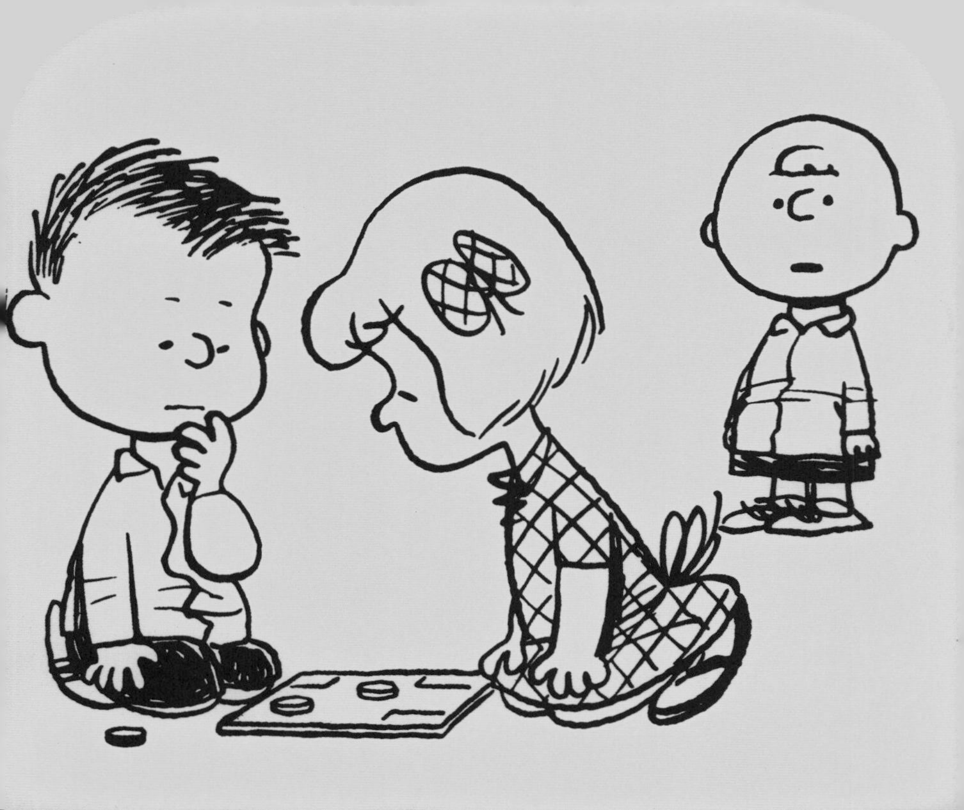

‘I said, I hate to spoil all the fun.
but I have to be going.”

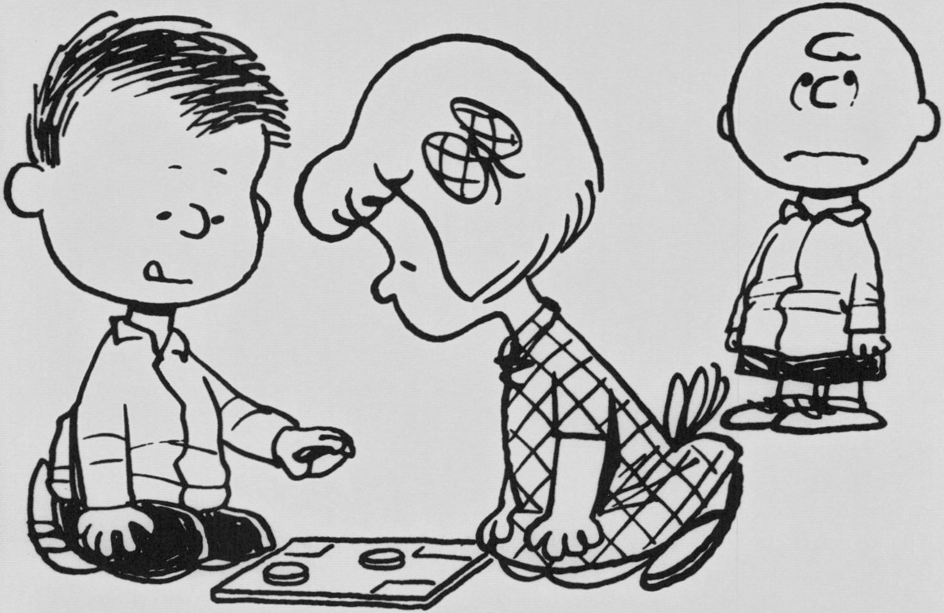

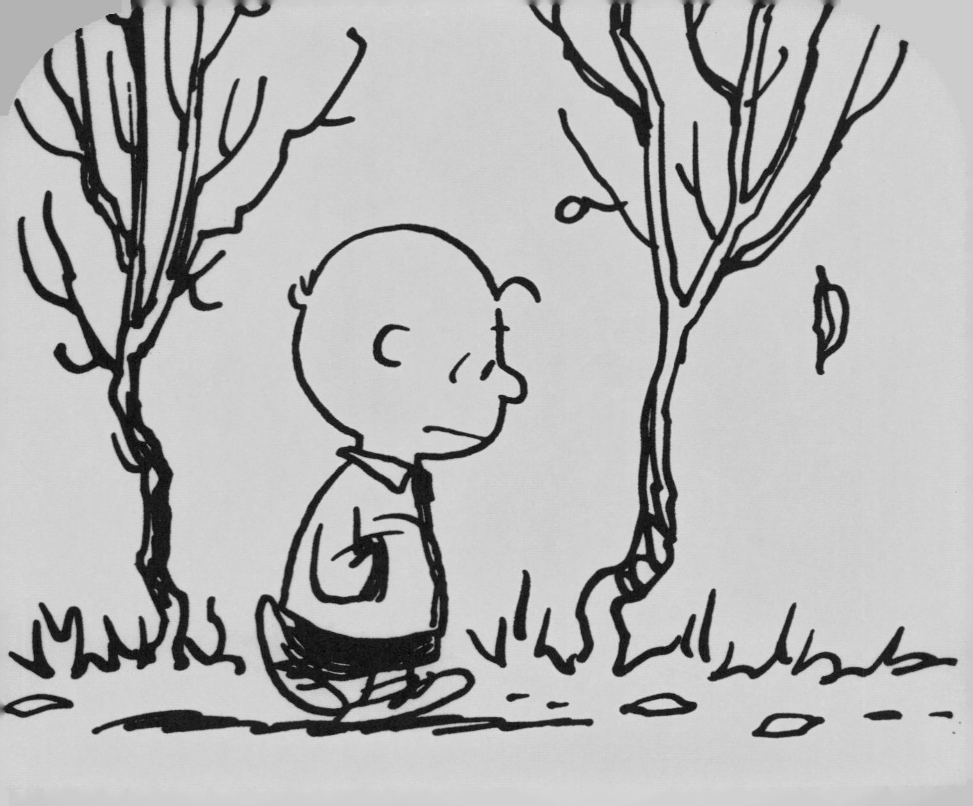

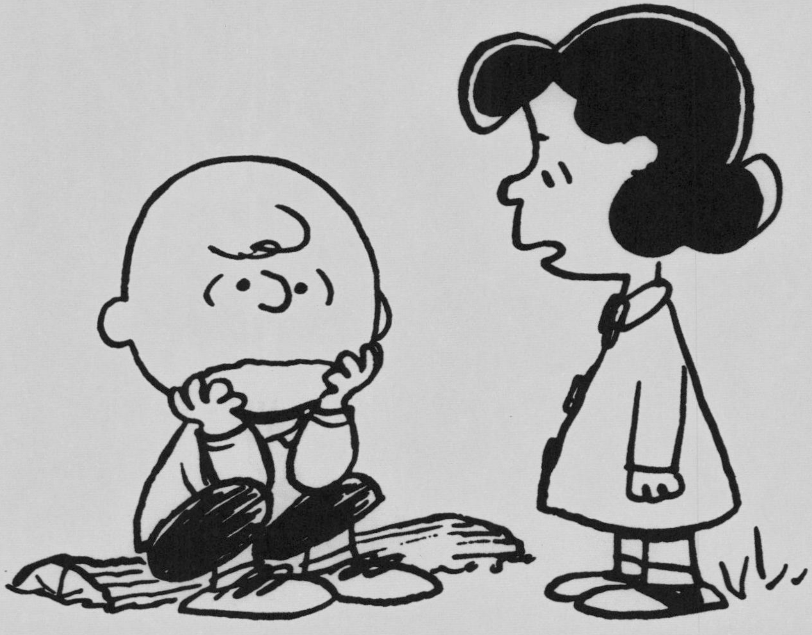

“What’s the matter with you?”

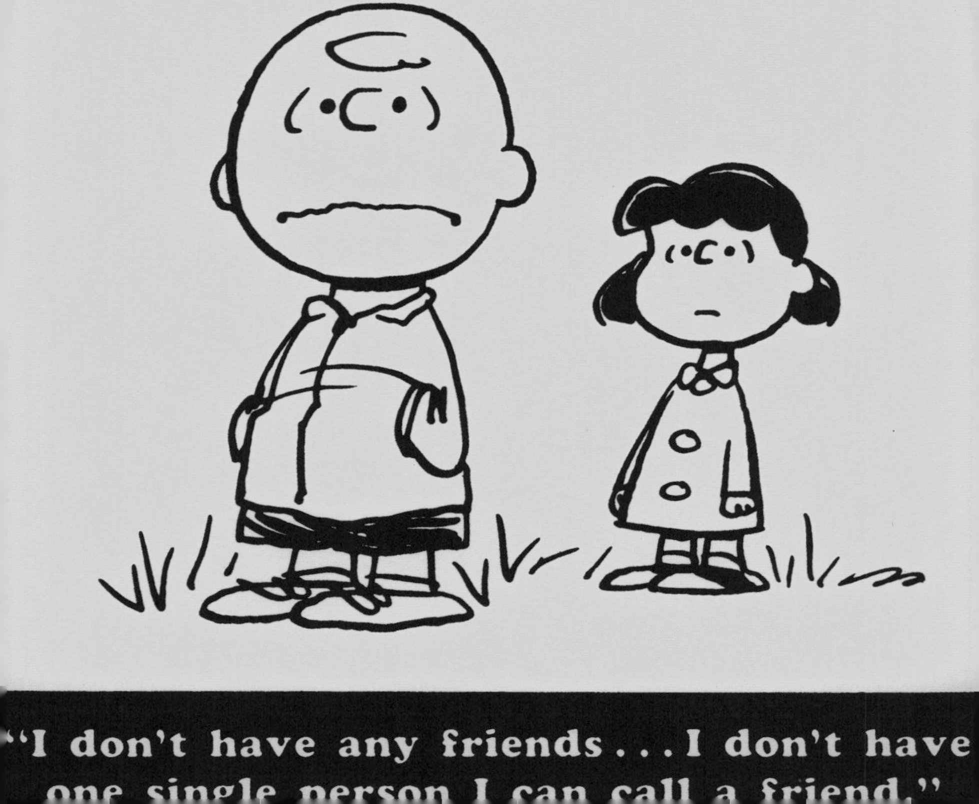

"I don't have any friends . . . I don't have one single person I can call a friend."

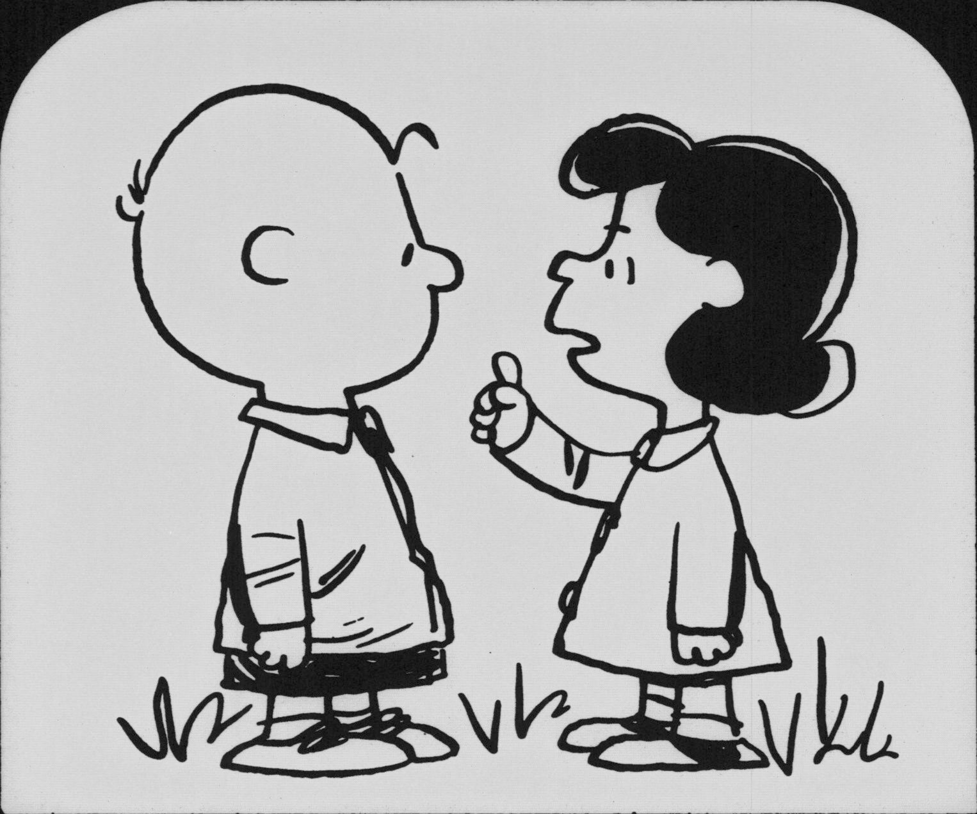

“Define ‘Friend’!”

"A friend is someone you can sock on the arm!"

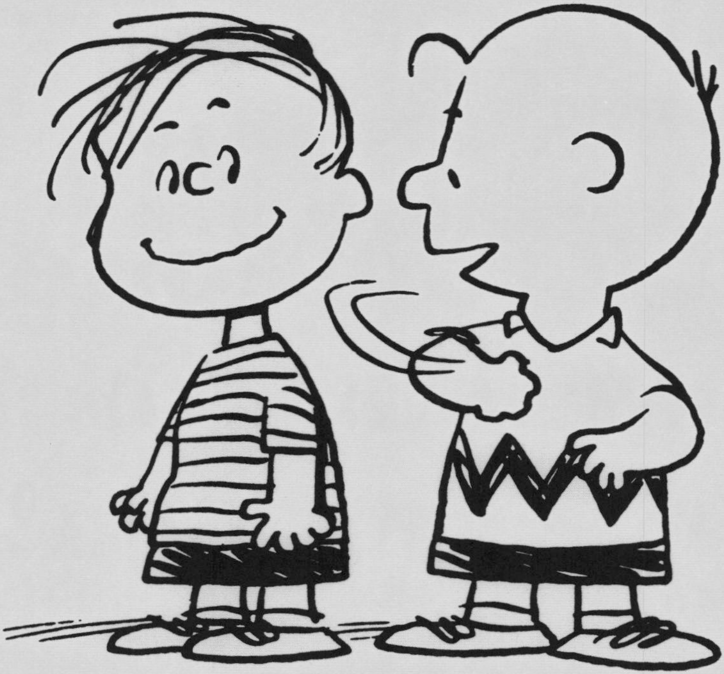

"A friend is someone who will take the side with the sun in his eyes."

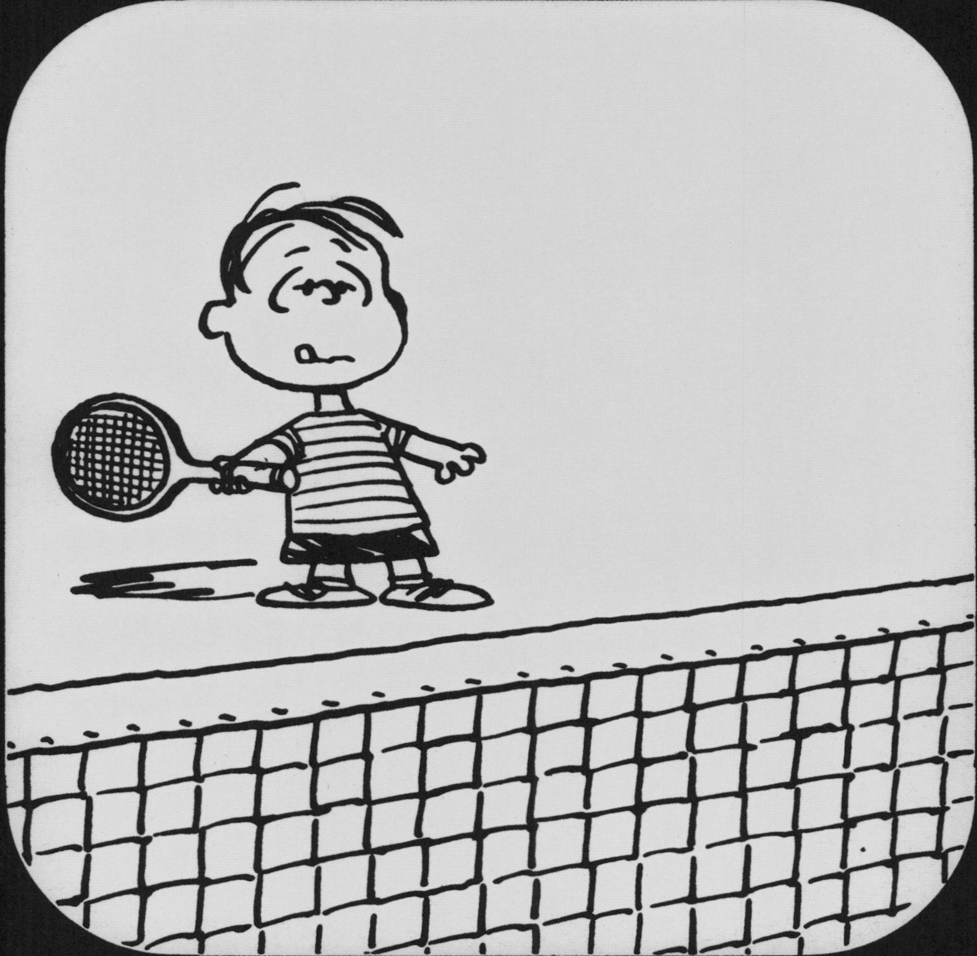

"A friend
is someone
who's willing to
watch the program
you want to
watch!"

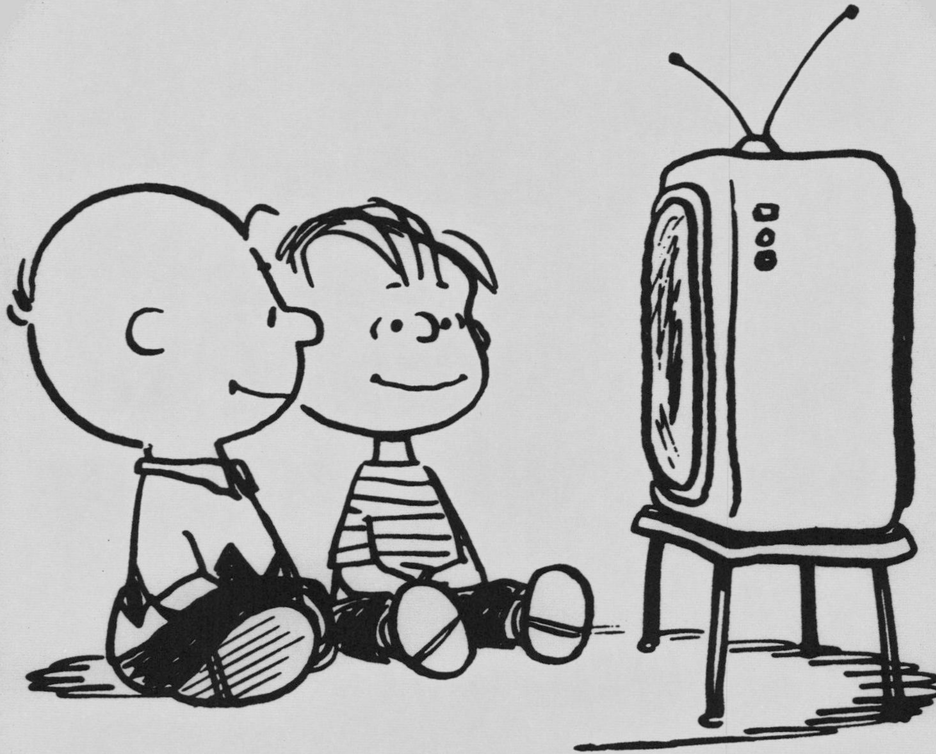

"A friend is someone who likes you even when the other guys are around."

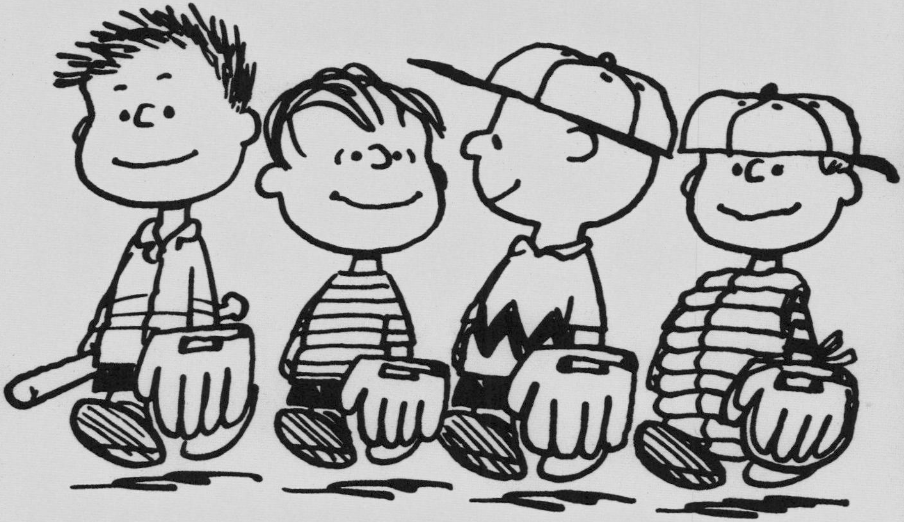

"A friend is someone who will share his home with you."

"A friend is someone who will trade you an Alvin Dark for a Luis Aparicio."

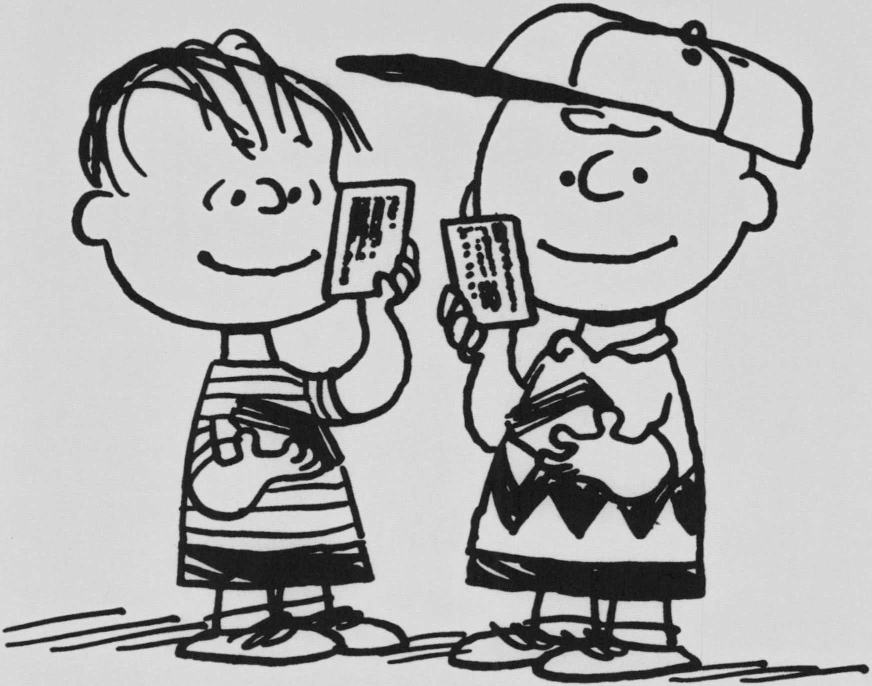

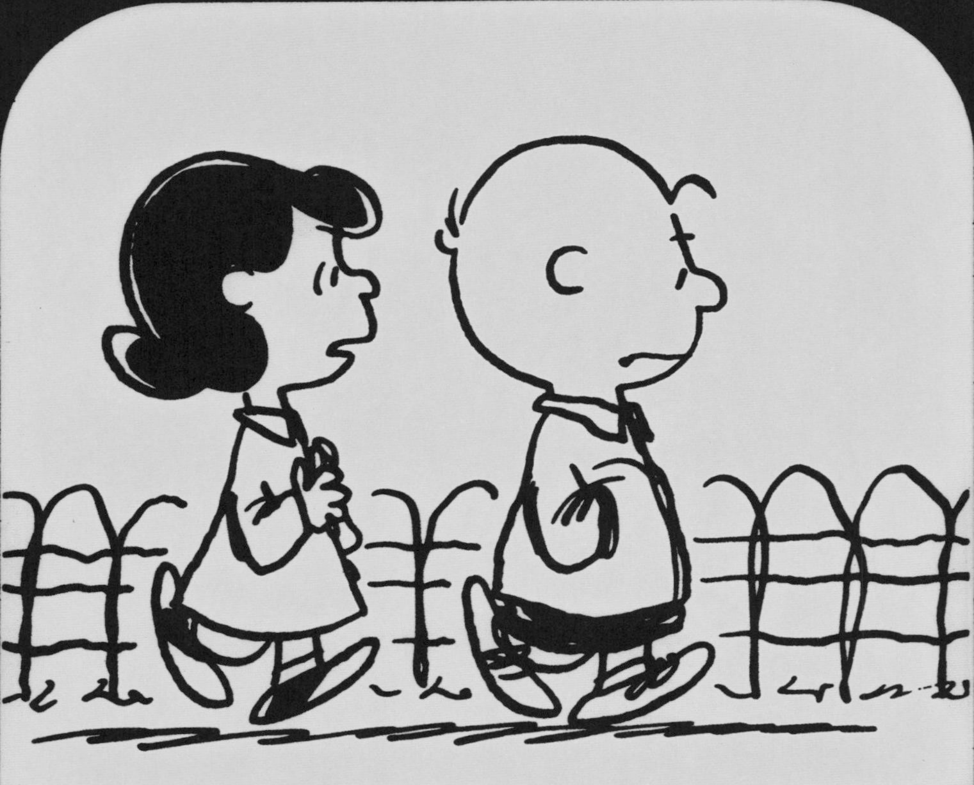

"I think you try too hard, Charlie Brown . . .
Be like me. I don't need any friends . . .
I'm self-sufficient!"

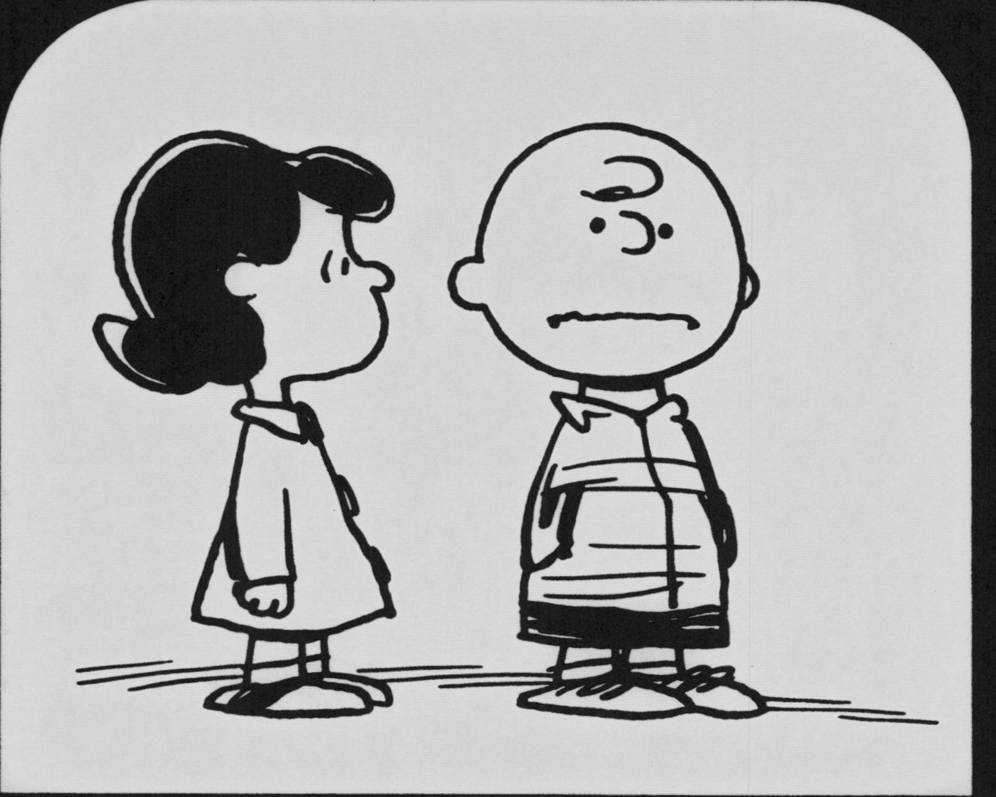

"Not me . . . I need
all the friends I can get!"

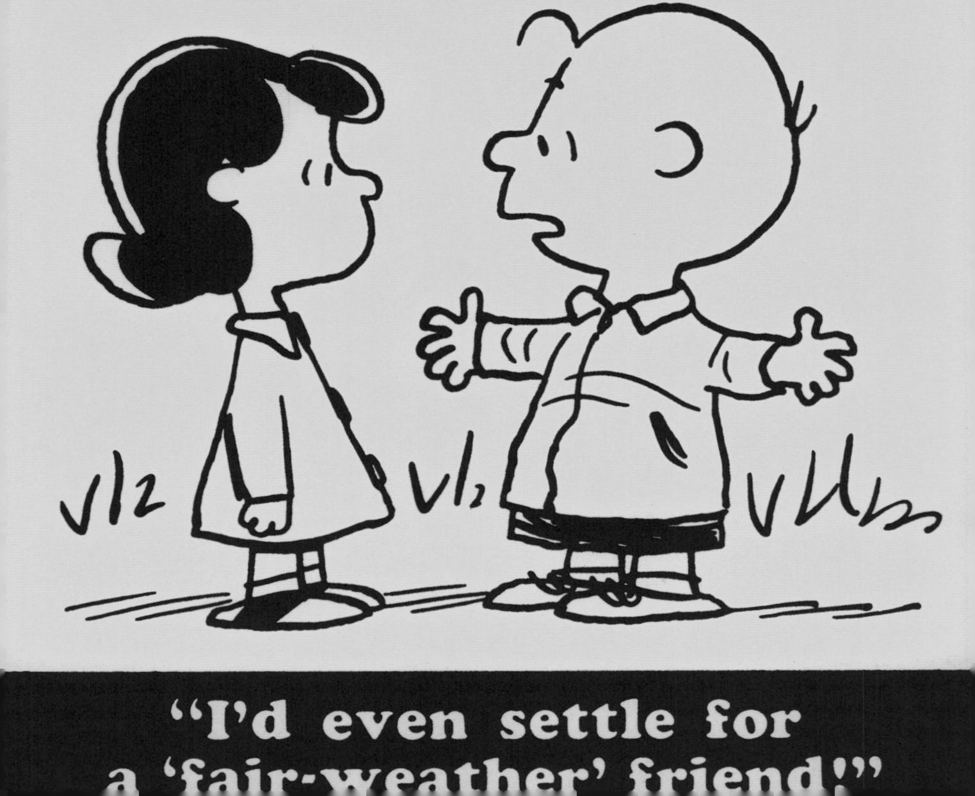

"I'd even settle for a 'fair-weather' friend!"

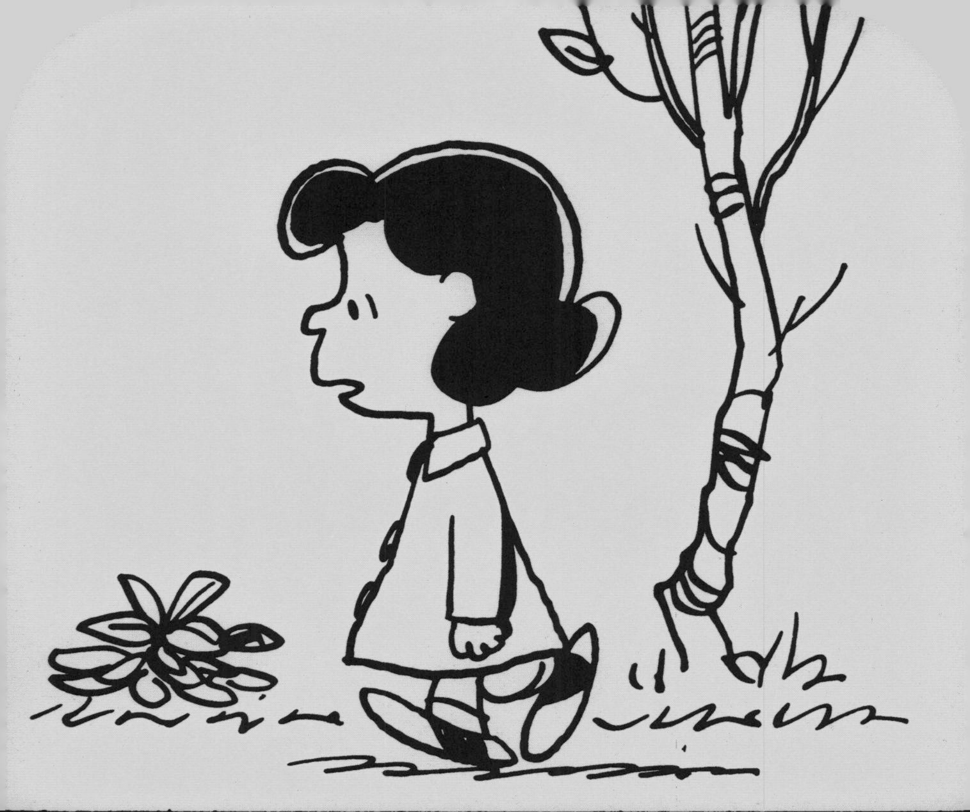

"Poor ol' Charlie Brown...
He really should try to be like me.
I don't care if I have any friends or not..."

"Just so
I'm popular!"

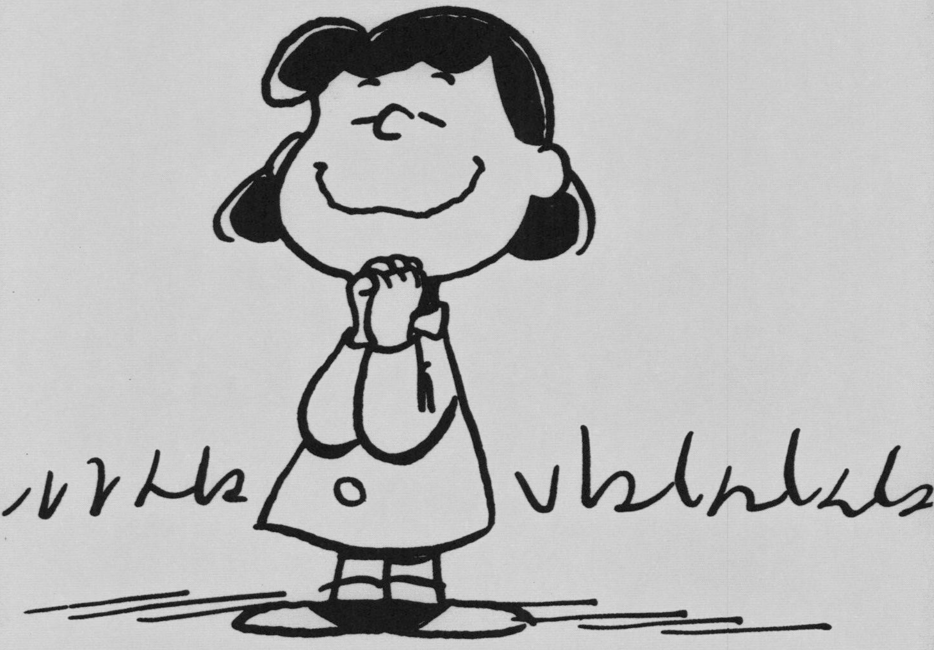

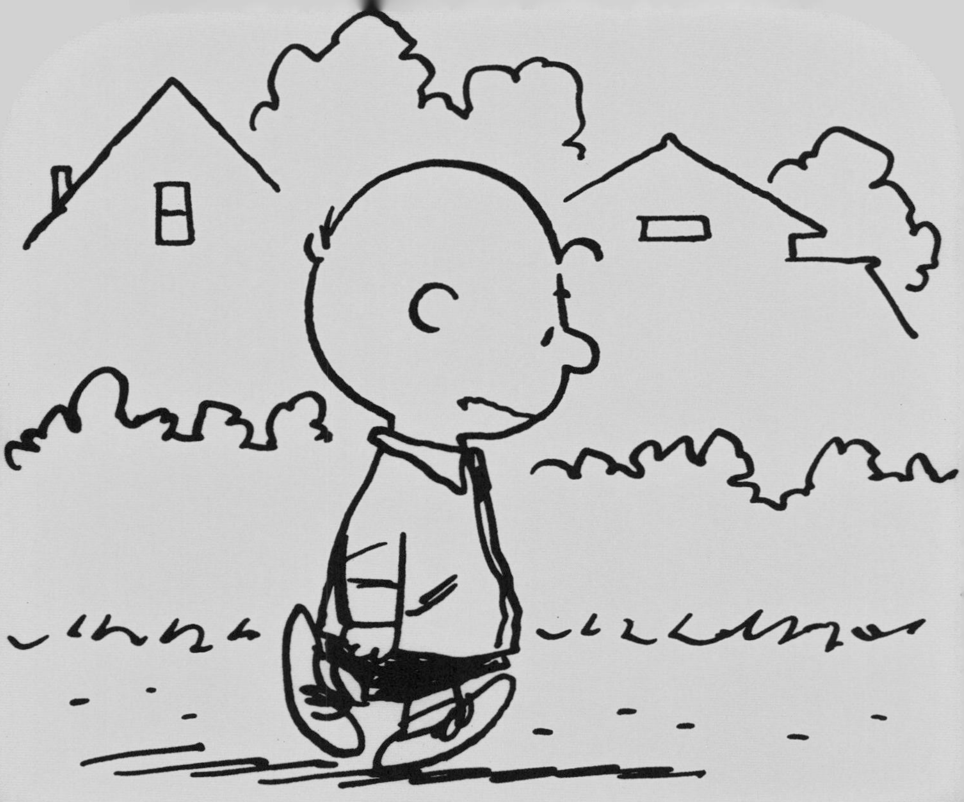

"I don't know...Talking to her never does much for me...."

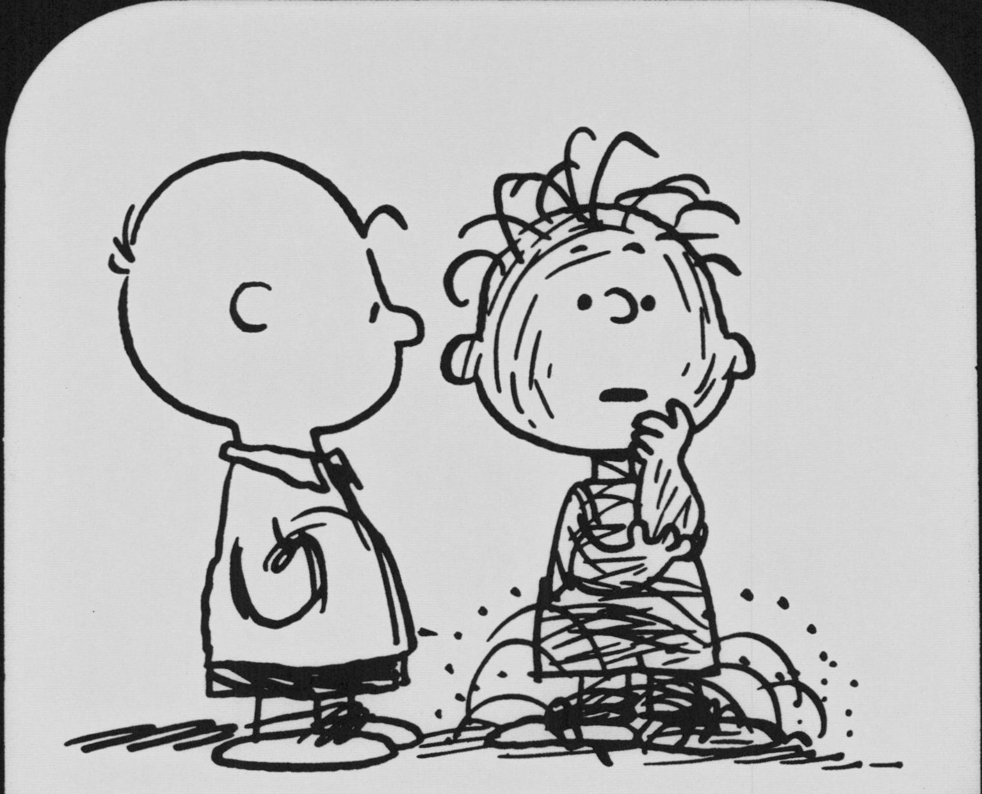

"You know what I think
a friend is, Charlie Brown?"

"A friend
is someone
who accepts
you for what
you are."

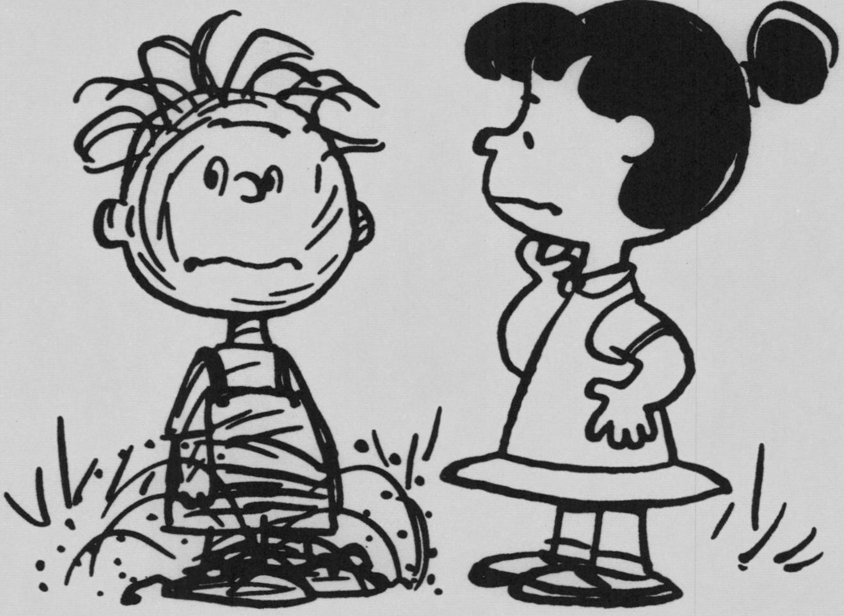

"A friend is someone who is not jealous if you have other friends."

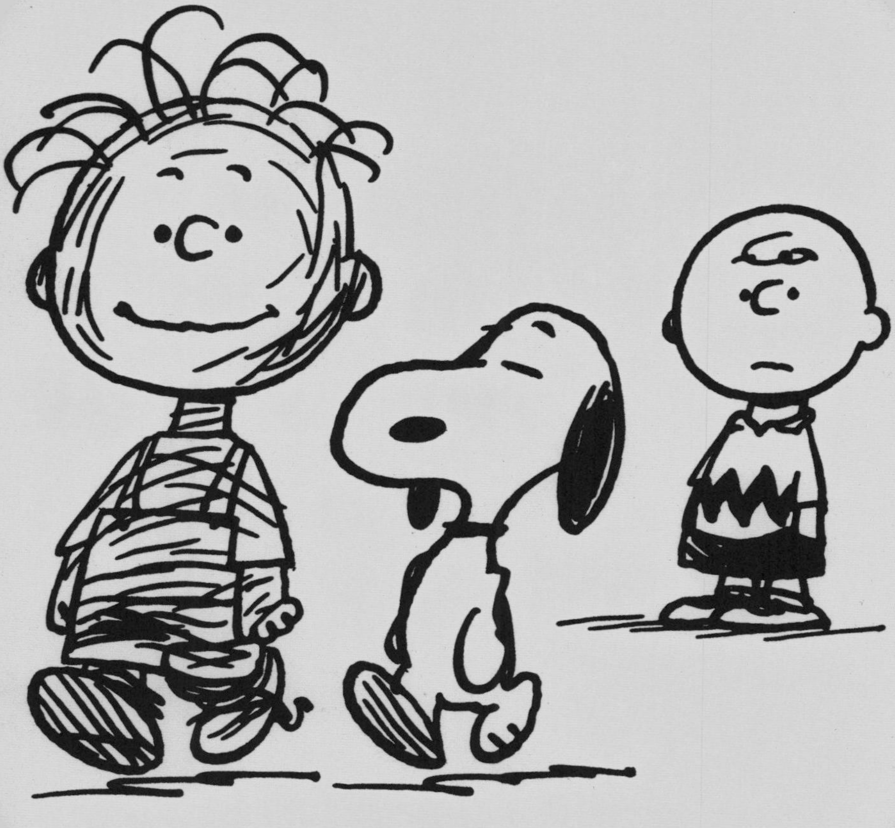

"A friend
is someone
you have things
in common with,
Charlie Brown."

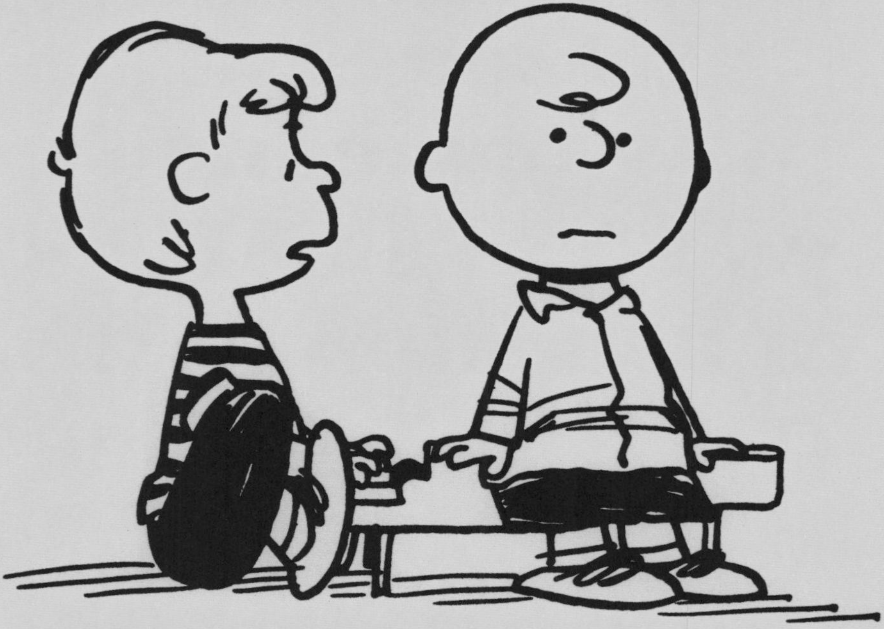

"A friend
is someone
who understands
why you like your
strawberry sodas
without any
strawberries
in them."

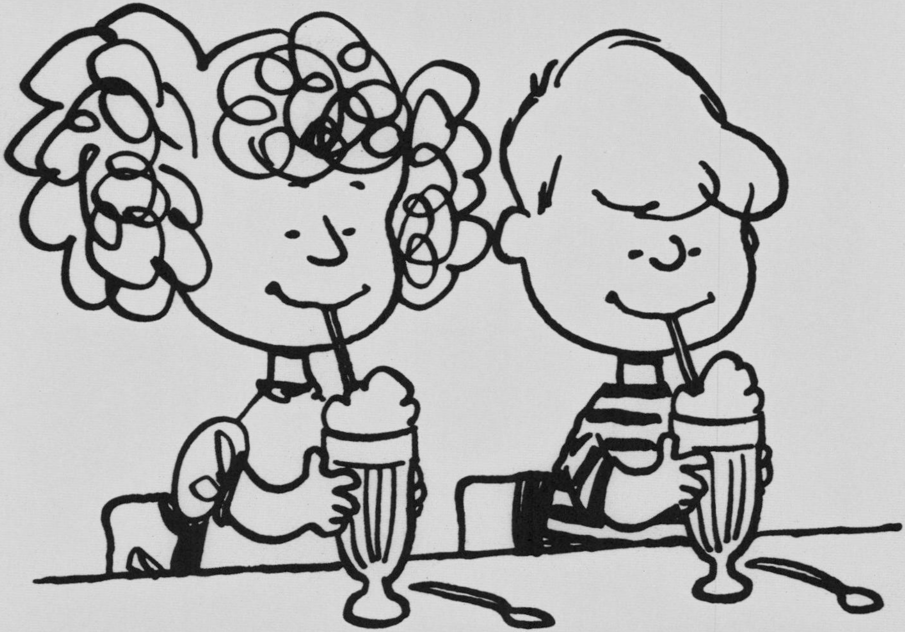

"A friend
is someone
who doesn't think
it's crazy to collect
old Henry Busse
records!"

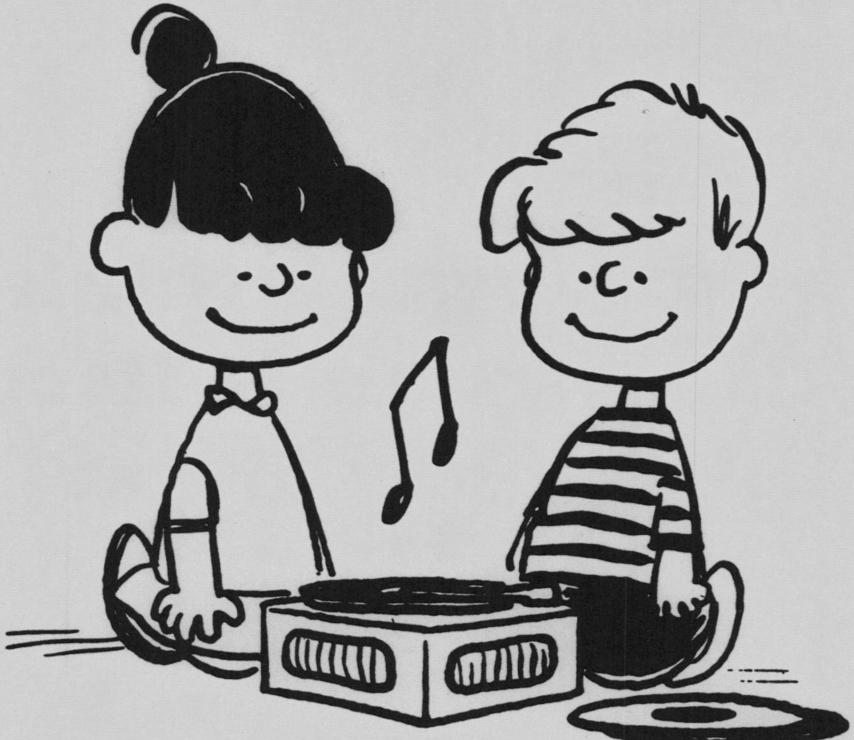

"A friend is someone who likes the same music you like."

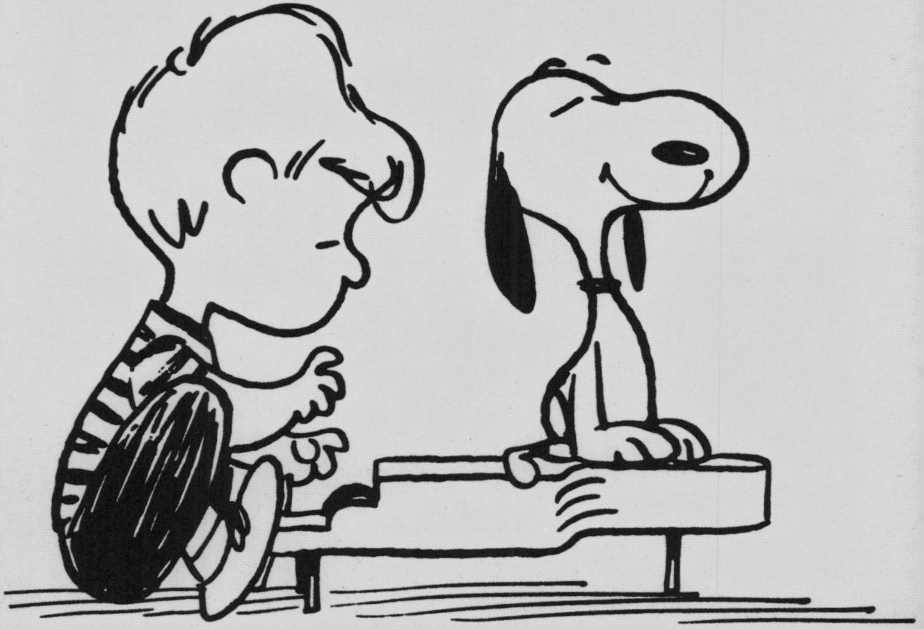

"A friend is someone who can't stand the same sort of music you can't stand!"

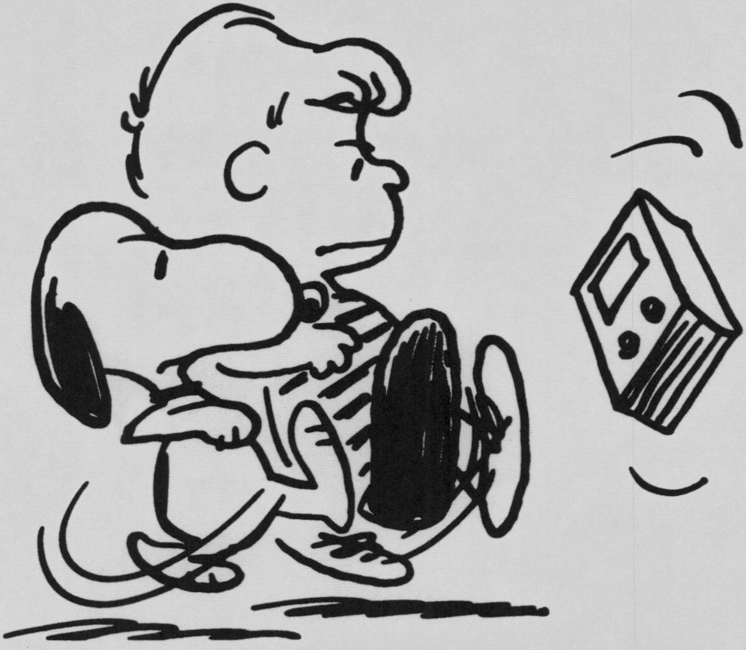

"A friend is someone who will hold a place in line for you."

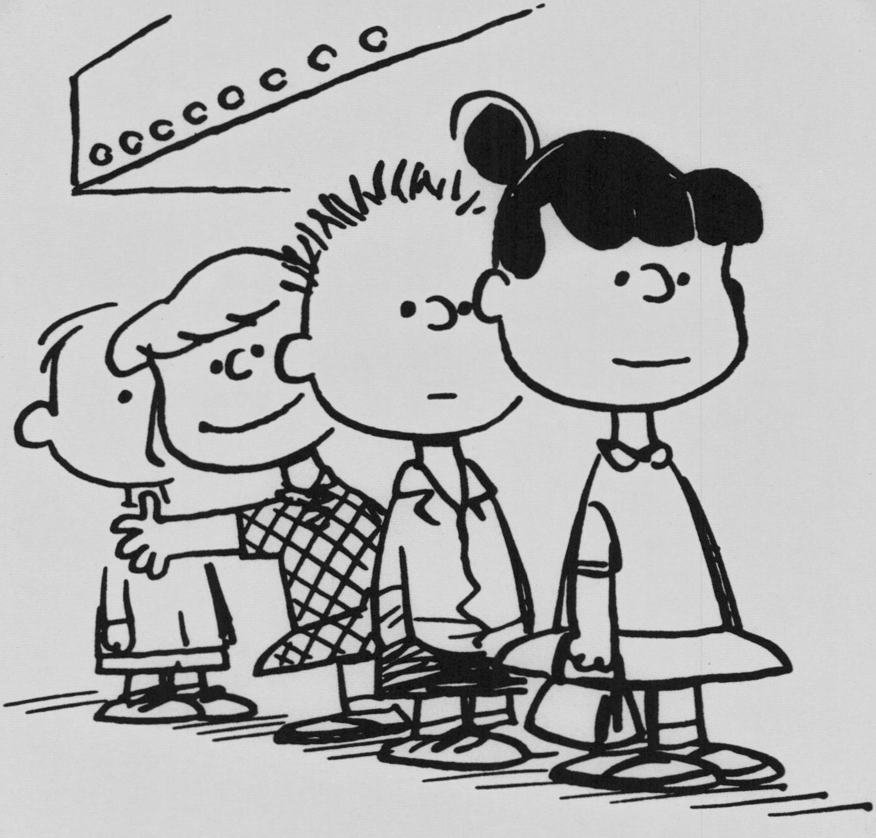

"A friend
is someone who
sticks up for you
when you're
not there."

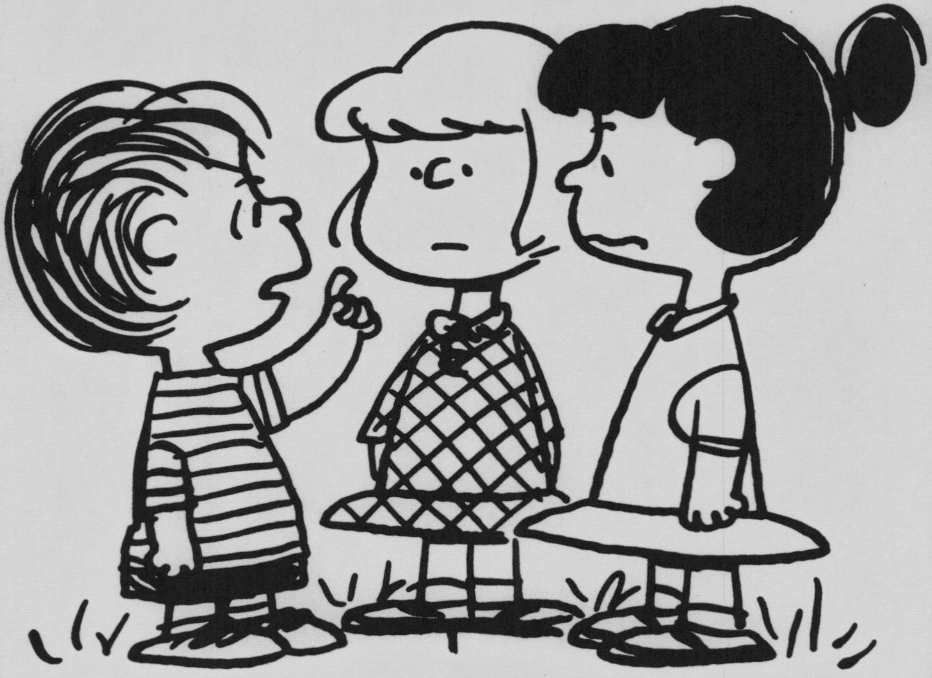

"A friend is someone who sends you a postcard when he's on vacation."

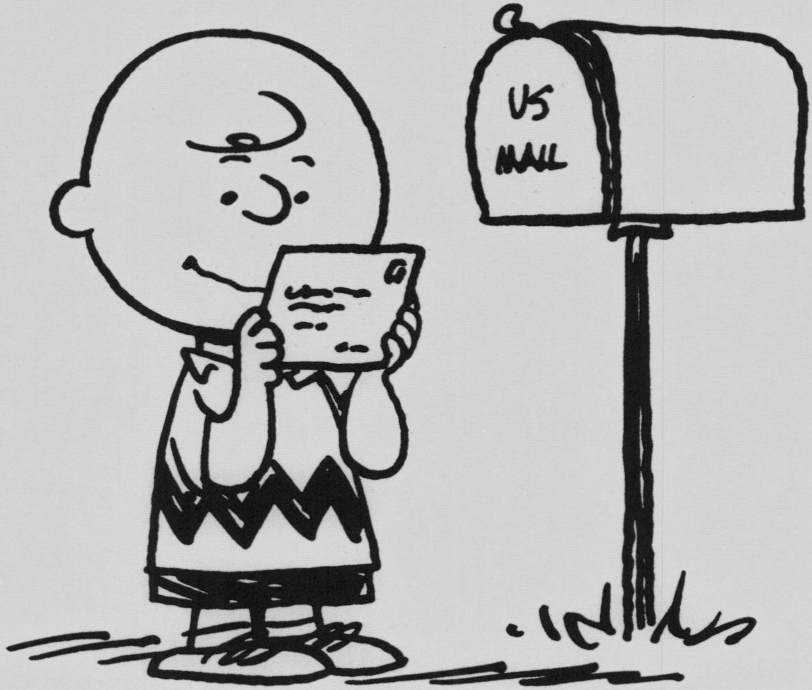
US
MAIL

"A friend is someone who doesn't criticize something you just bought."

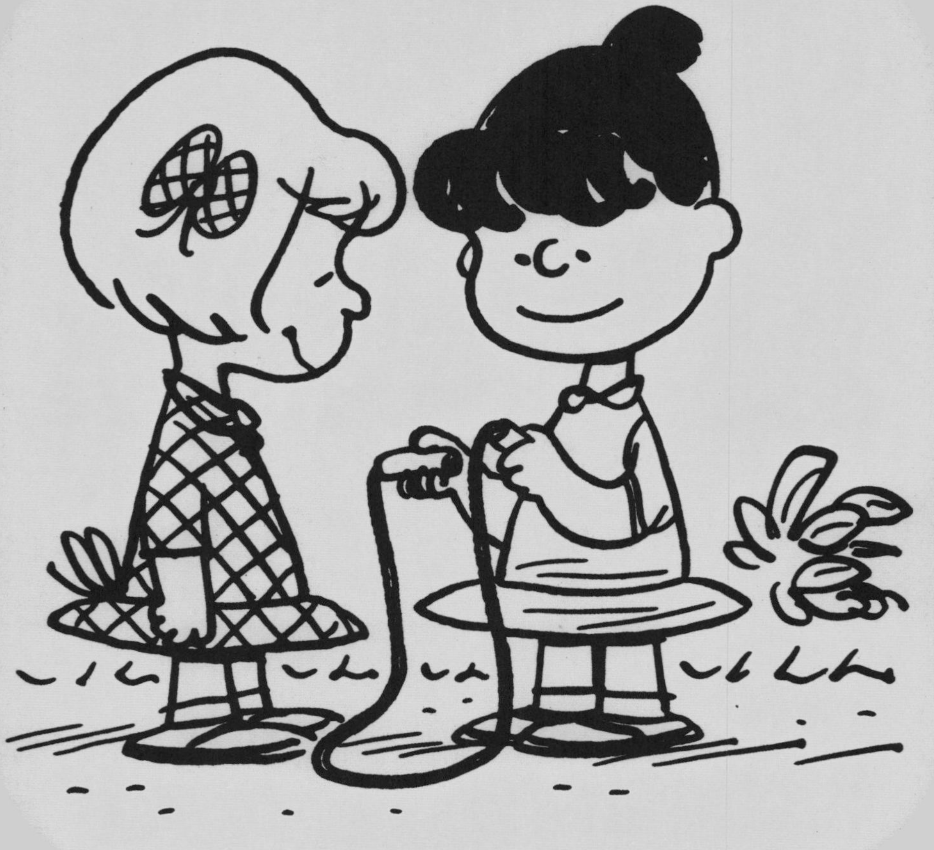

"A friend is someone who takes off the leash!"

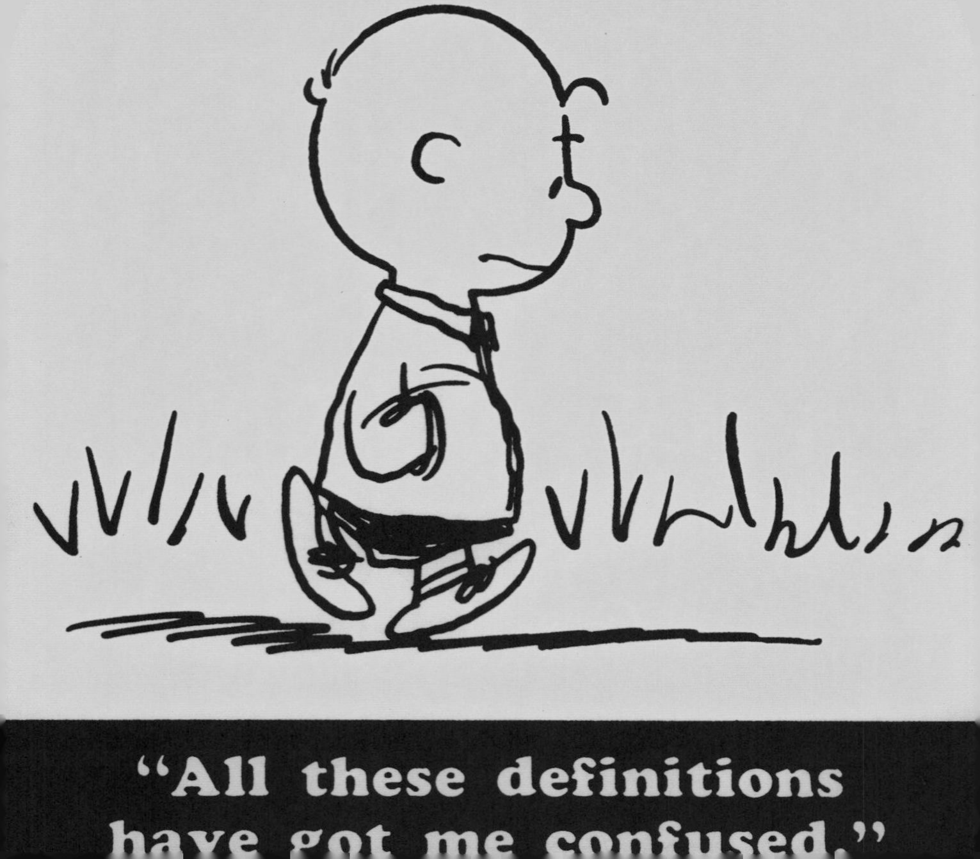

"All these definitions have got me confused."

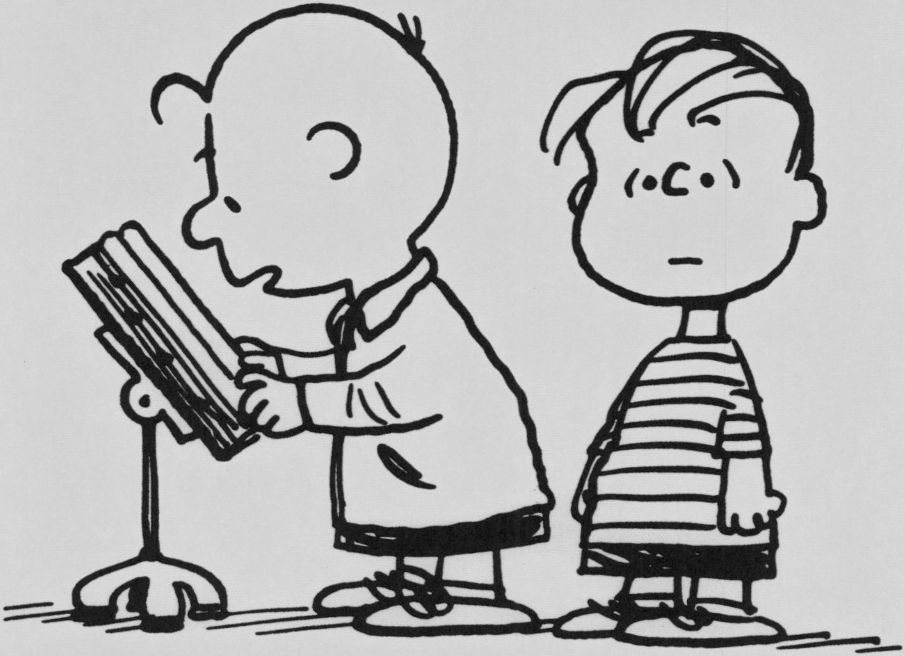

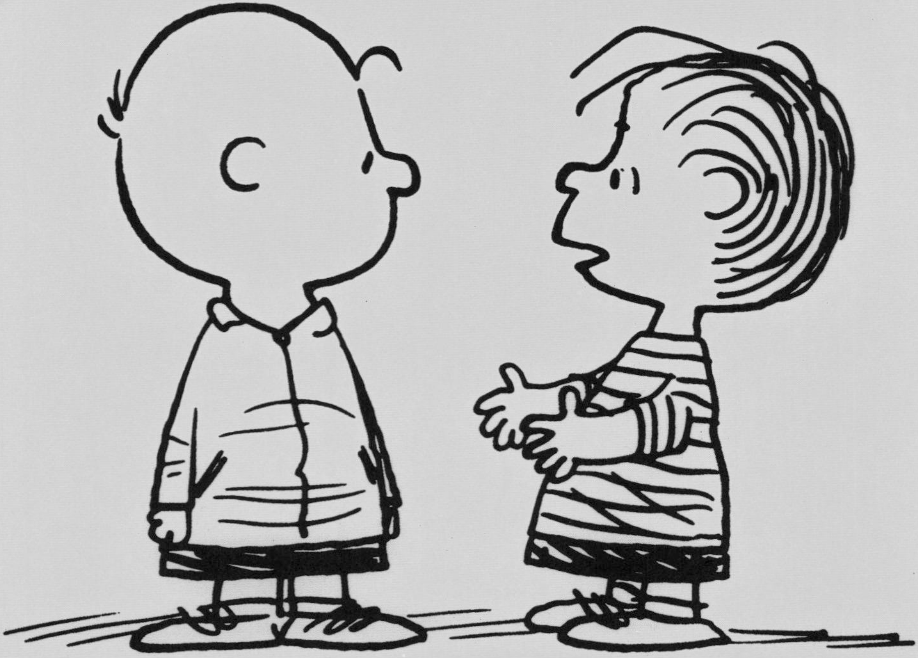

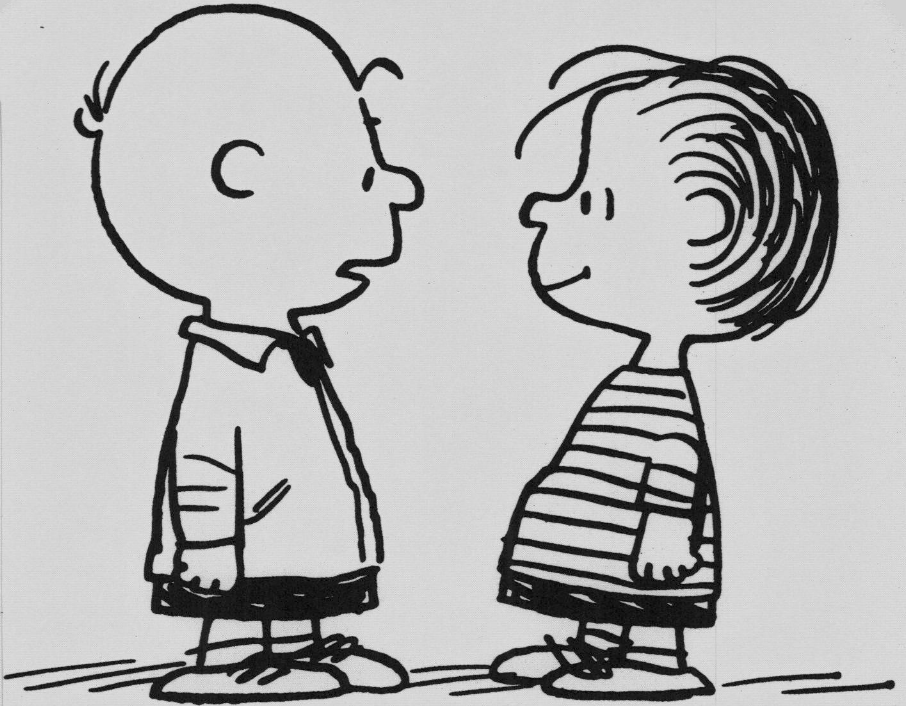

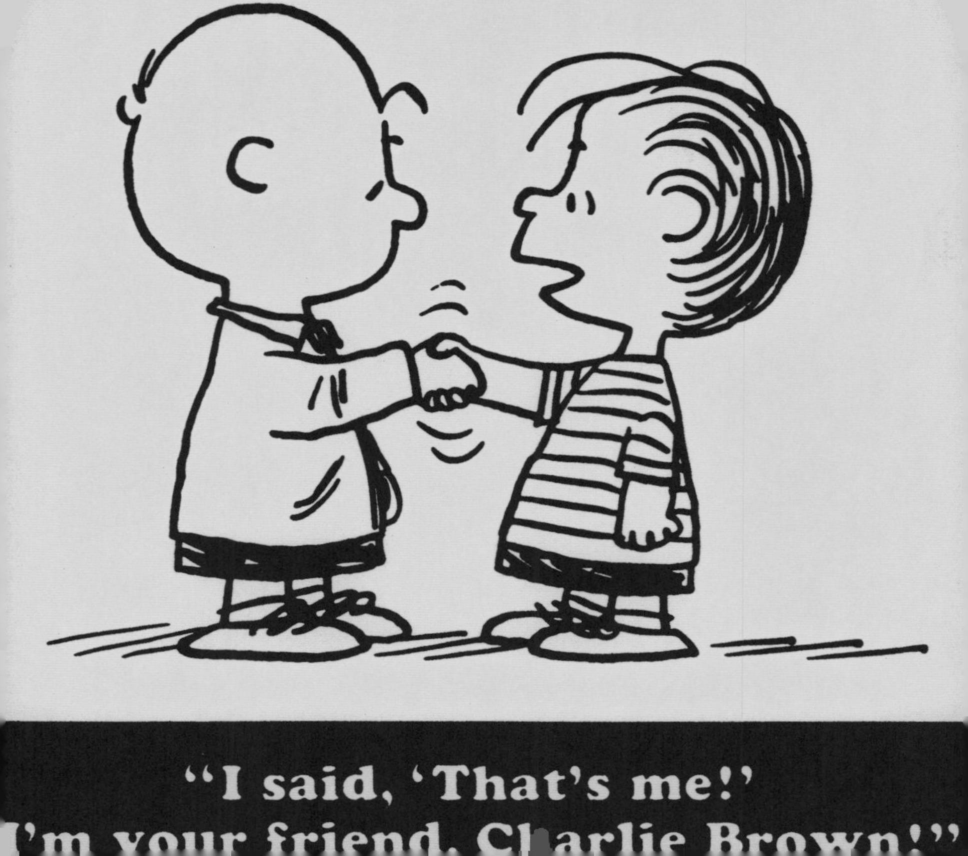

"I said, 'That's me!'
I'm your friend, Charlie Brown!"

"Well, what do you know?"

Love is
mussing up
someone's
hair

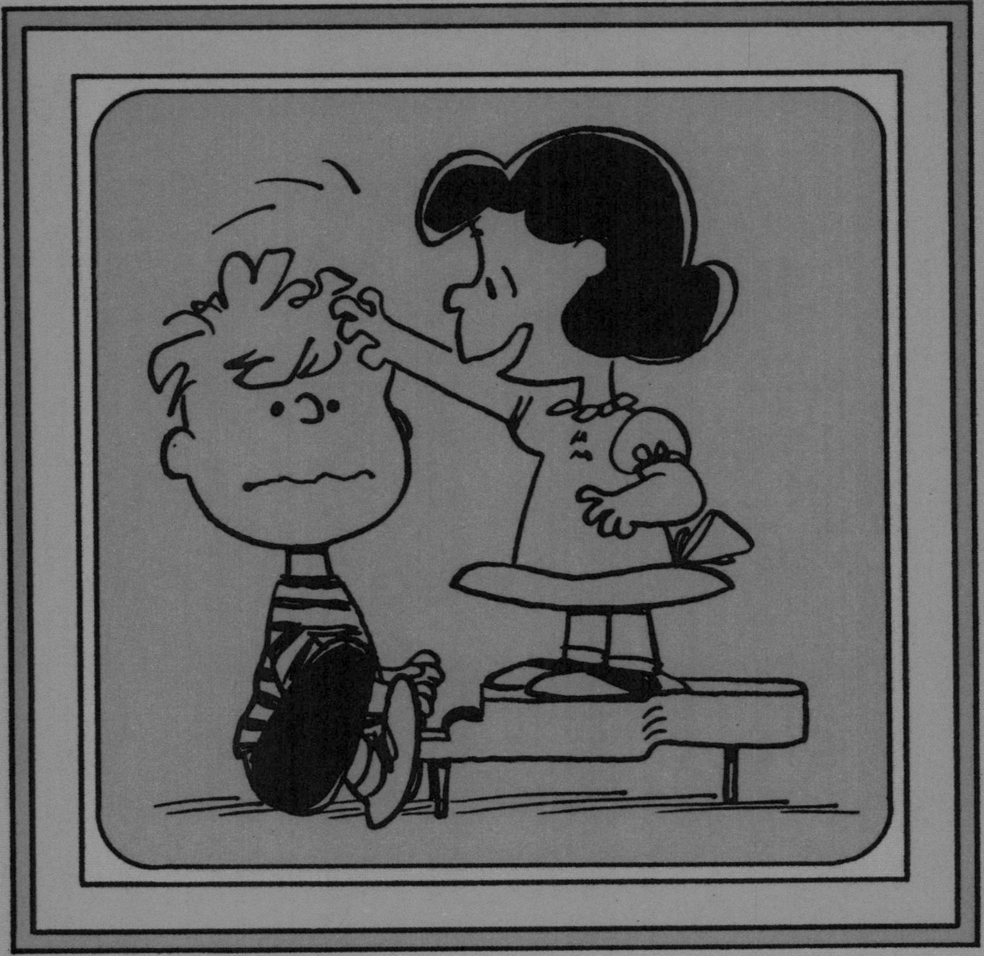

Love is
loaning your
best comic
magazines

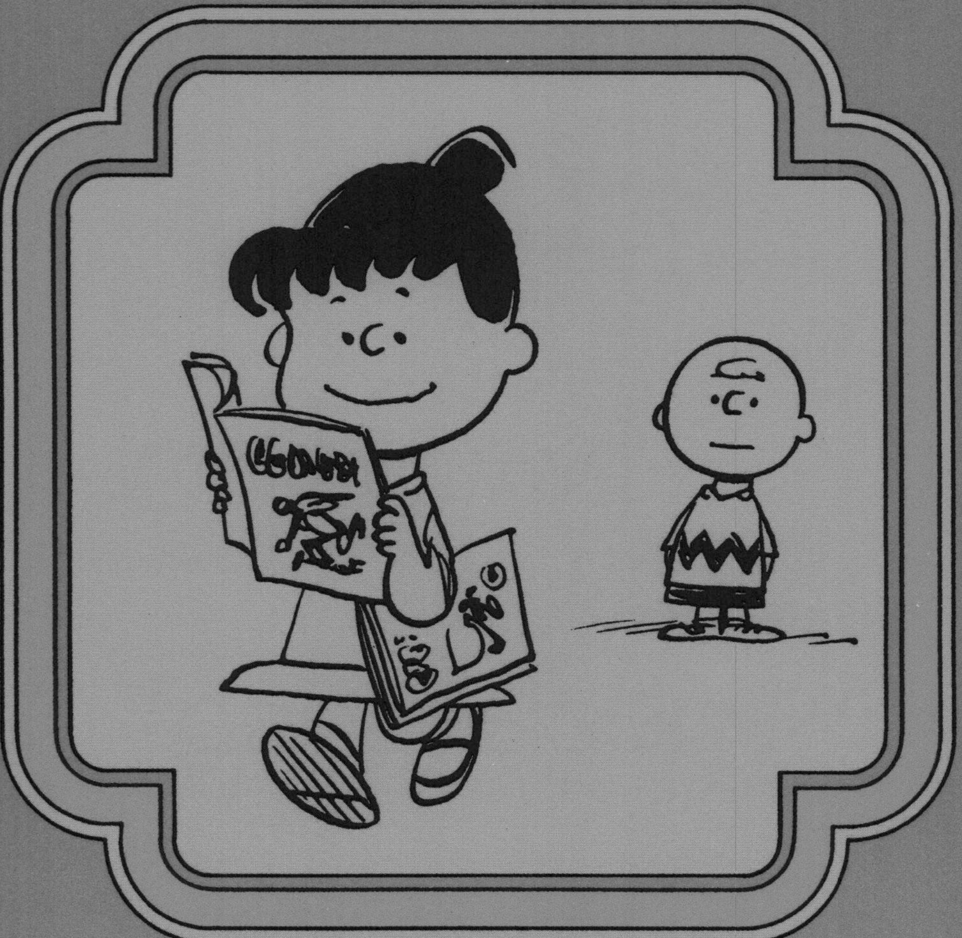

Love
is
having
a
special song

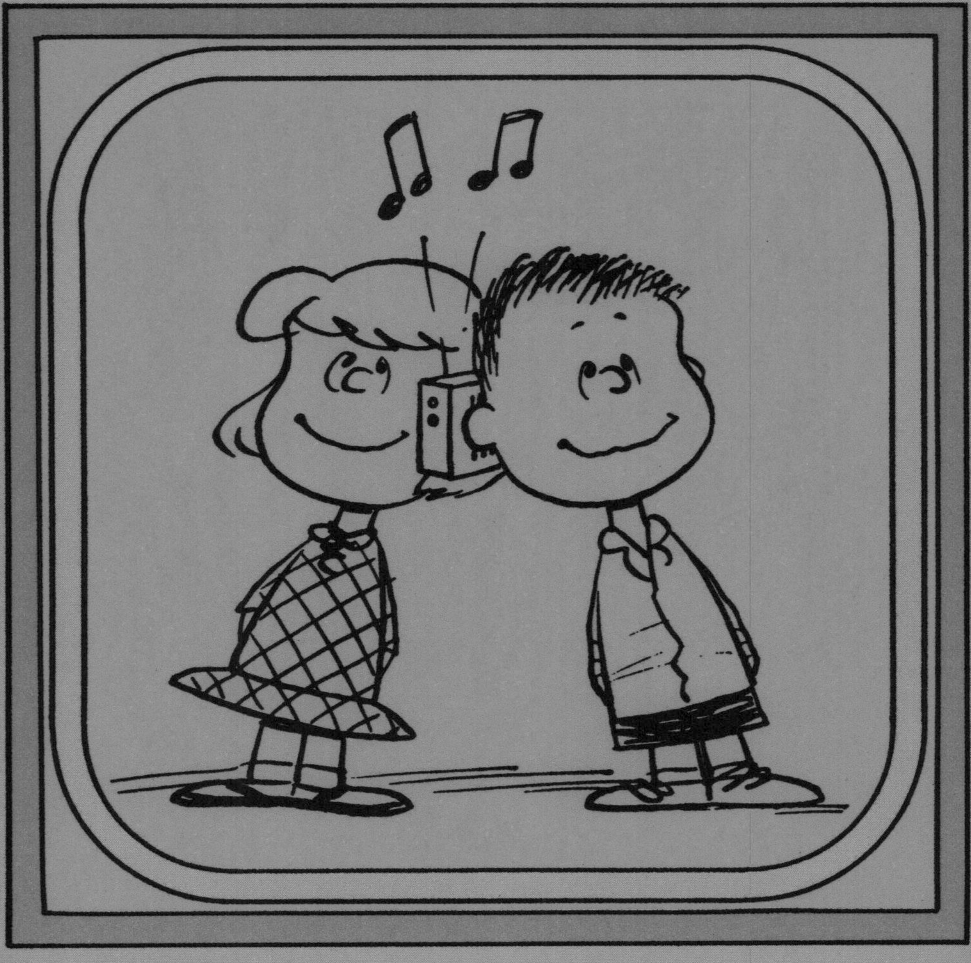

Love

is

tickling

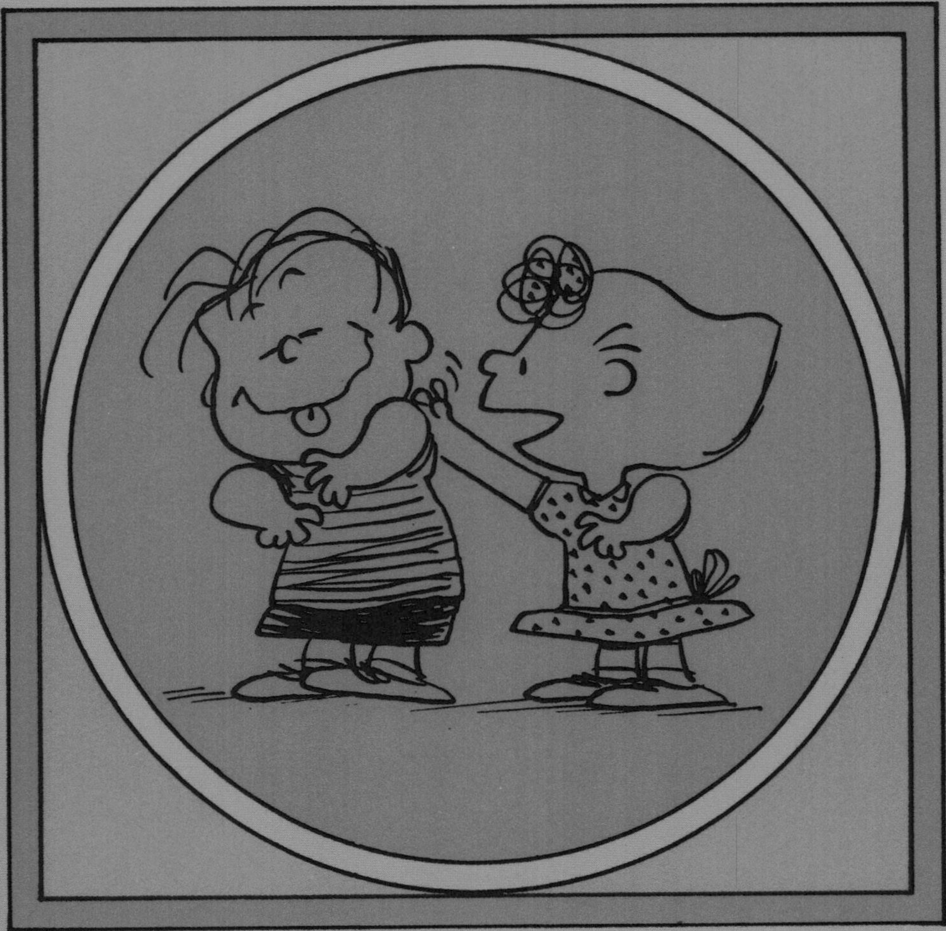

Love is
a valentine
with lace
all around
the edges

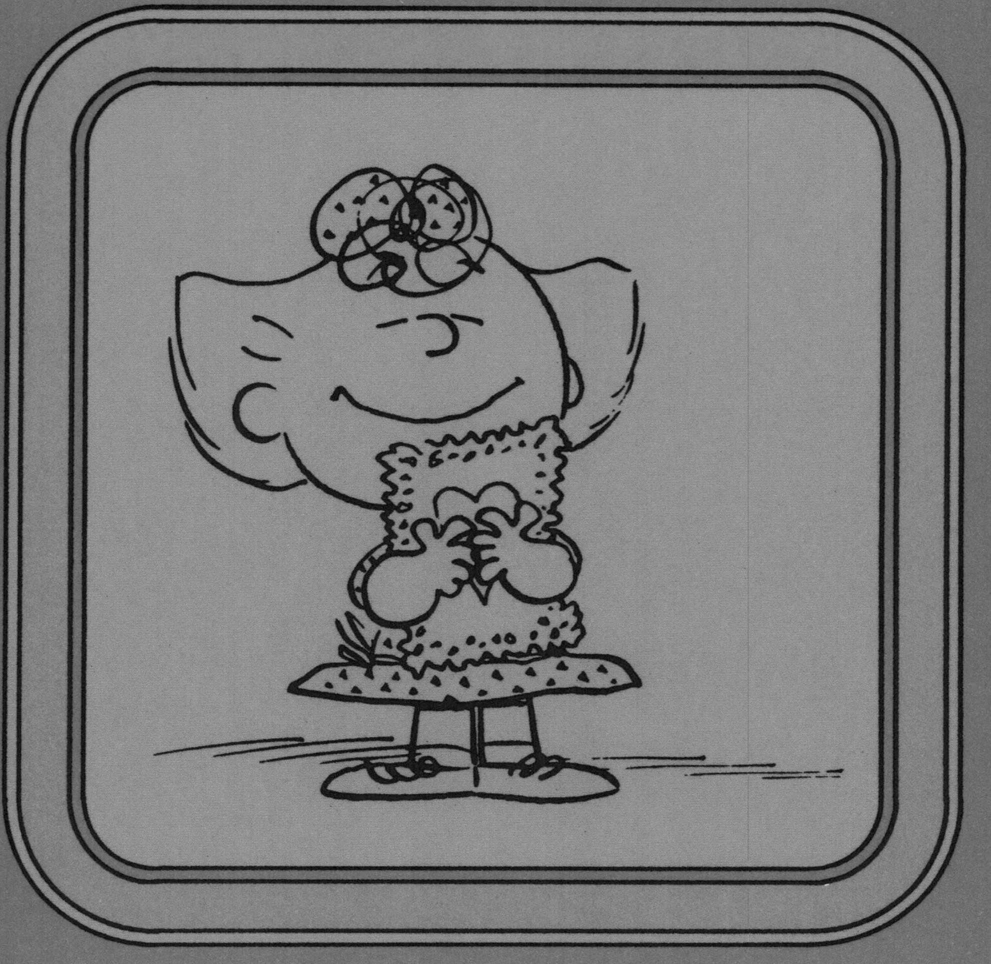

Love is
wishing you had
nerve enough to
go over and
talk with that little girl
with the red hair

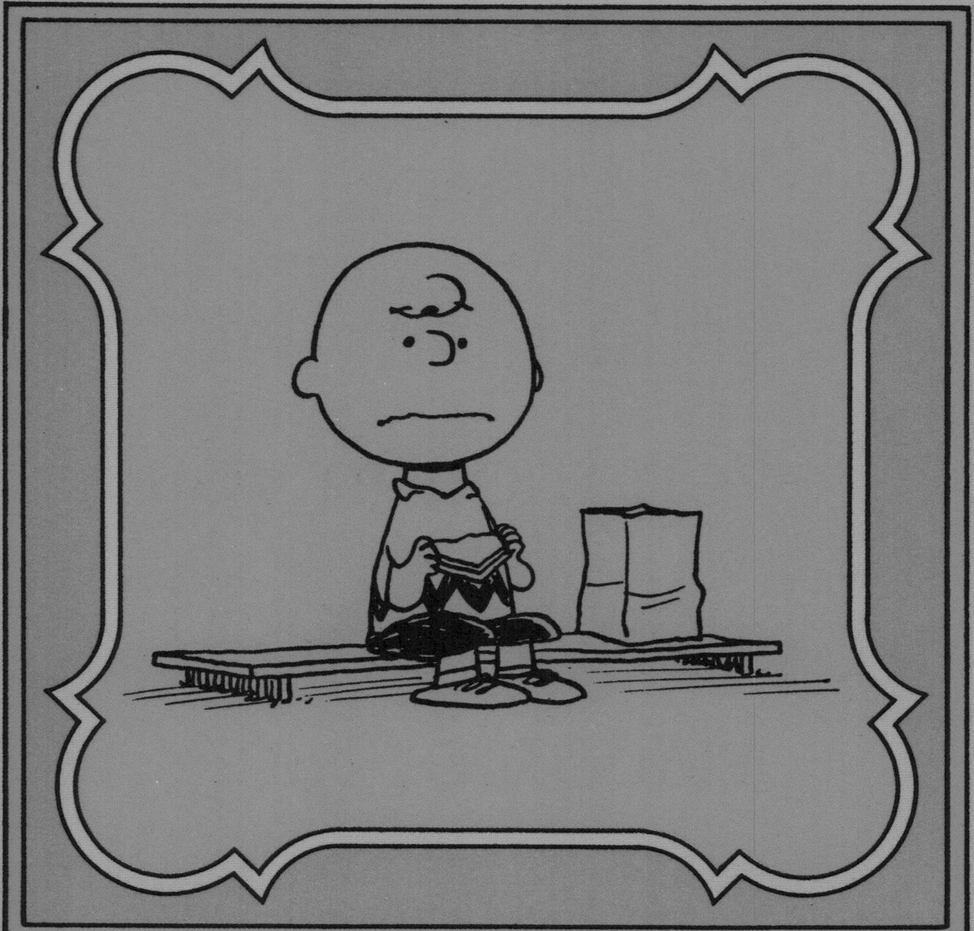

Love is
letting him win
even though you
know you could
slaughter him

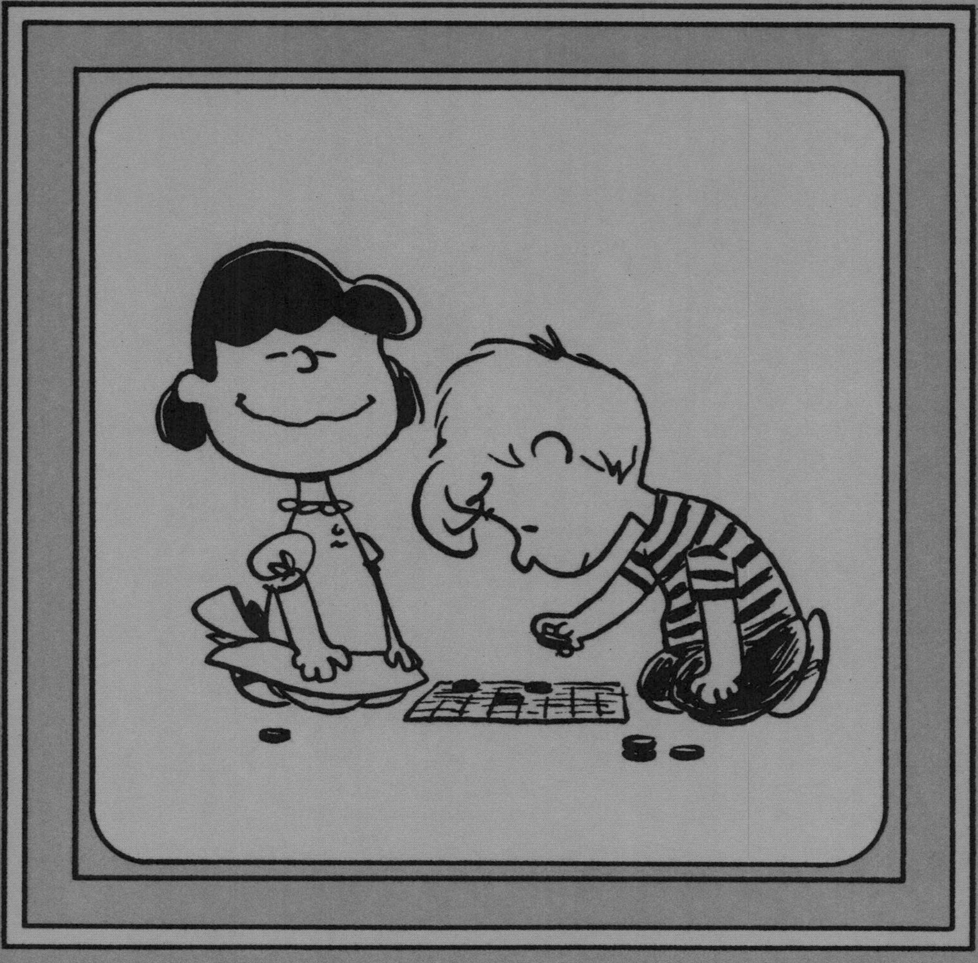

Love is
sharing
your
popcorn

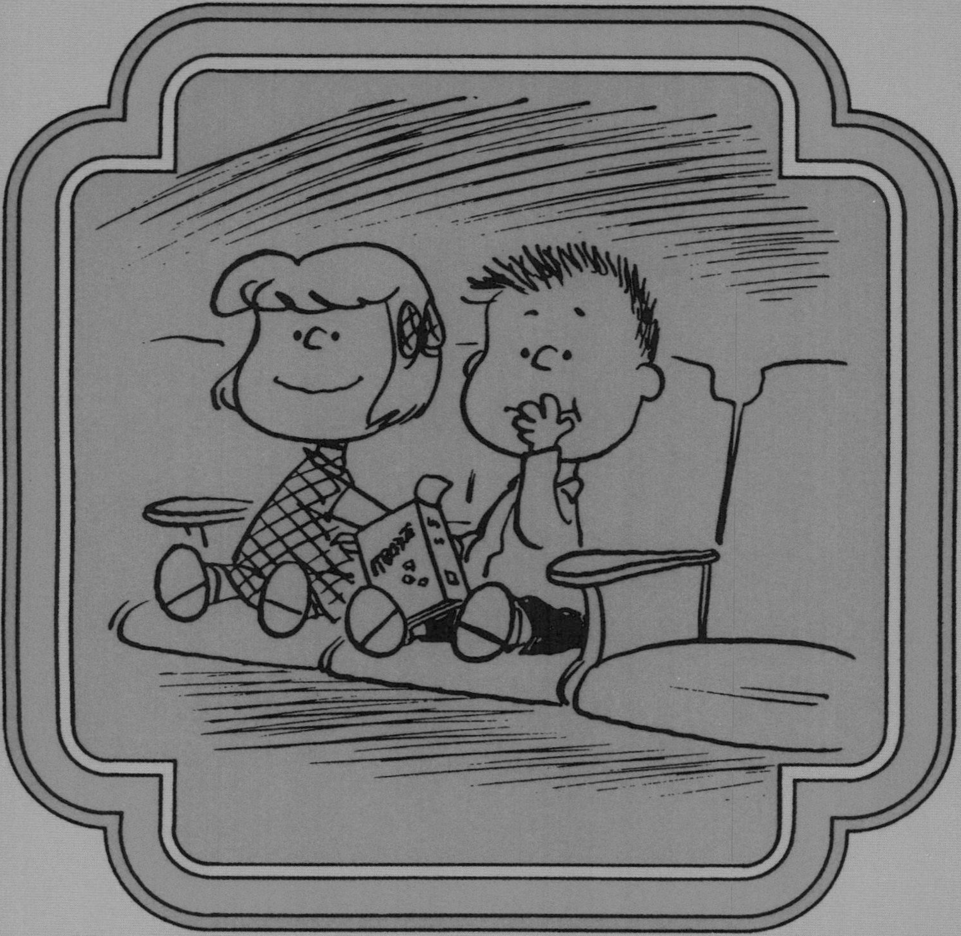

Love is
hating
to say
good-bye

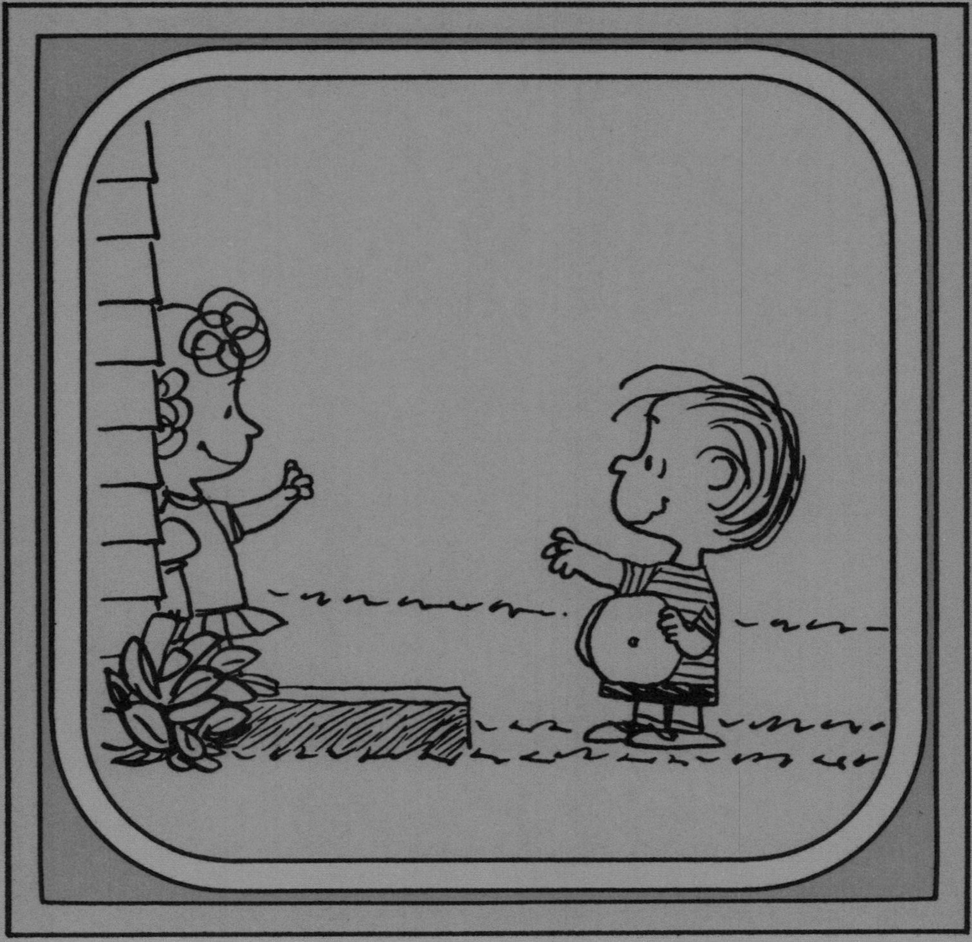

Love is walking hand-in-hand

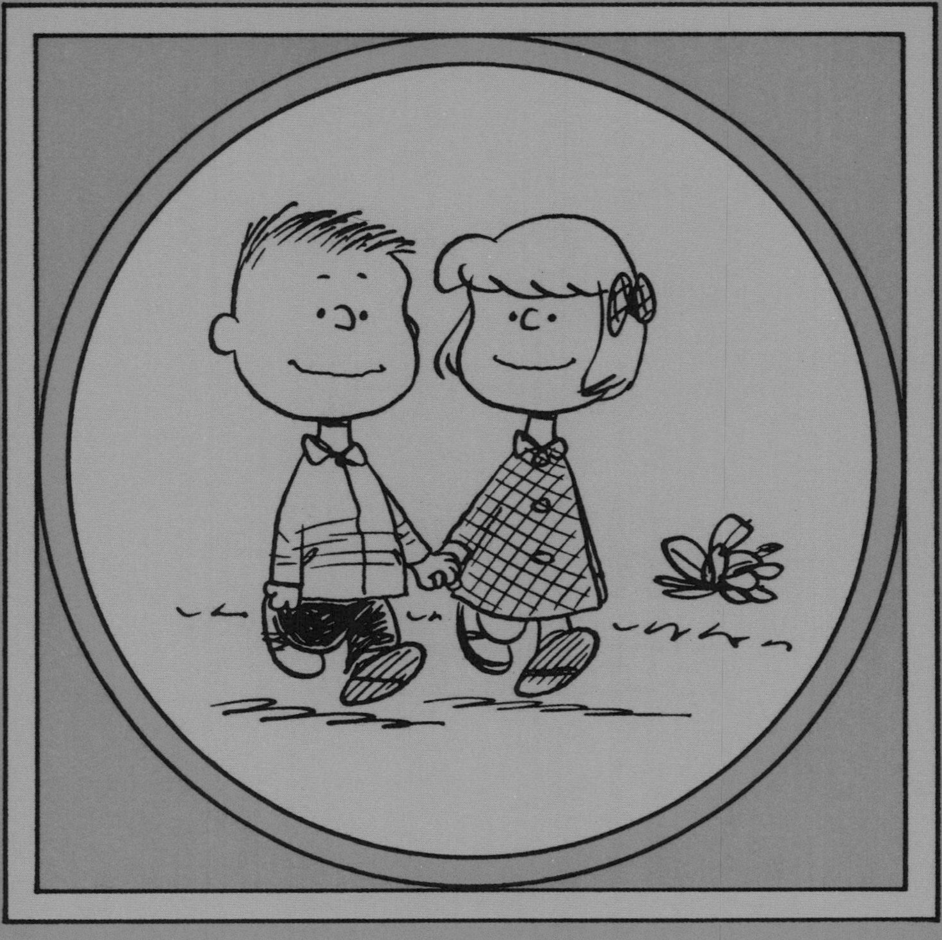

Love is
a letter
on pink
stationery

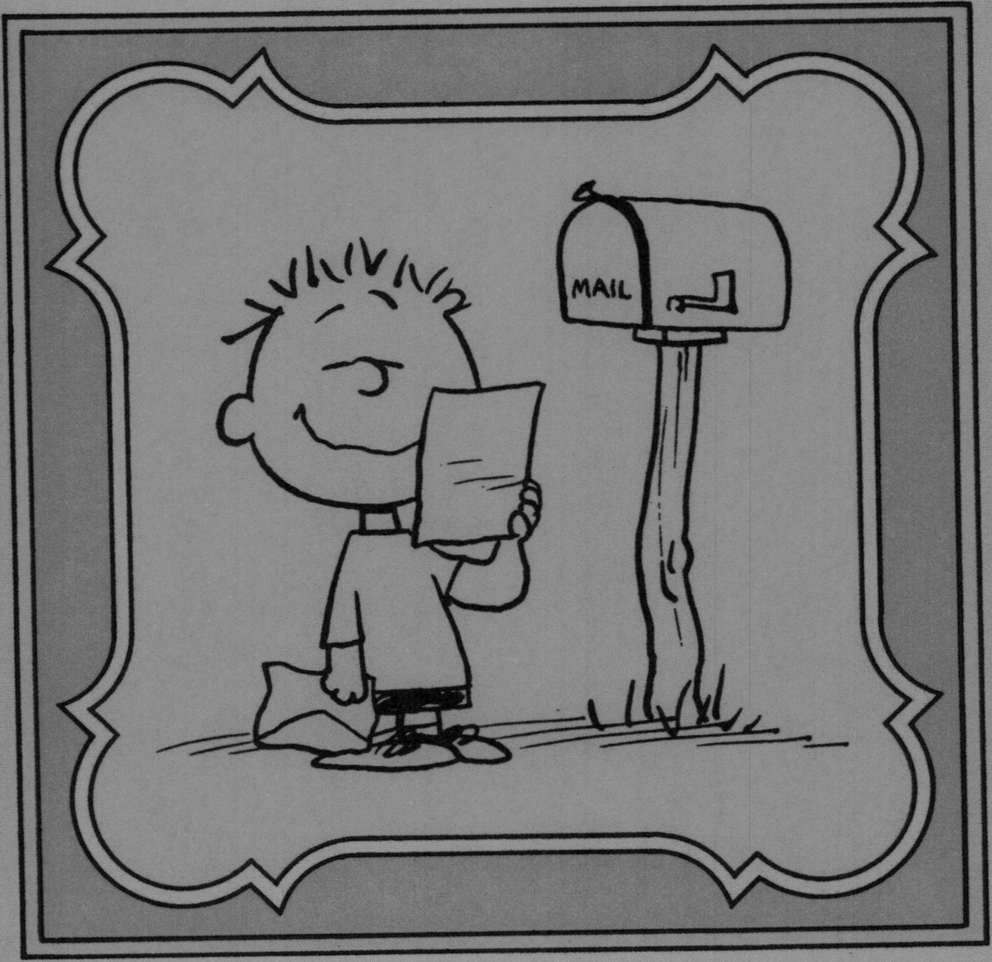
MAIL

Love is
getting someone
a glass of water
in the middle
of the night

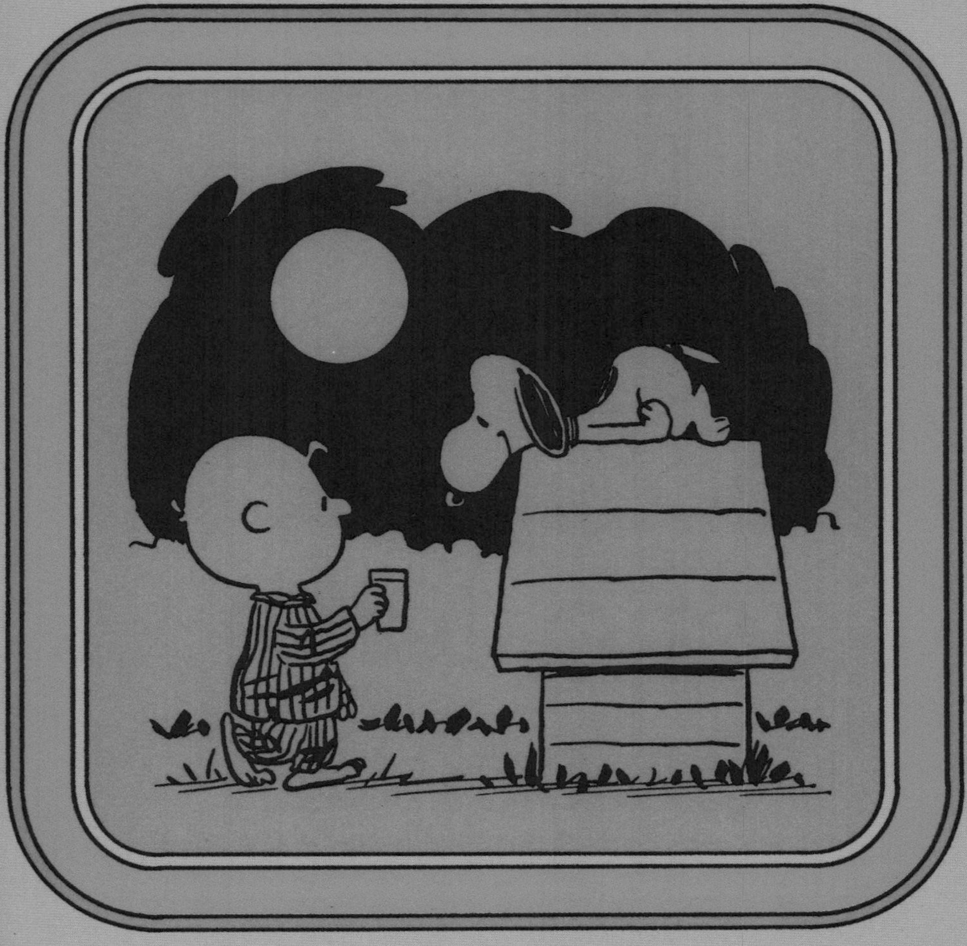

Love is
passing
notes back
and forth
in school

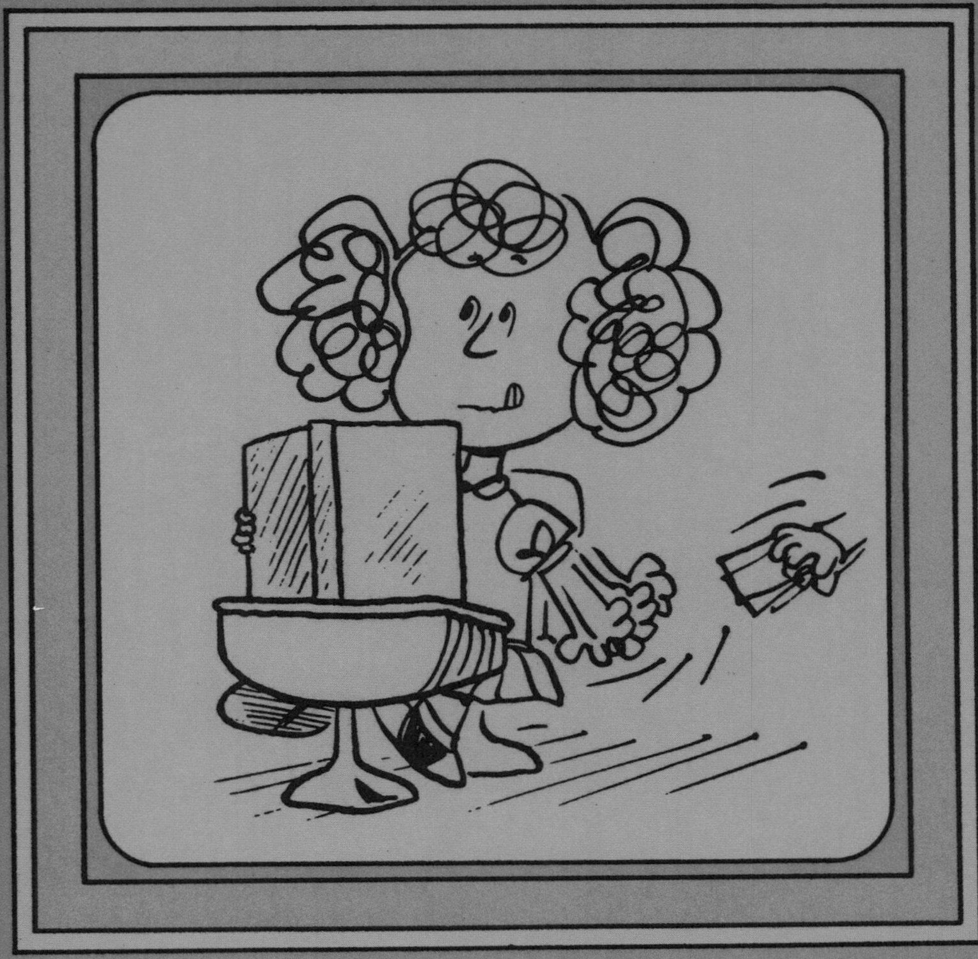

Love is
standing in
a doorway just
to see her
if she comes
walking by

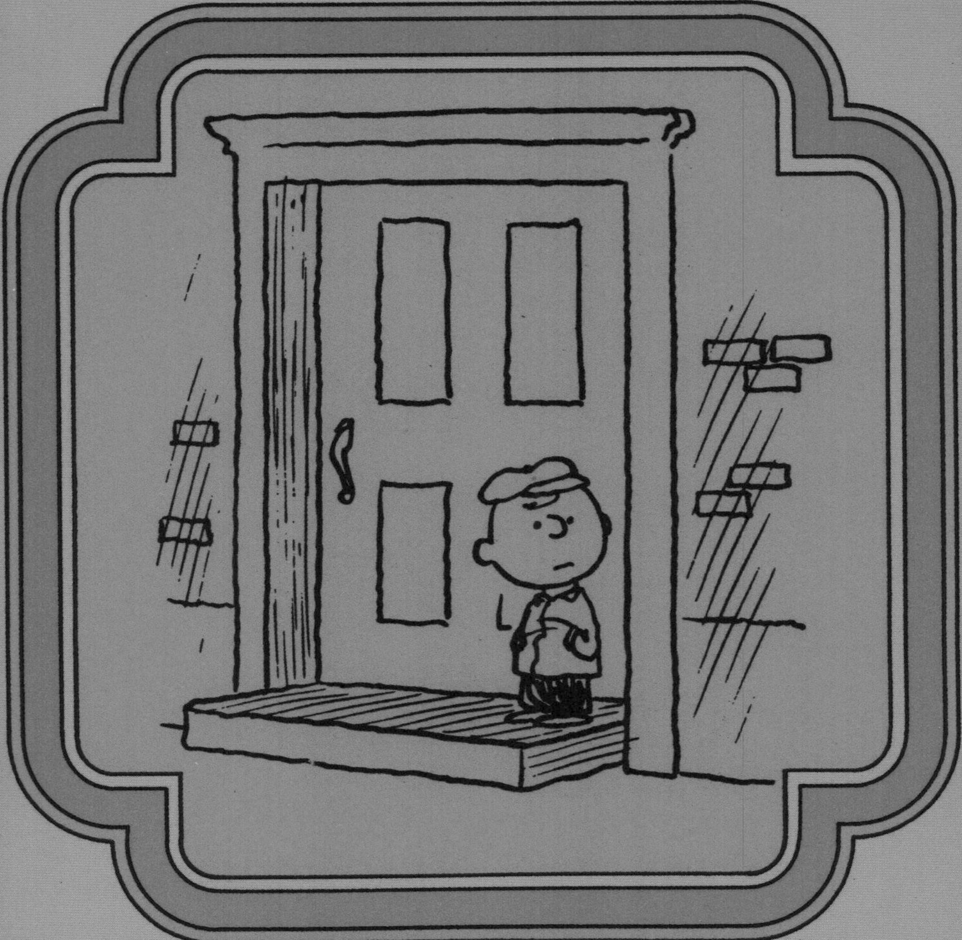

Love is
making
fudge
together

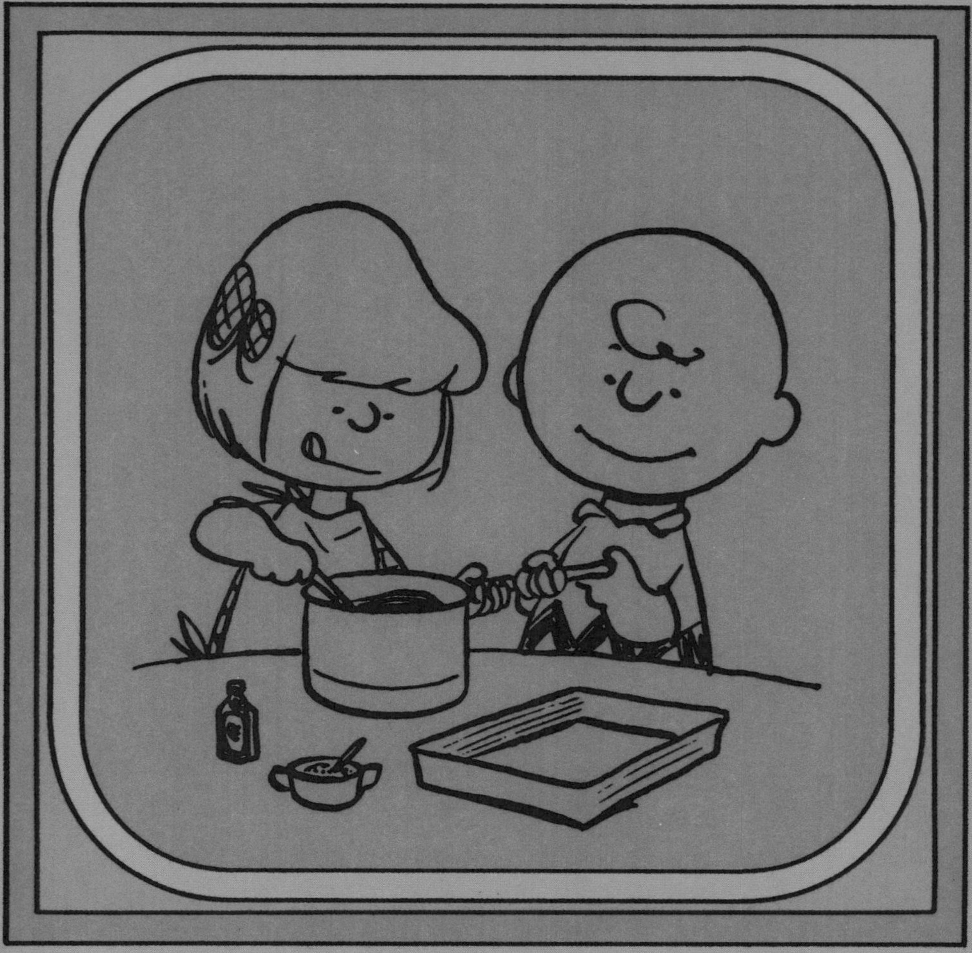

Love is
wondering
what he's doing
right now this
very moment

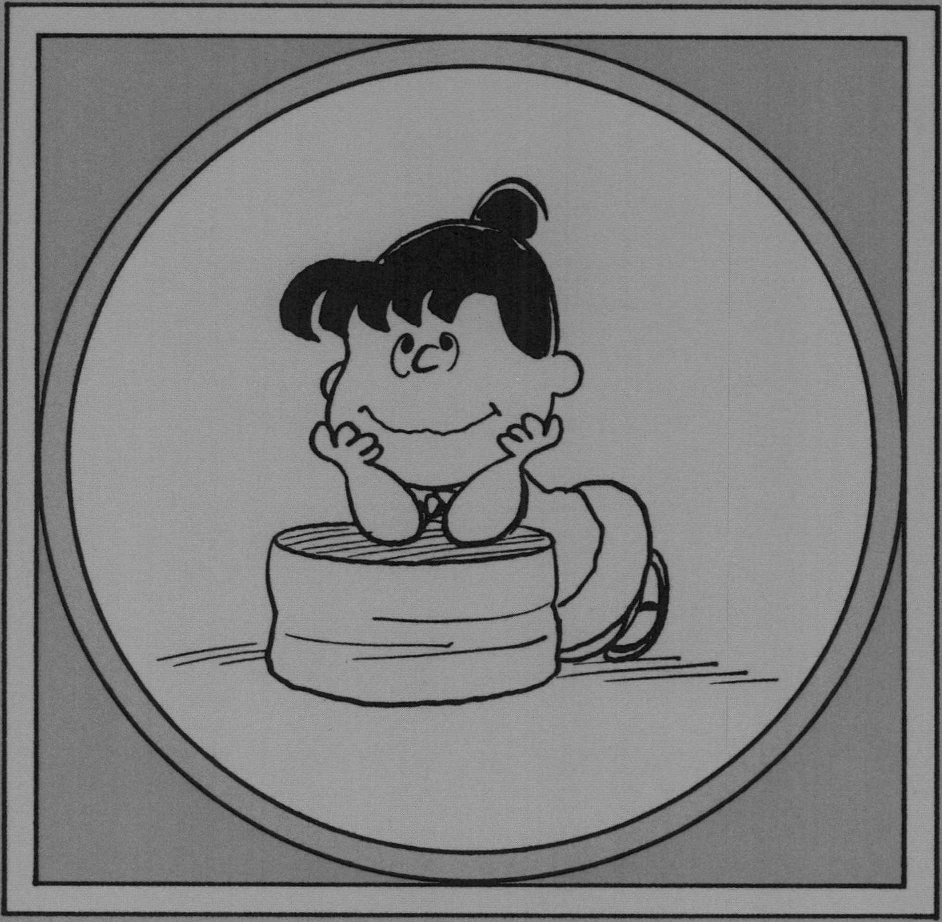

Love is
buying
somebody
a present
with your
own money

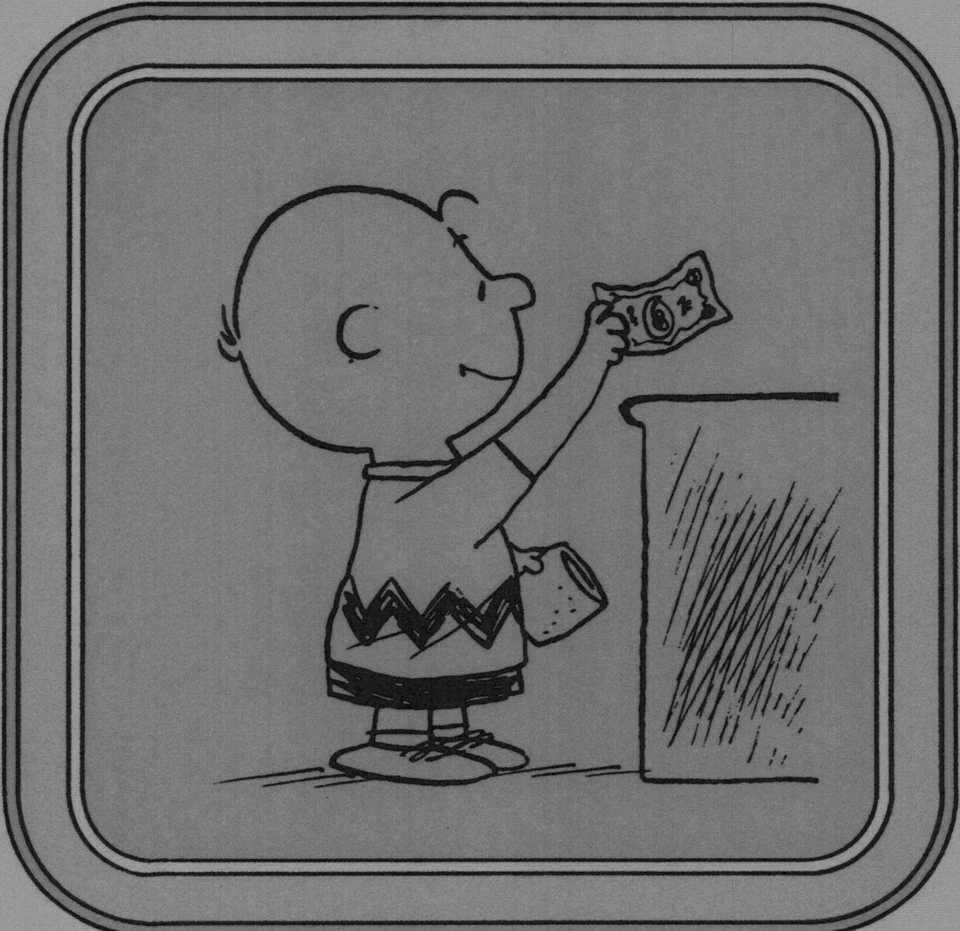

Love is
not
nagging

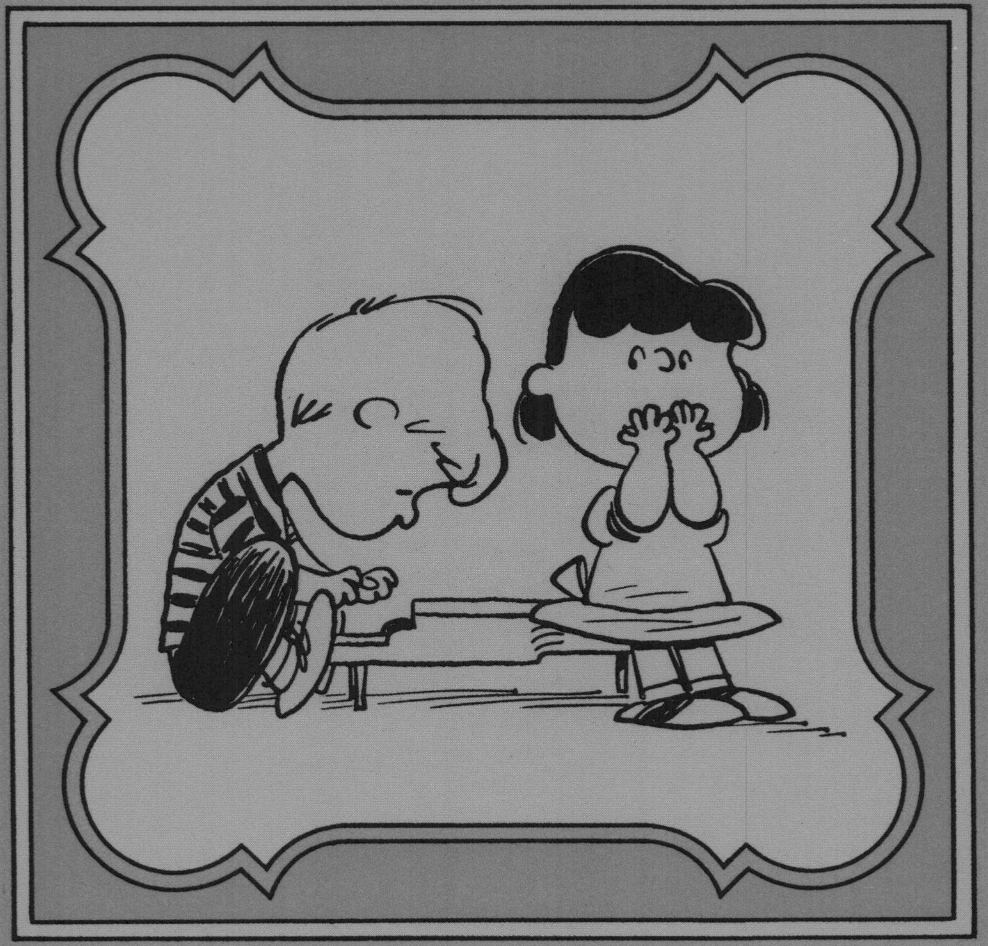

Love is
visiting
a sick
friend

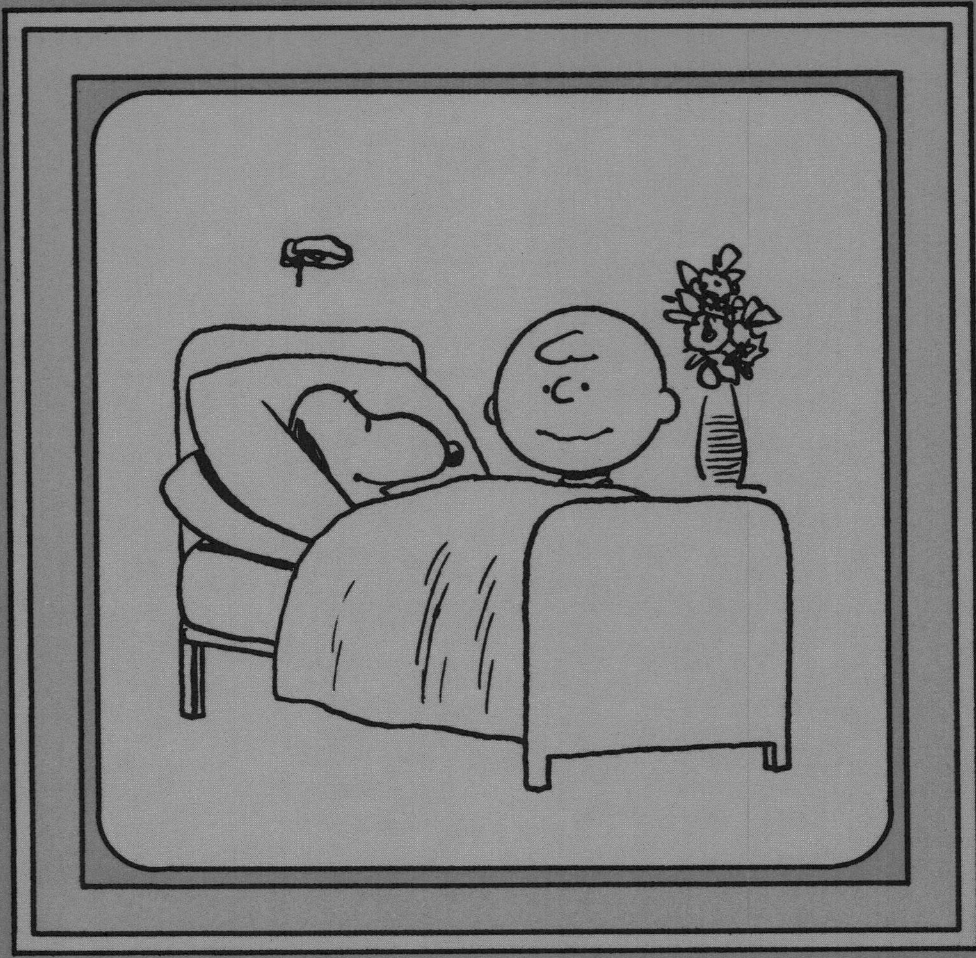

Love is
a
phone
call

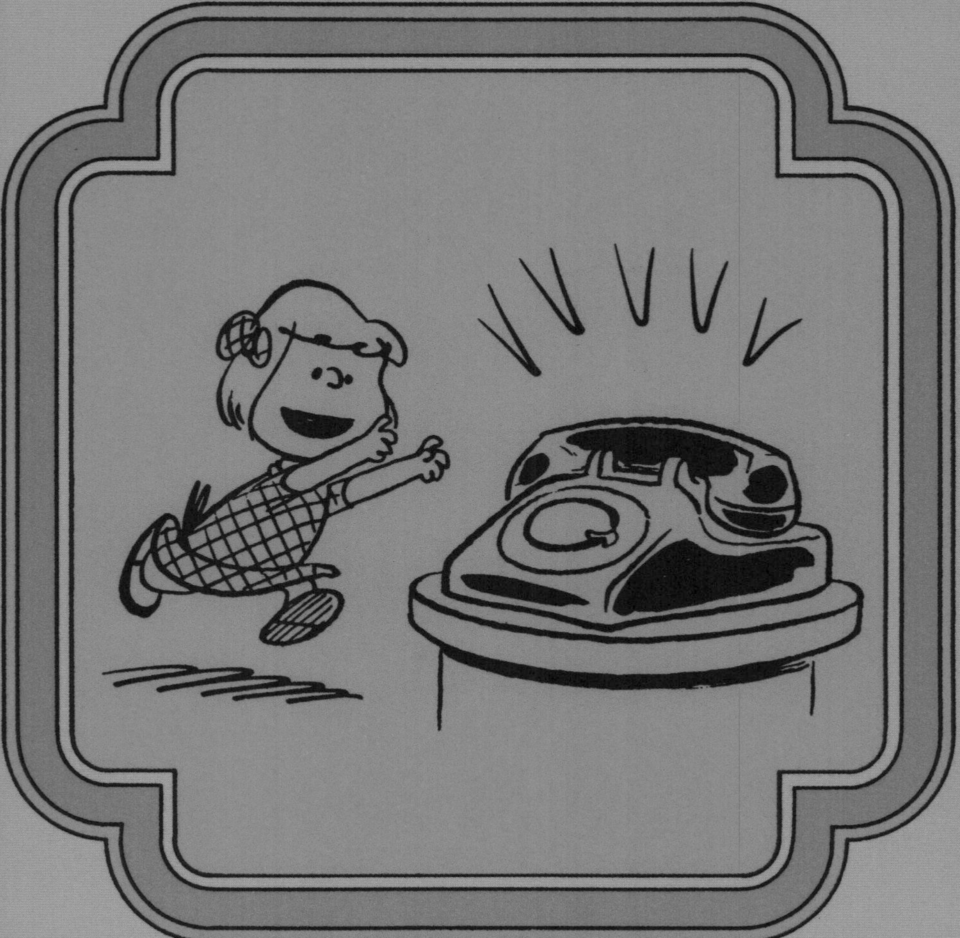

Love is
walking
in the rain
together

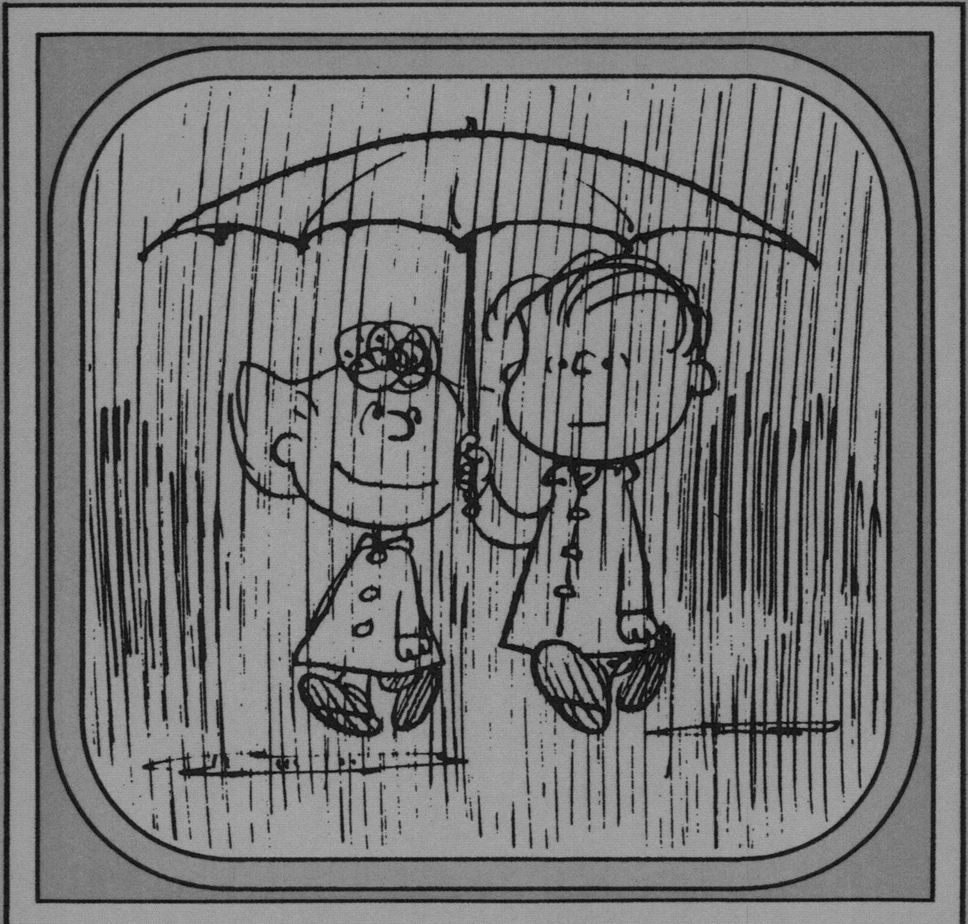

Love is
eating out
with your
whole family

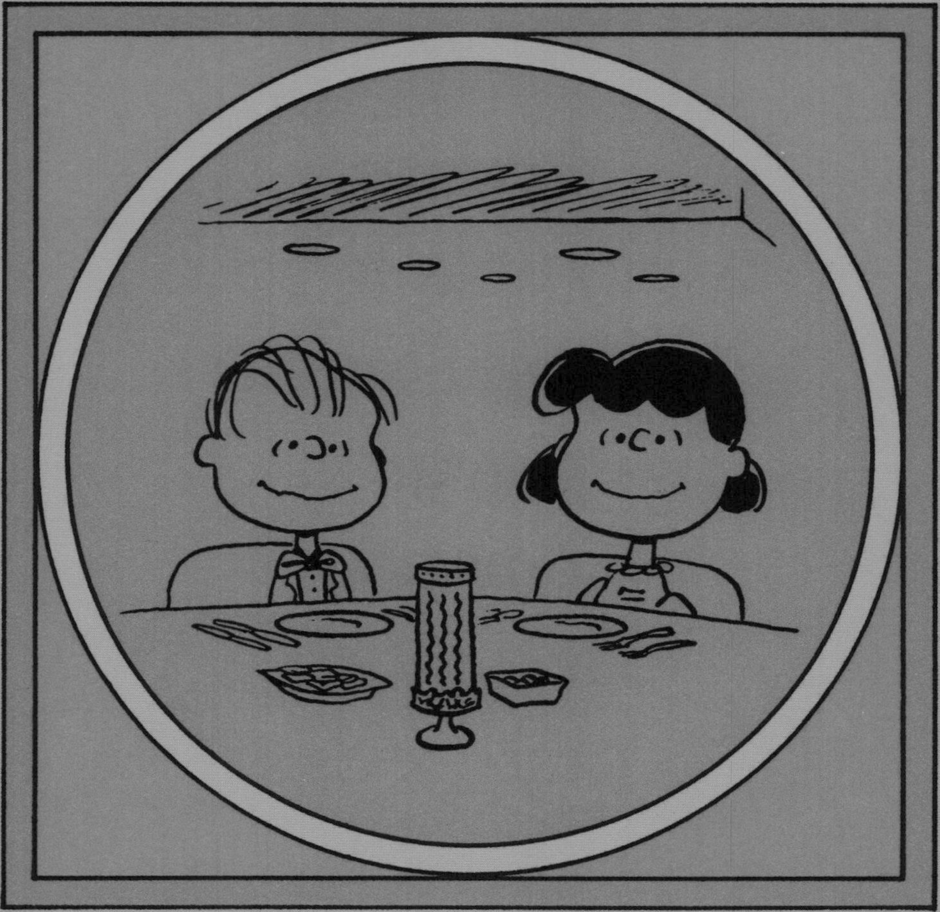

Love is
being able to spot
her clear across
the playground
among
four hundred
other kids

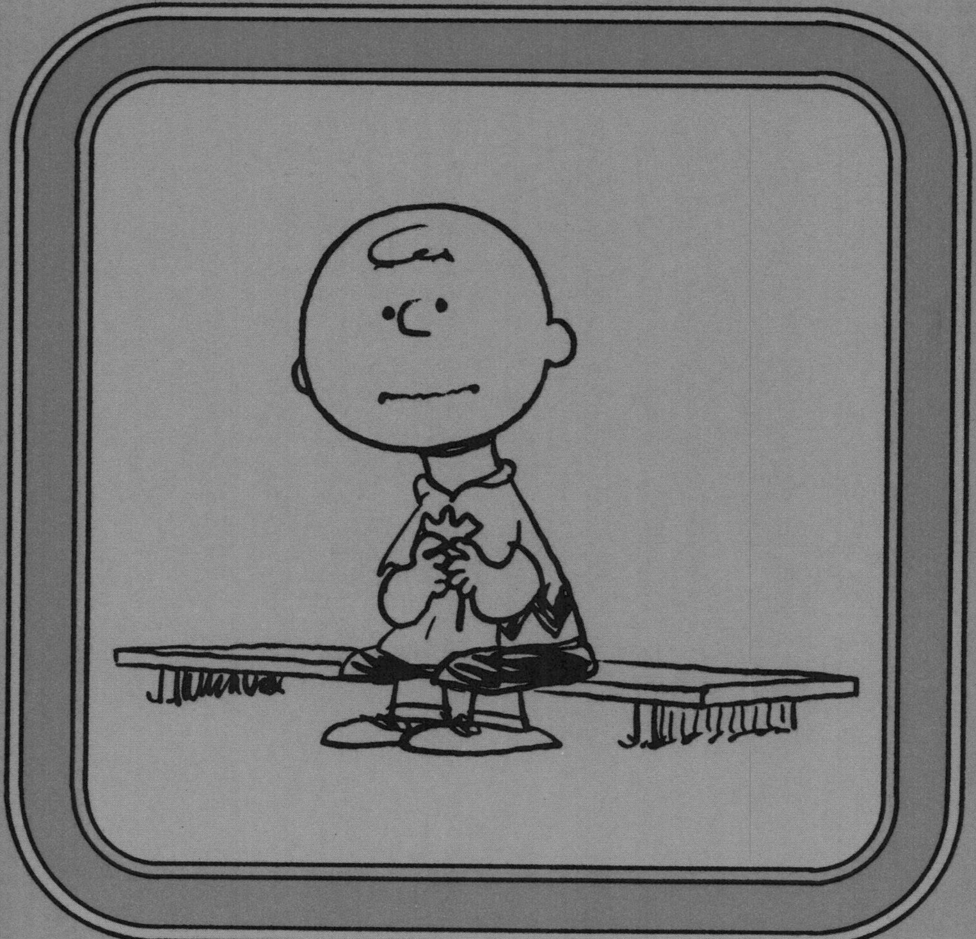

Love is
committing
yourself
in writing

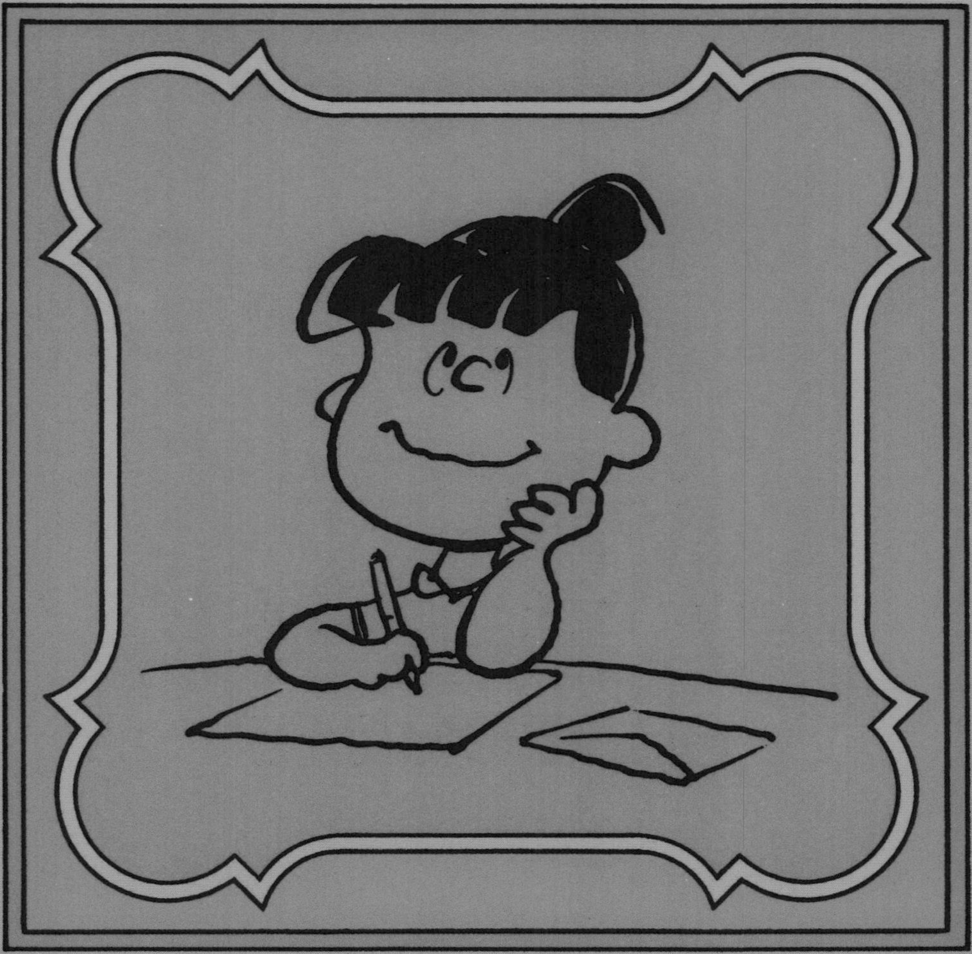

Love is
meeting
someone
by the pencil
sharpener

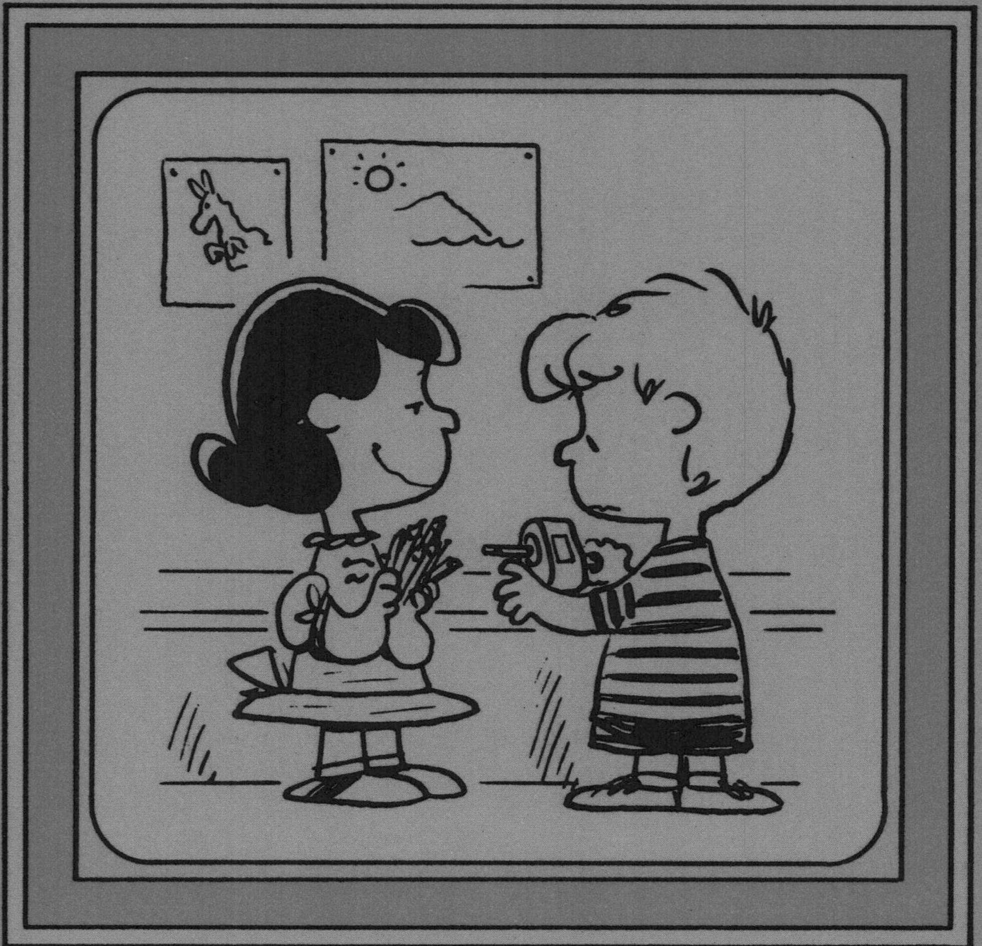

Love is
being happy
just knowing
that she's
happy...but
that isn't so easy

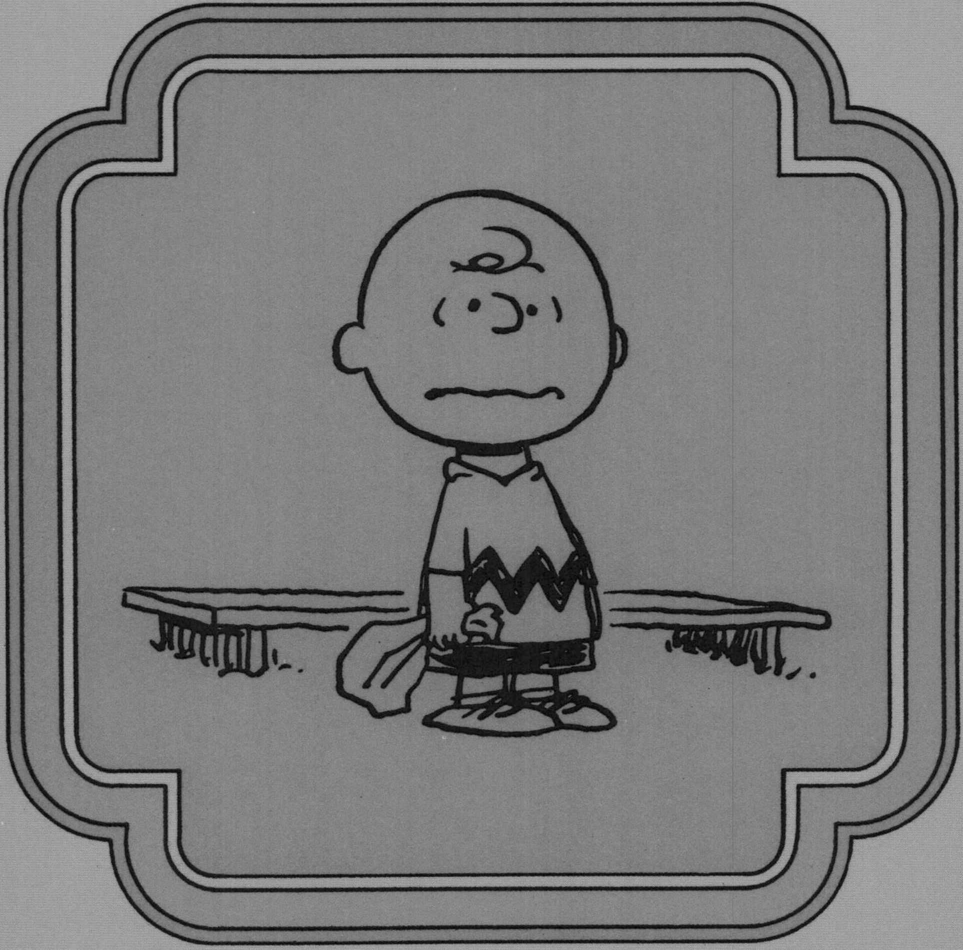

Love

is a

flag

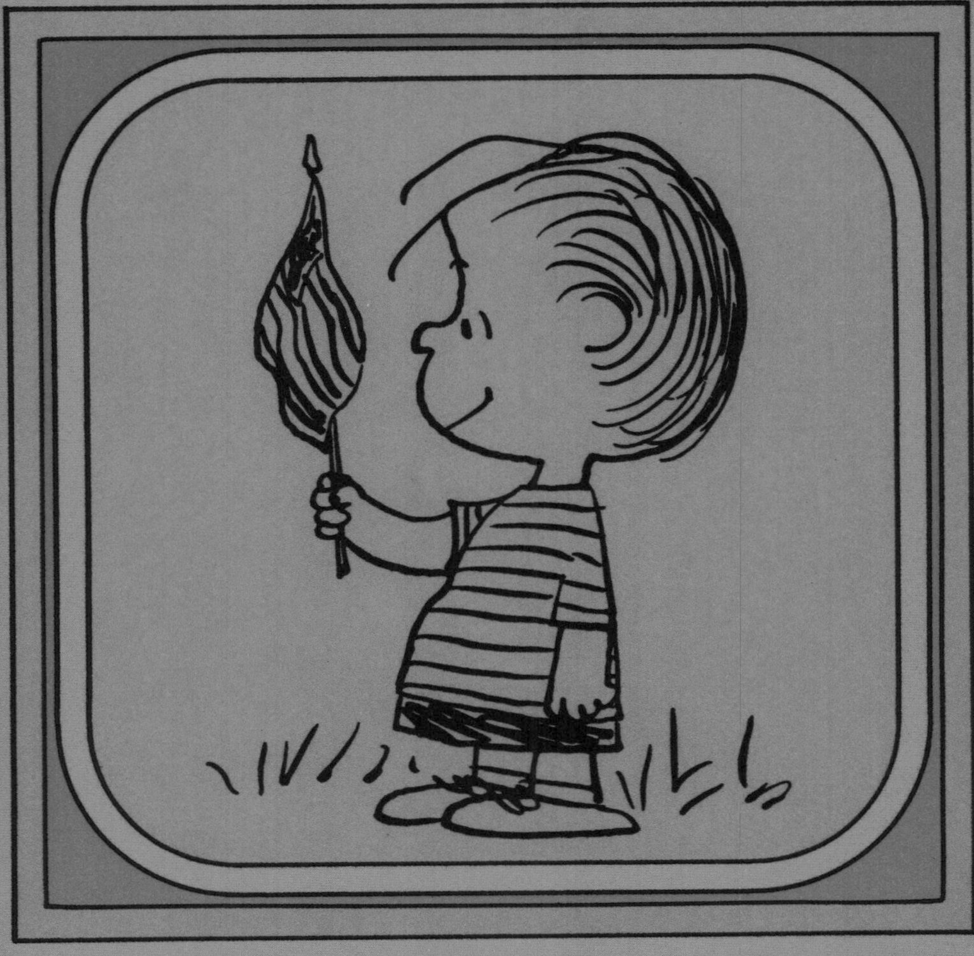

Love is
liking
people

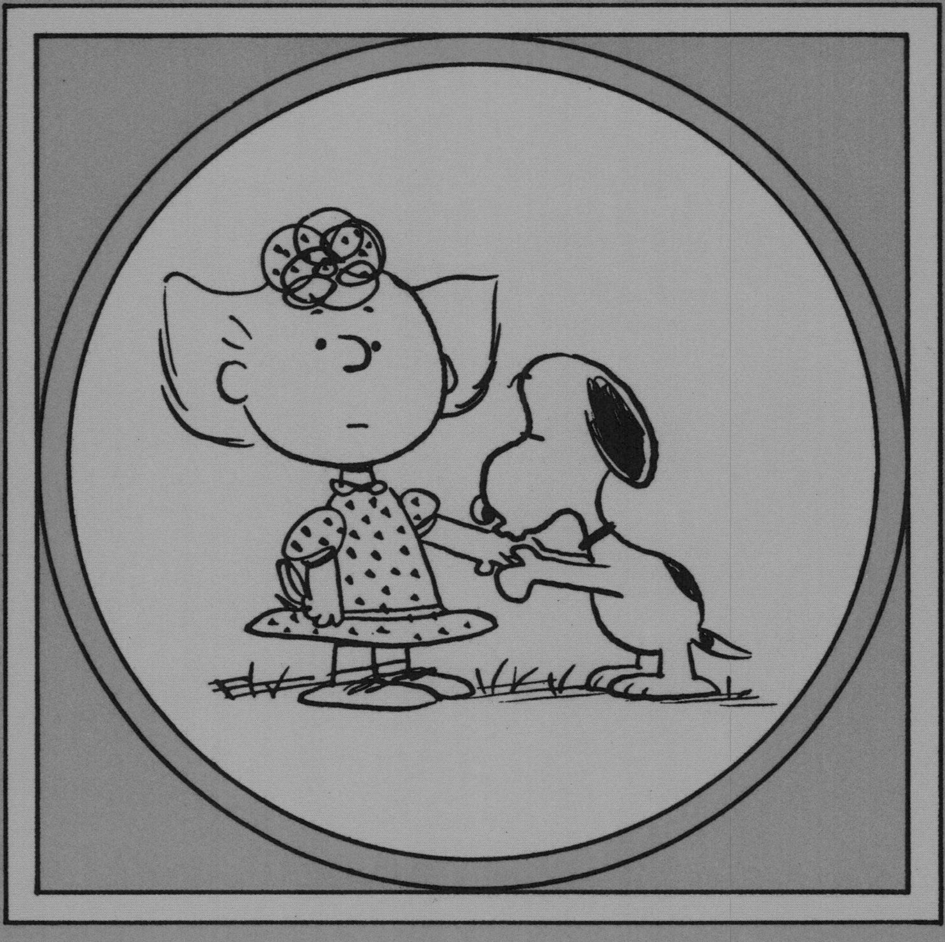

Love is
liking
ideas

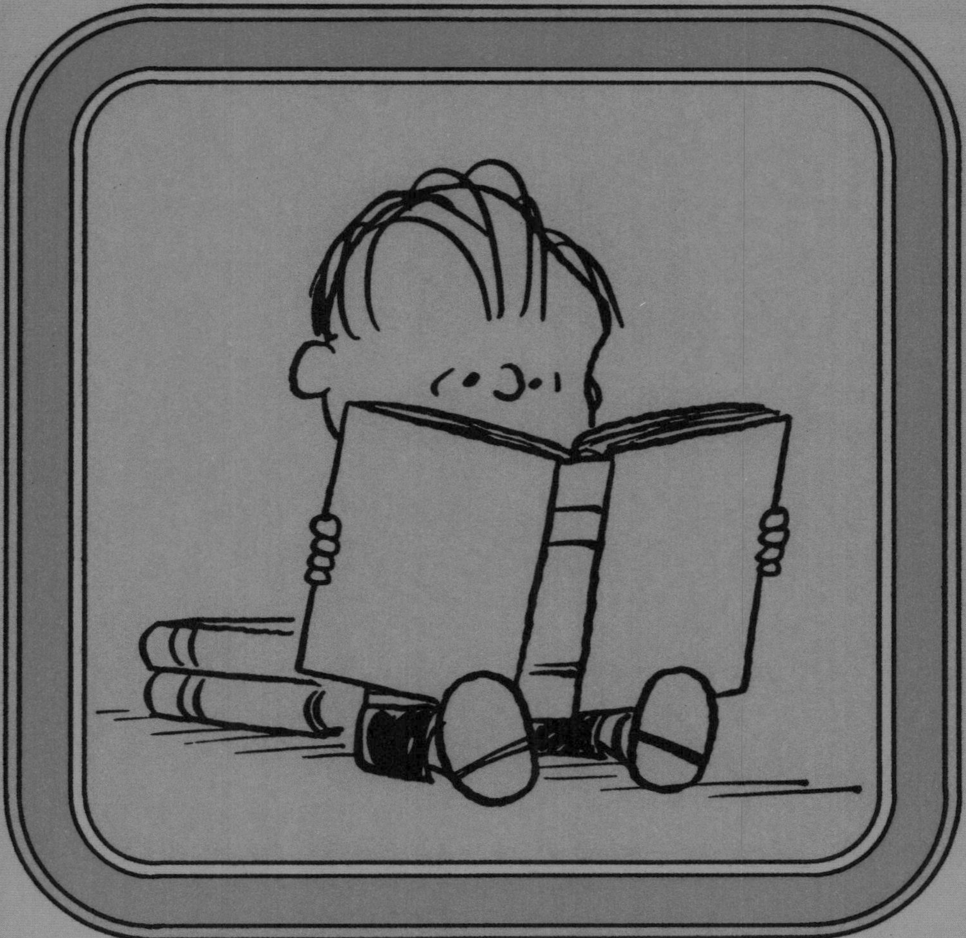

Love is
the
whole
world

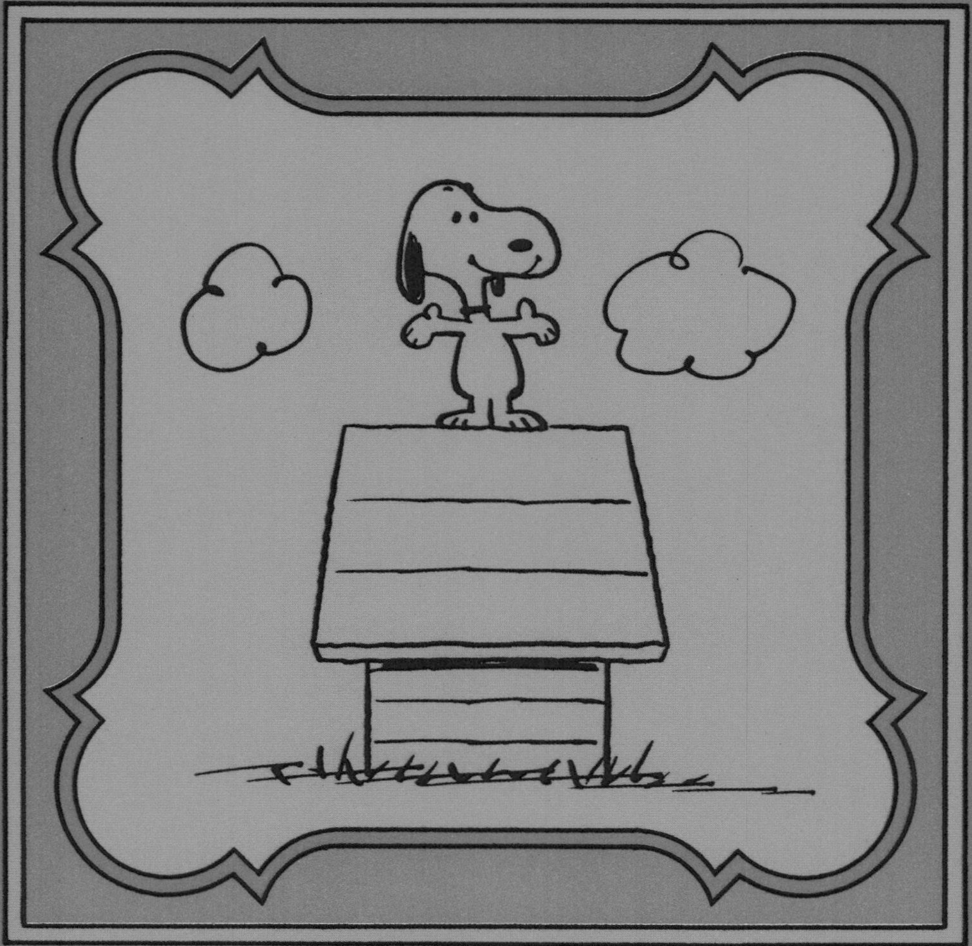

It must be suppertime... my stomach-clock just went off!

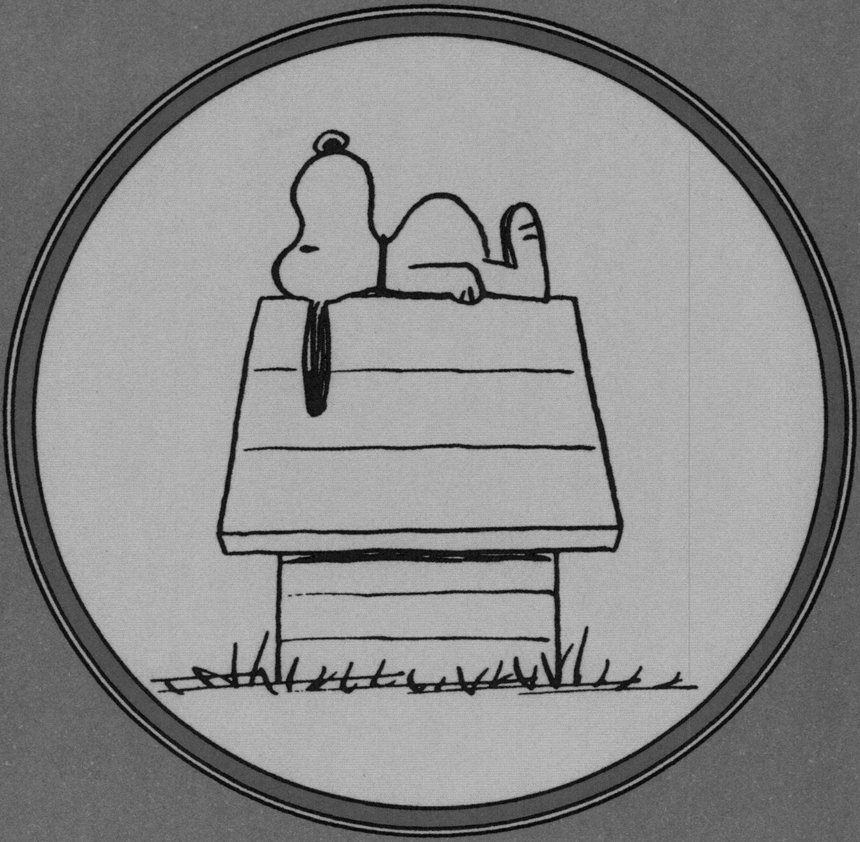

THREE HUNDRED AND FIFTY MILLION DOLLARS A YEAR IS SPENT ON DOG FOOD! I WONDER IF THAT INCLUDES TIPS!

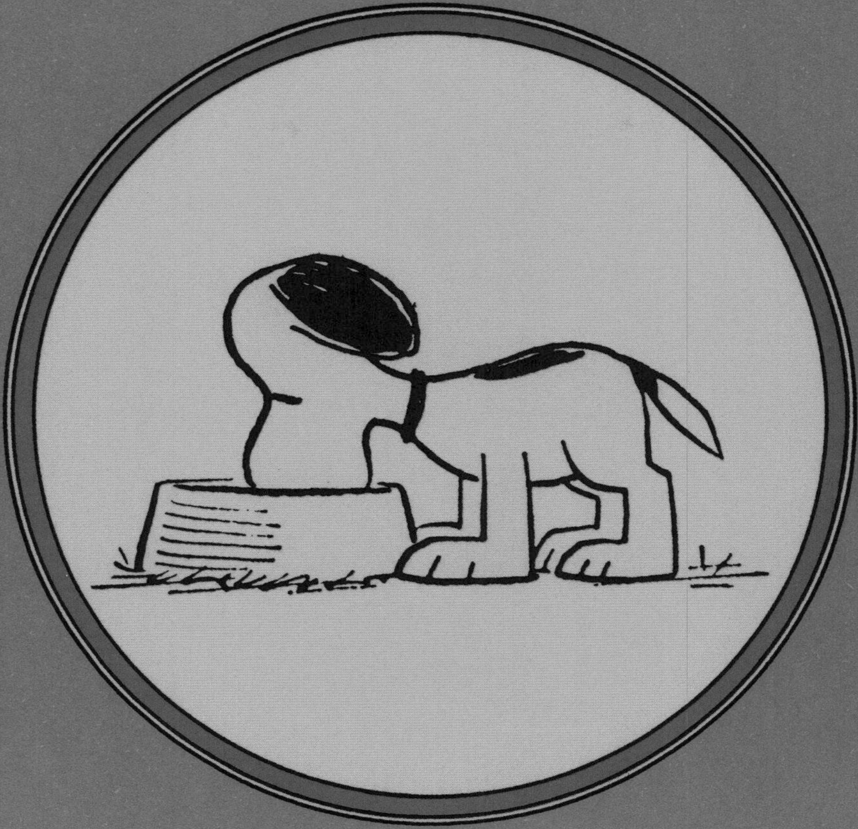

N⁰

AFTER-DINNER

SPEAKER?

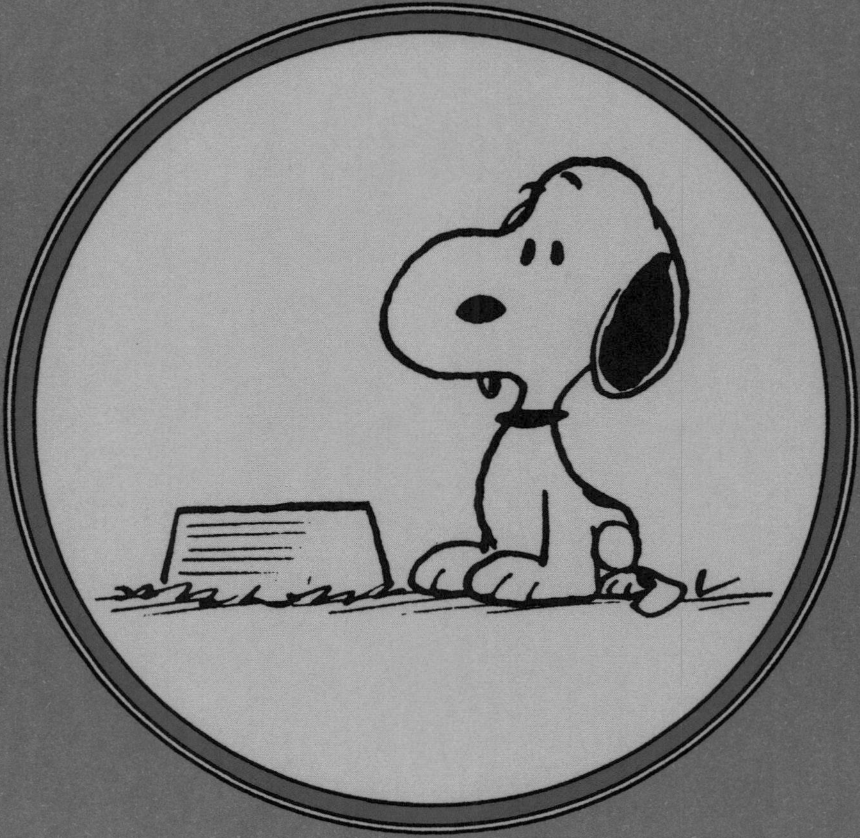

THIS IS
GOOD HOT
CHOCOLATE,
BUT IT WOULD
TASTE EVEN BETTER
WITH A SKI LODGE
AROUND IT!

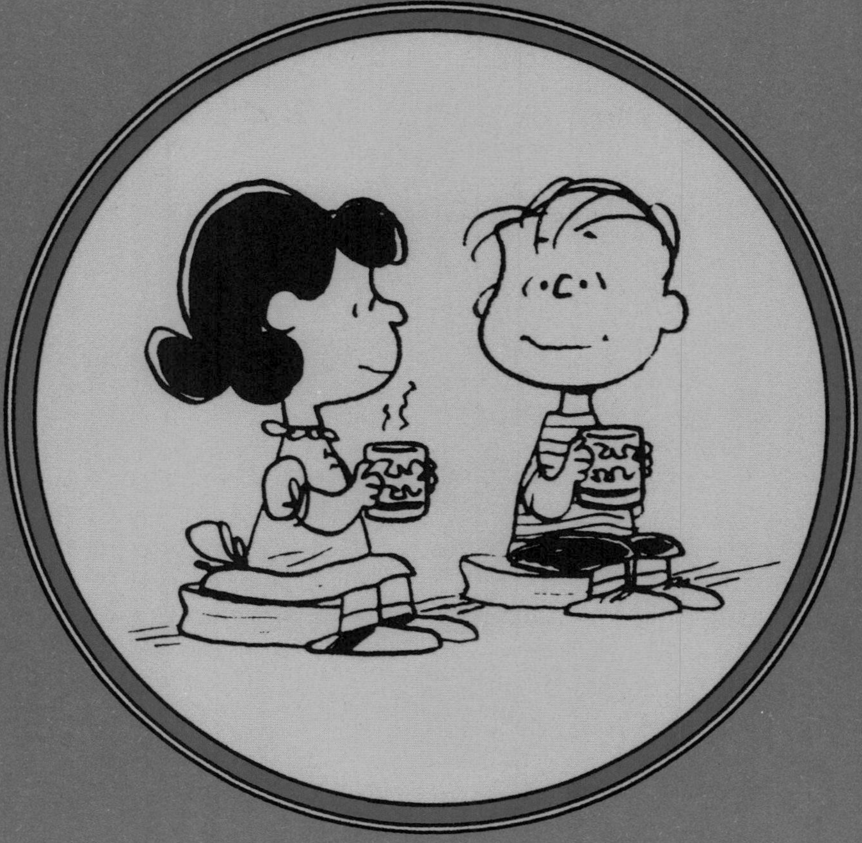

TO ME, THE UGLIEST SIGHT IN THE WORLD IS AN EMPTY DOG DISH!

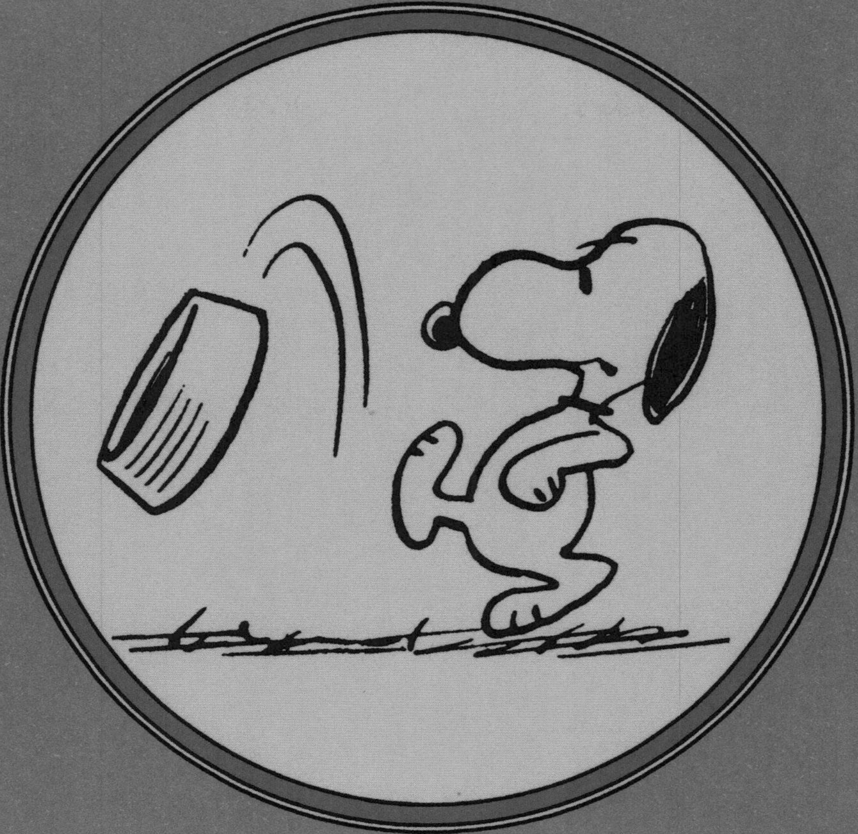

A

WATCHED

SUPPER DISH

NEVER

FILLS!

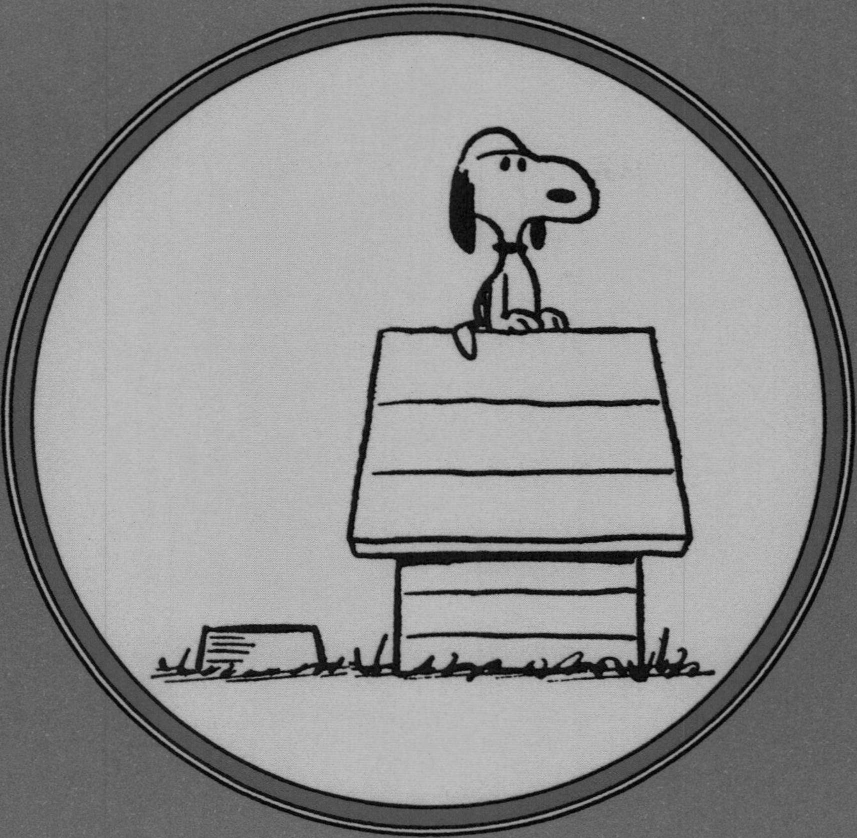

My
STOMACH
TELLS ME IT'S
SUPPERTIME BUT
I KNOW IT ISN'T.
I HATE
A STOMACH
THAT TELLS
LIES!

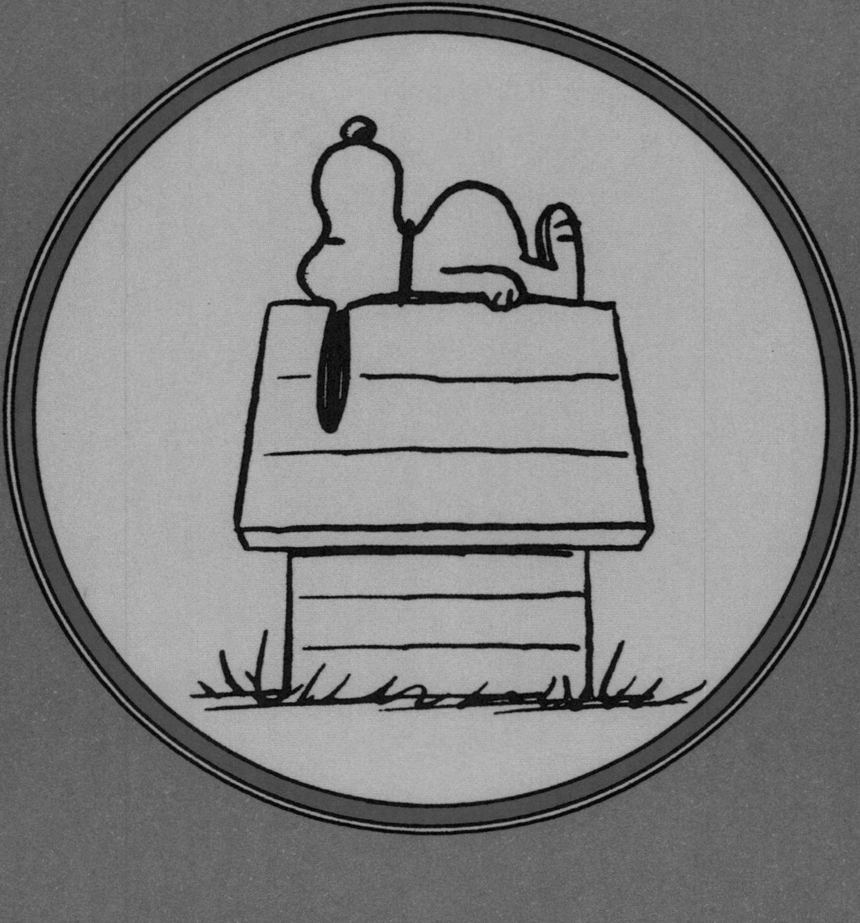

WITHHOLD MY COMPLIMENTS TO THE CHEF!

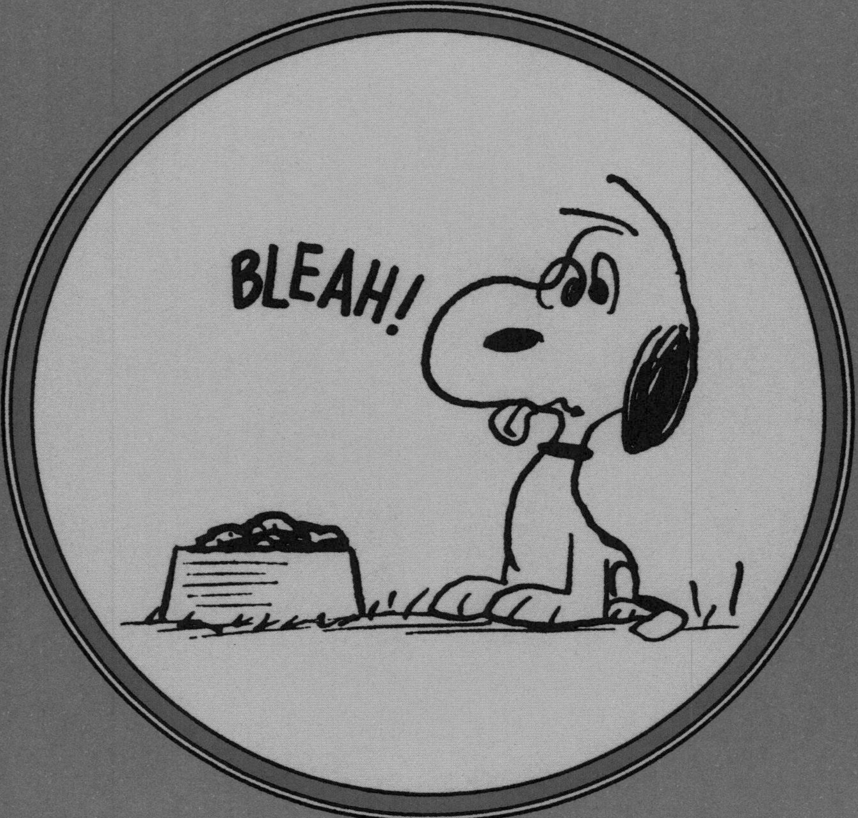
BLEAH!

I KNOW YOU HAVE A COLD, SO I PUT A MENTHOL COUGH DROP ON TOP!

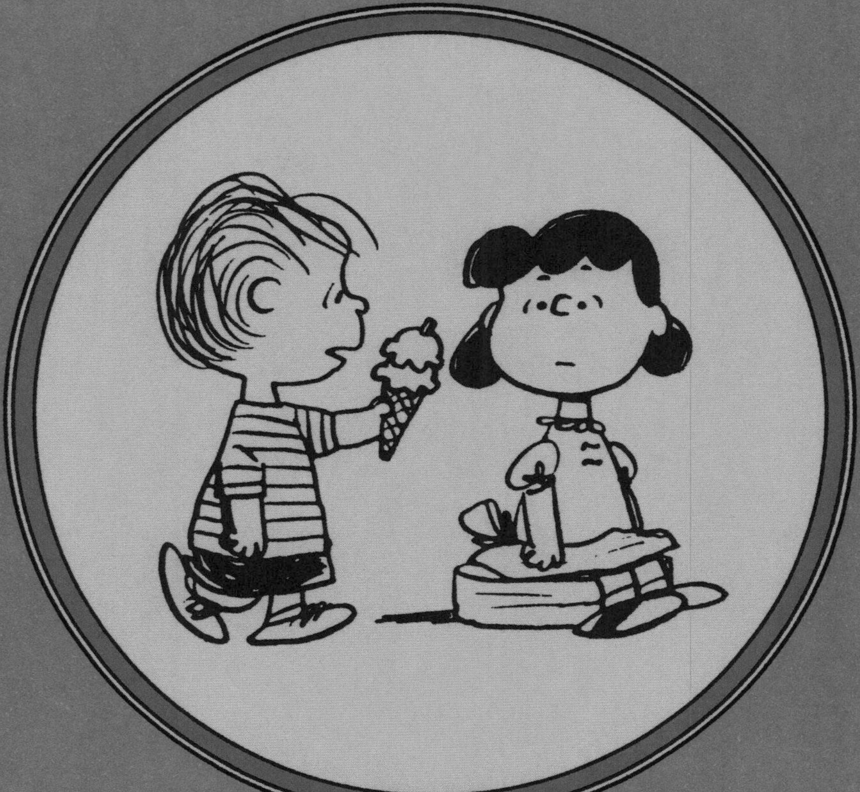

ACTUALLY, WORLD WAR I FLYING ACES VERY SELDOM DRANK ROOT BEER.

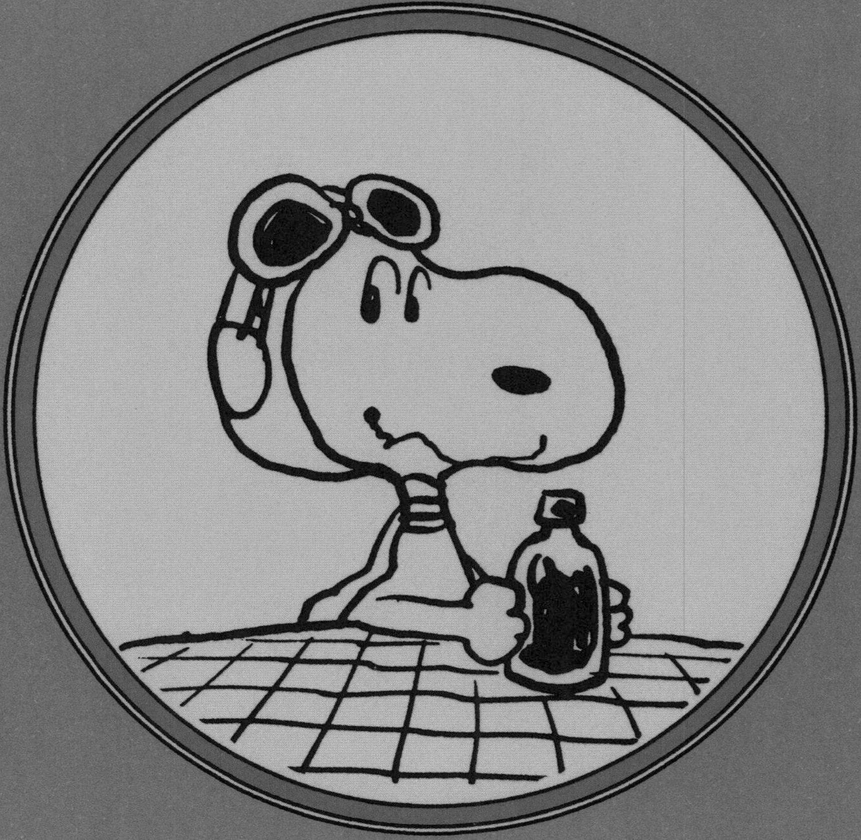

I KNEW
I SMELLED
A PICNIC
GOING BY!

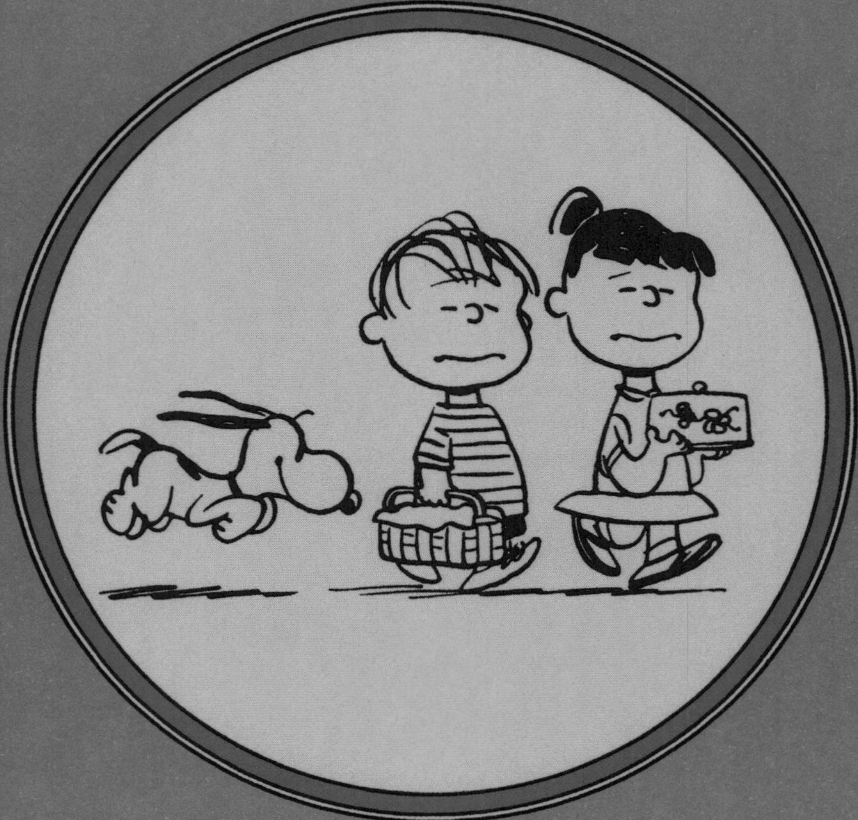

I HATE IT WHEN IT SNOWS ON MY FRENCH TOAST!

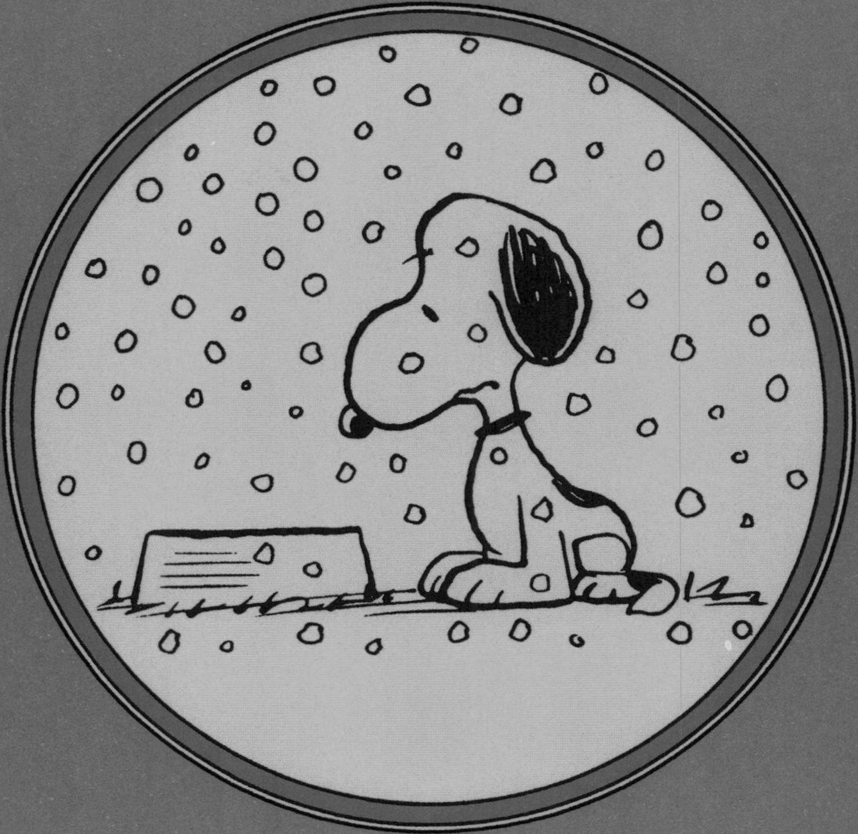

ROQUEFORT OR THOUSAND ISLAND?

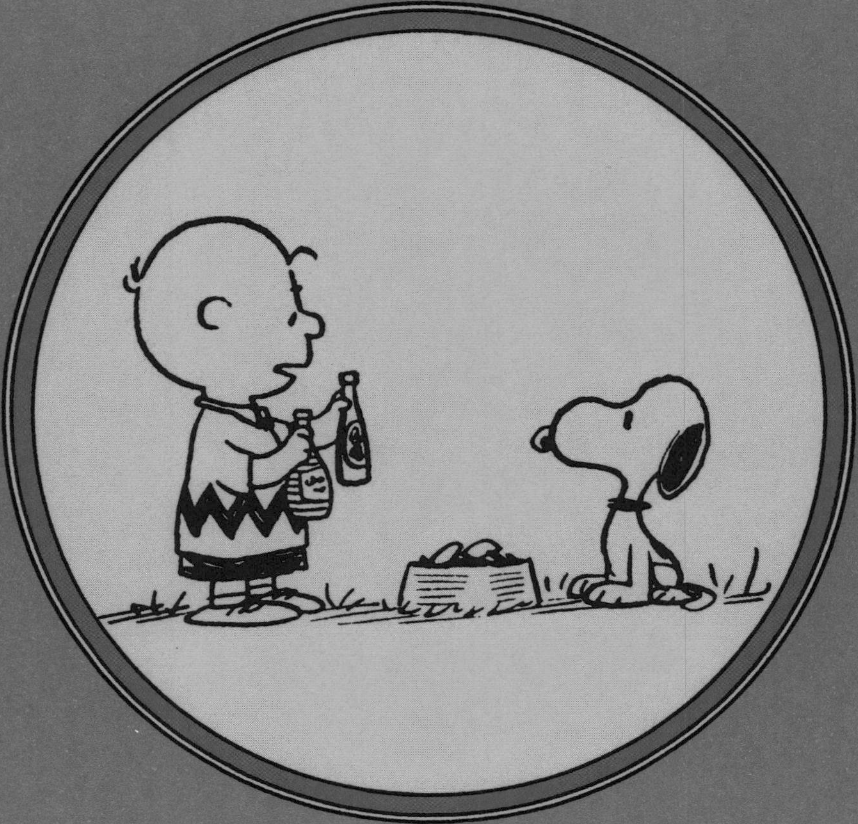

I'VE JUST GOT TO KEEP EATING UNTIL I'VE FORGOTTEN OL' "WHAT'S-HER-NAME"?

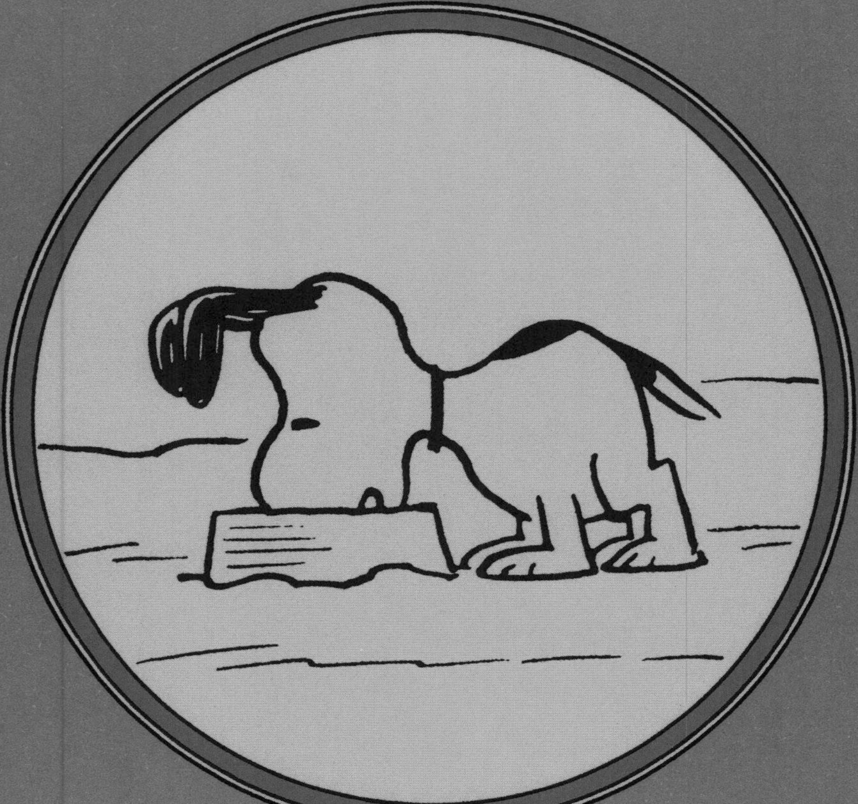

Twenty-three pounds... how humiliating!

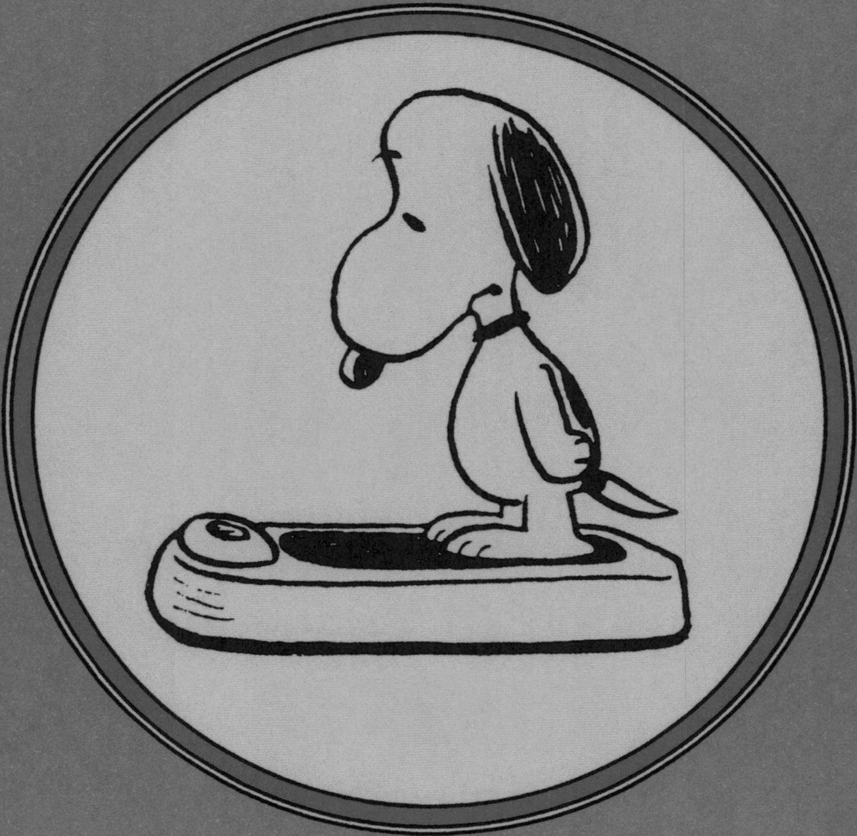

EATING OUT CAN BE FUN!

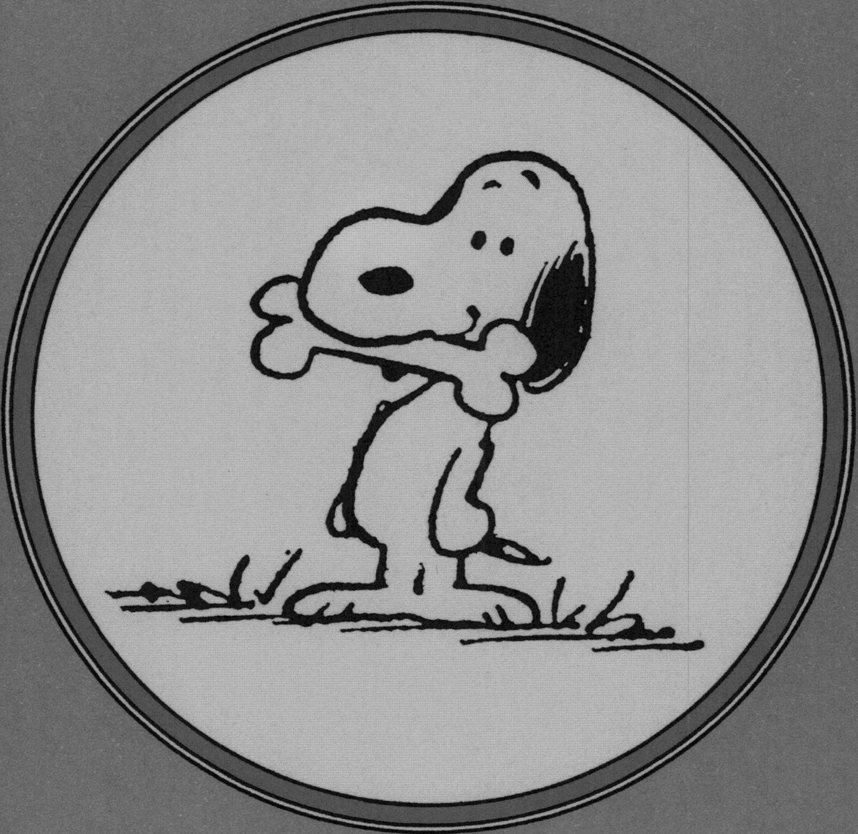

THUMB
A
LA
MODE!

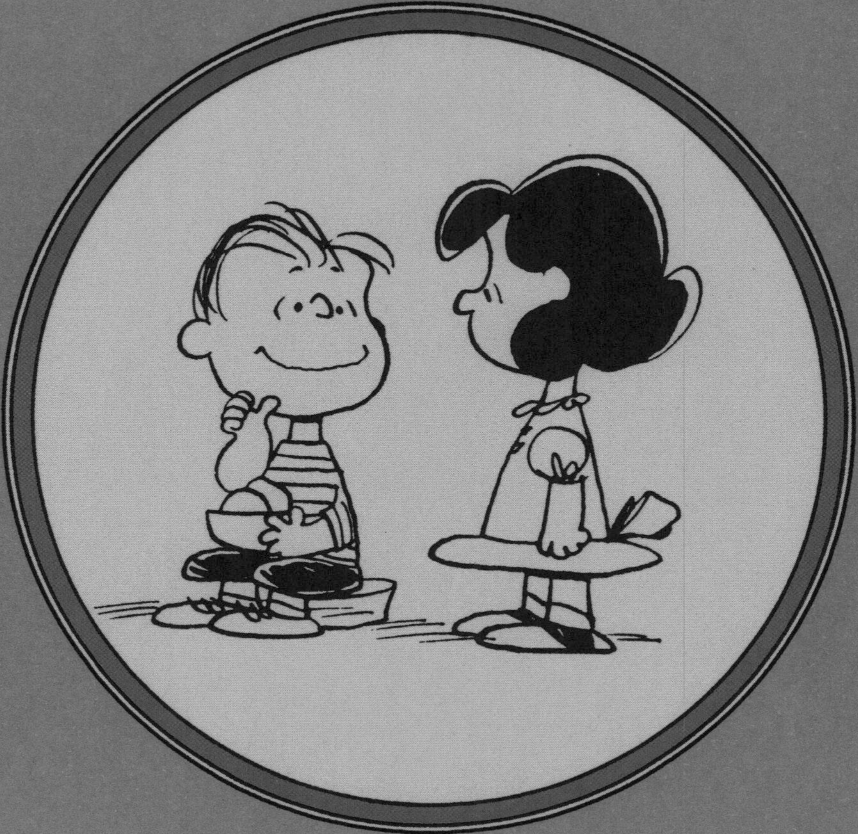

IT'S THE MIDDLE OF JANUARY! IT'S SNOWING! THE WEATHER IS FREEZING! ...AND WHAT DO I GET? COLD CEREAL.

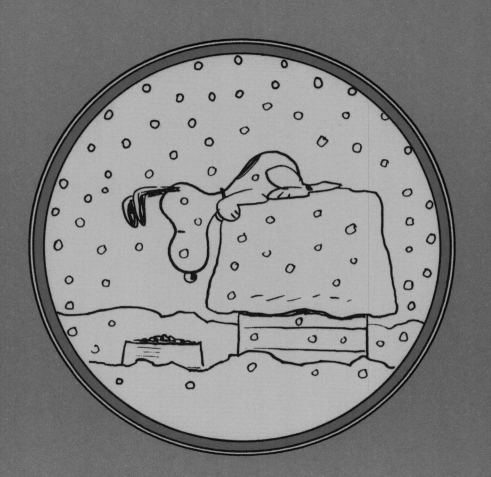

Tonight I THINK I'LL HAVE MY SUPPER IN THE YELLOW DISH AND MY DRINKING WATER IN THE RED DISH... LIFE IS TOO SHORT NOT TO LIVE IT UP A LITTLE!

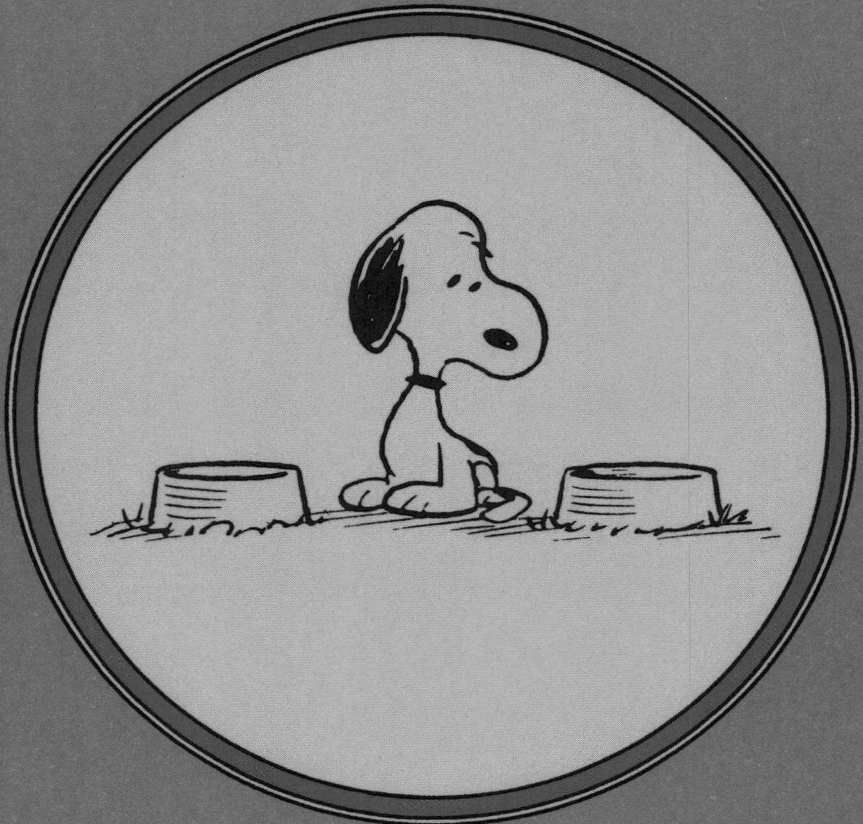

I WAS SITTING HERE WATCHING T.V., WHEN ALL OF A SUDDEN, I FELT A PIECE OF JELLY BREAD CALLING ME!

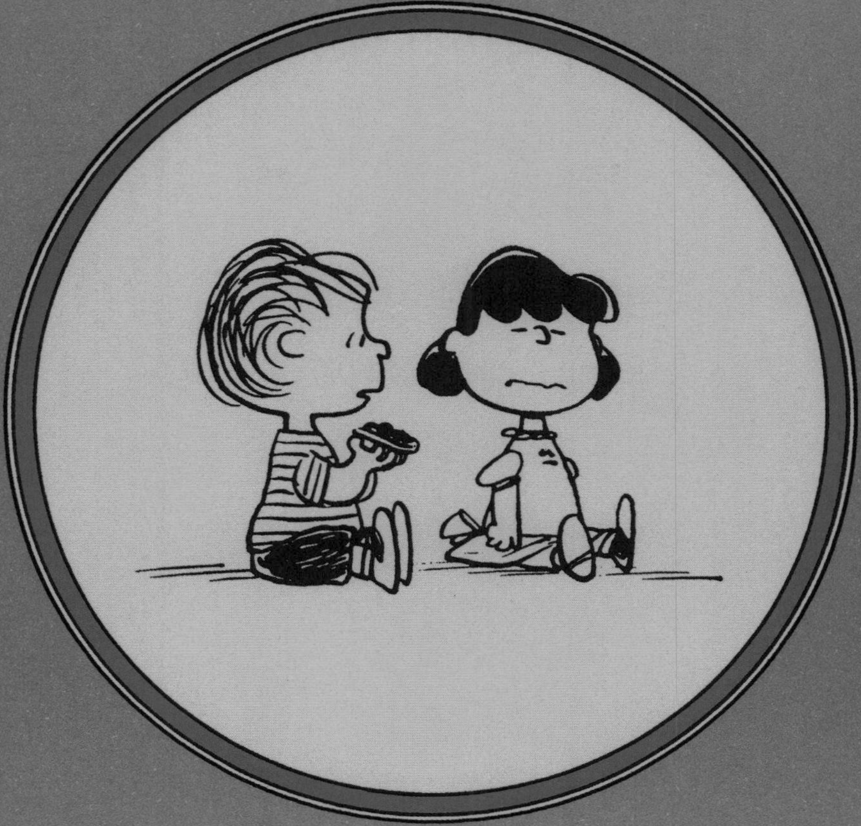

A GOOD WAY TO FORGET A LOVE AFFAIR IS TO EAT A LOT OF GOOP!

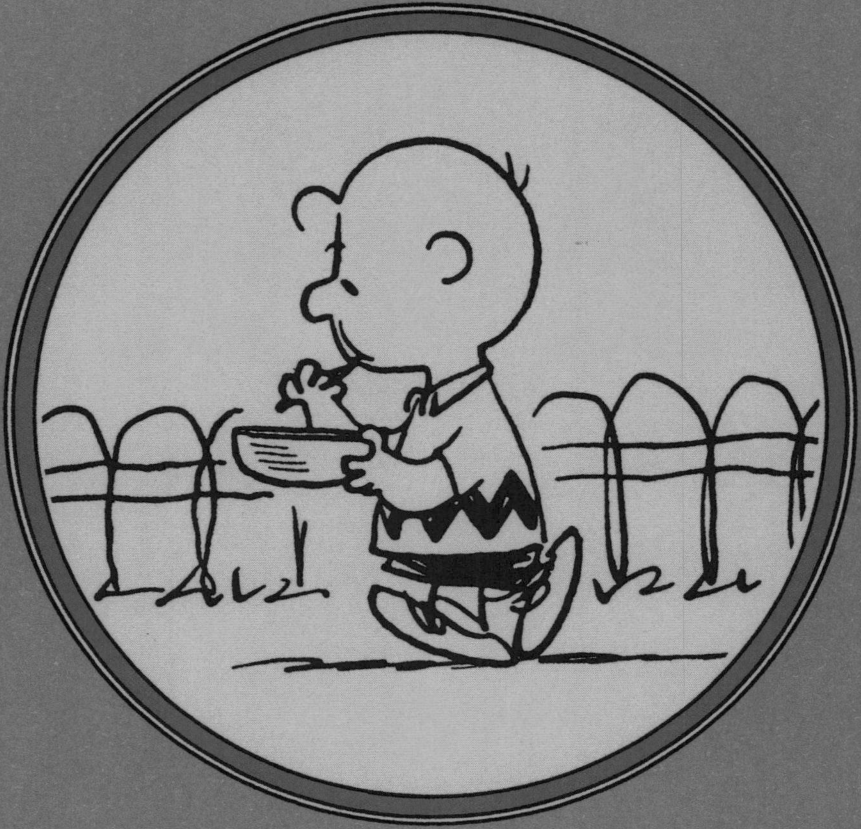

I NEVER KNOW WHAT TO DO WITH THE USED TEA BAG...

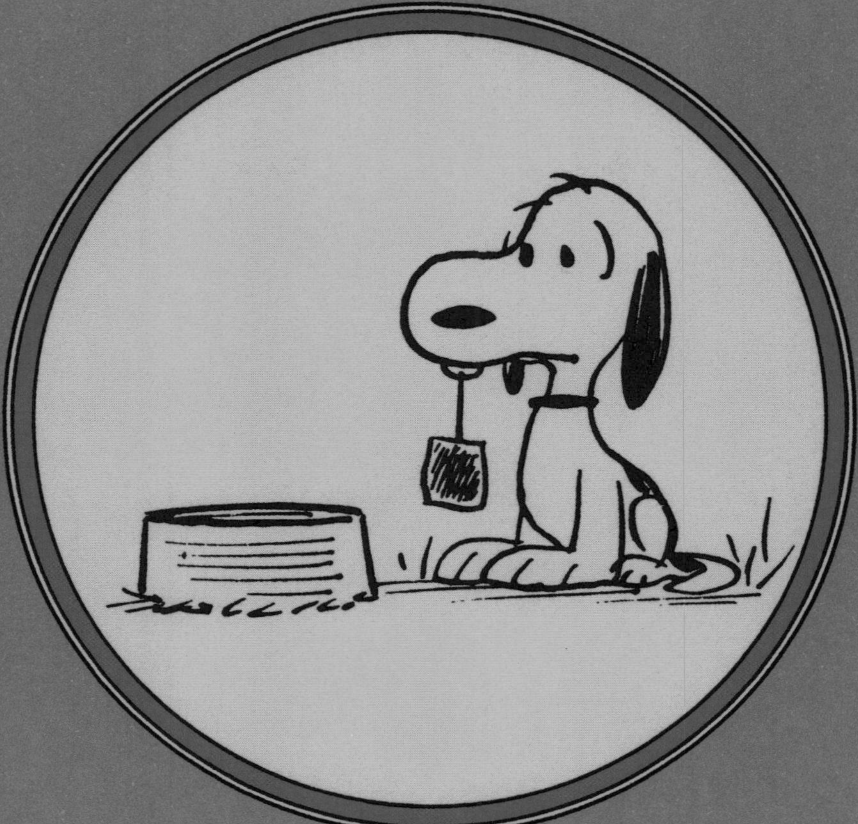

CRITICIZE ME ALL YOU WANT, BUT DON'T INTERFERE WITH MY FOOD-LIFE!

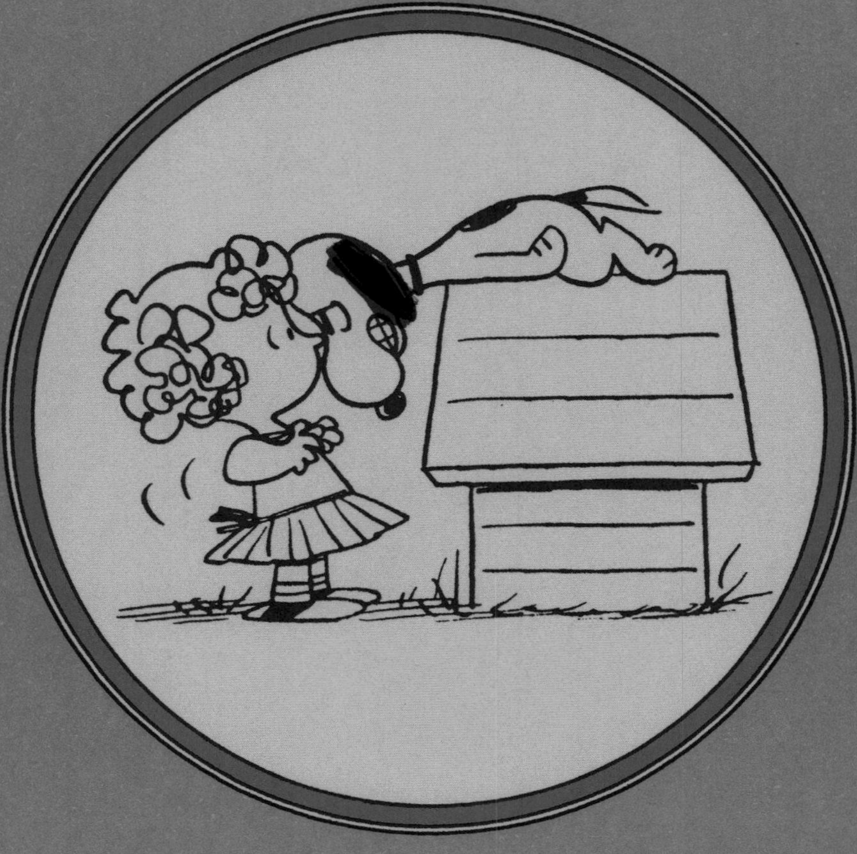

I

LOVE EATING IN A CAFETERIA... I'LL HAVE SOME OF THIS, AND SOME OF THAT, AND SOME OF THESE AND SOME OF THOSE!

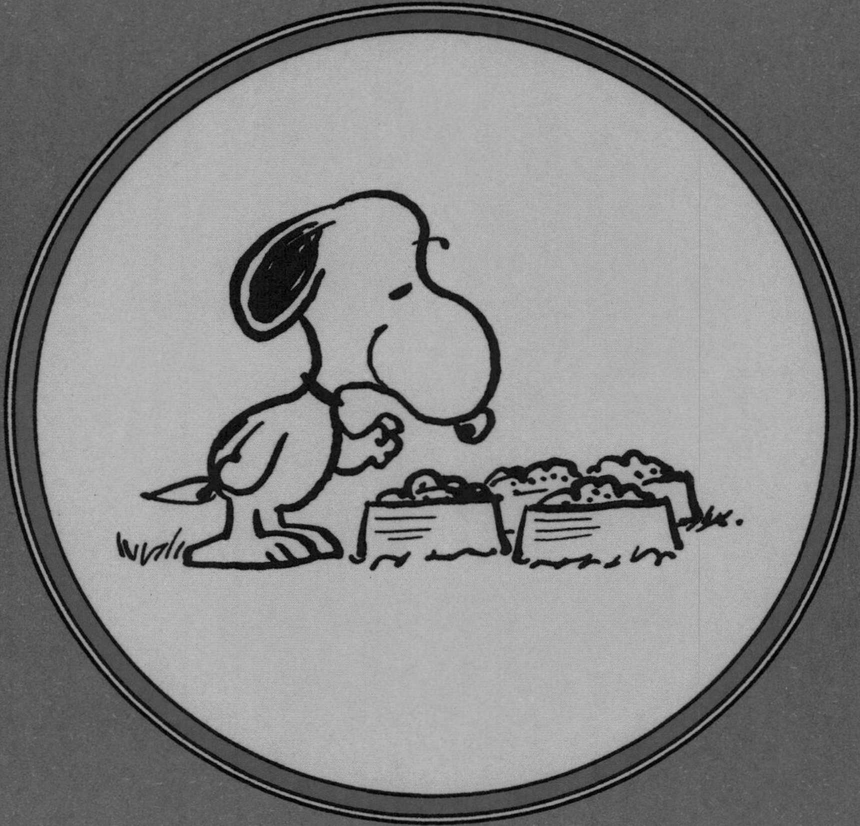

JUST AS I THOUGHT, HE'S CUTTING DOWN MY RATIONS!

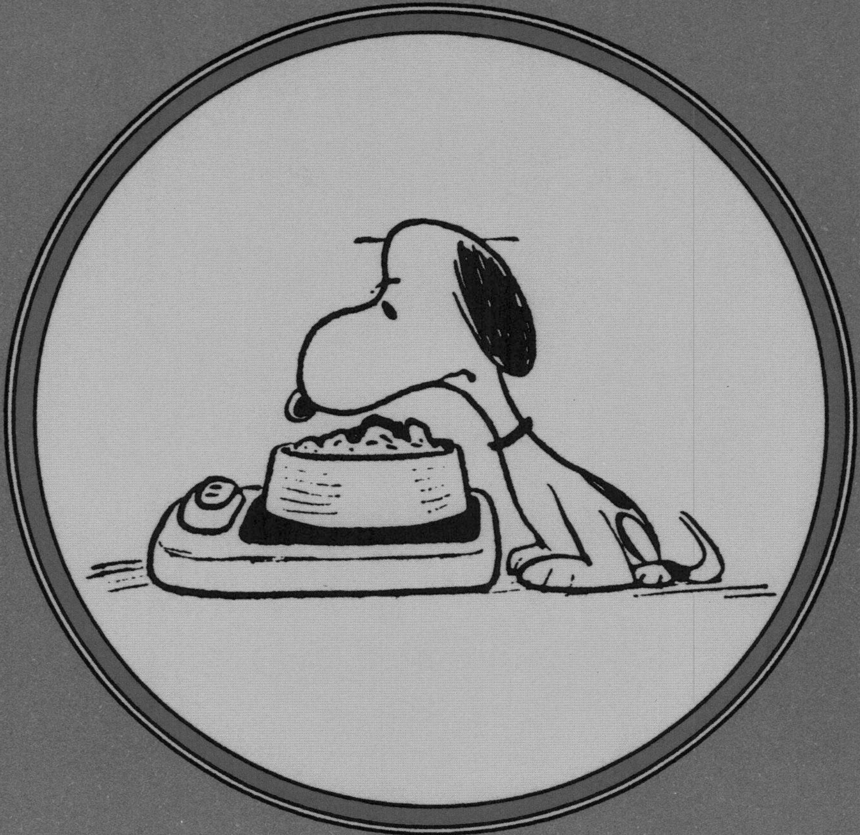

THAT'S THE ONLY DOG I KNOW WHO WORRIES ABOUT HIS CHOLESTEROL LEVEL!

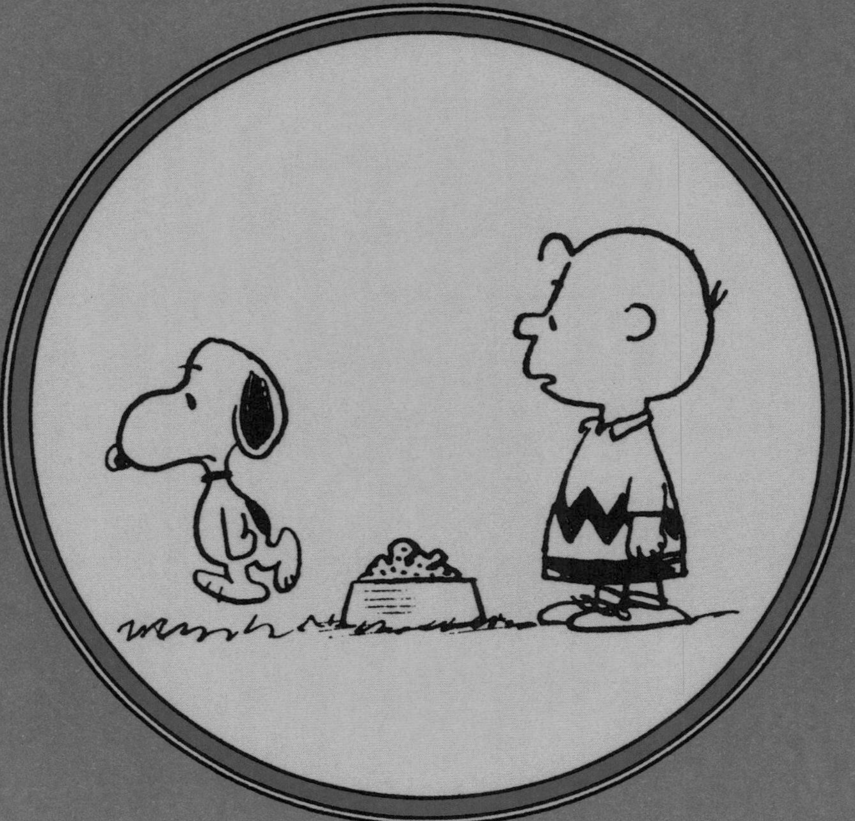

CHRISTMAS HAS BEEN OVER FOR TWO MONTHS AND I'M STILL GETTING " FIGGY PUDDING "!

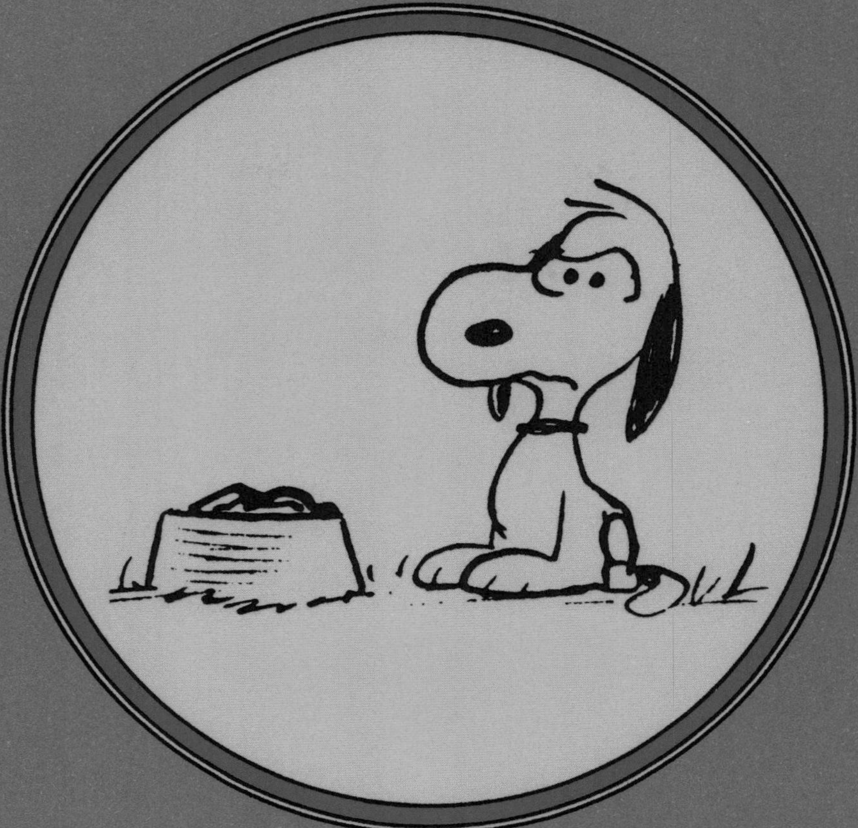

I EAT BECAUSE I'M FRUSTRATED... AND I'M FRUSTRATED BECAUSE I DON'T GET TO EAT ENOUGH!

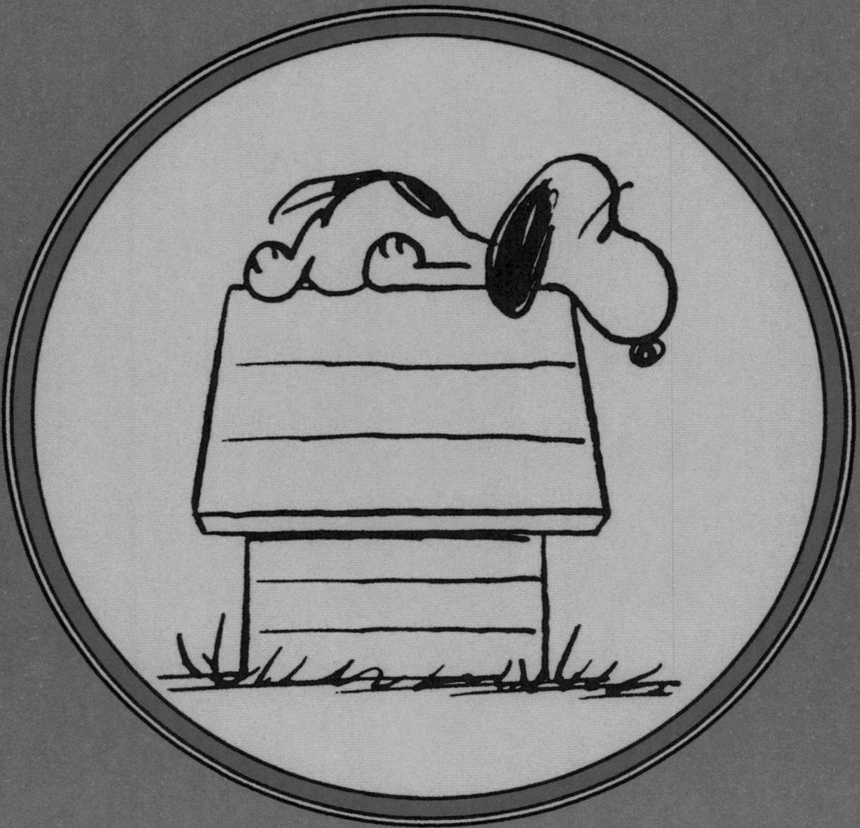

Rats...
HE ALWAYS PUTS TOO MUCH CINNAMON ON MY CINNAMON TOAST!

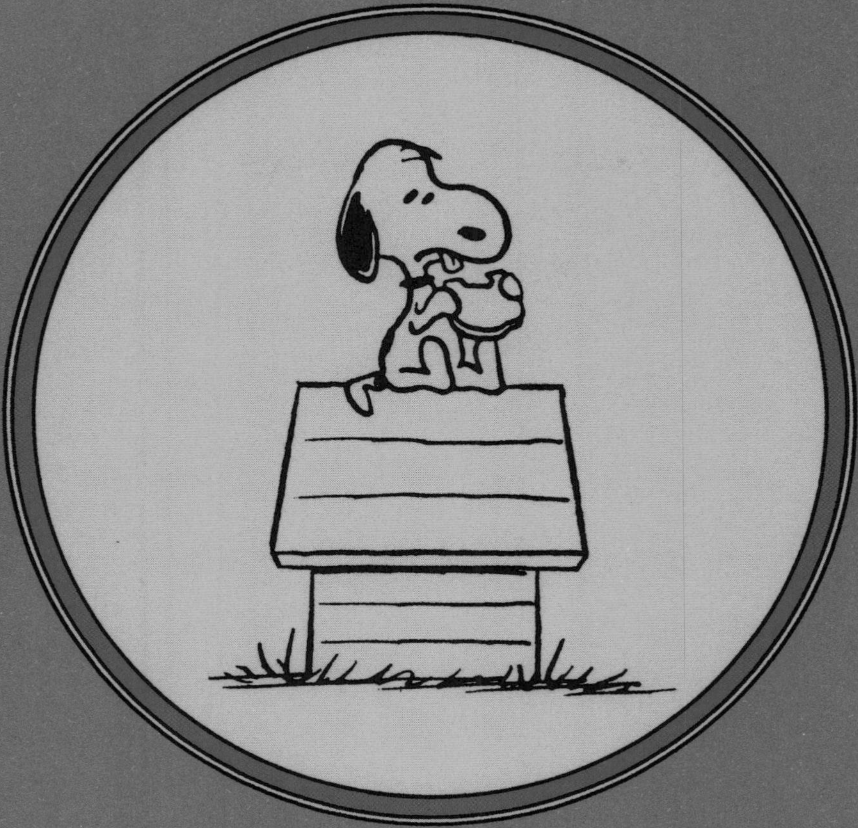

How can I eat when I feel guilty?

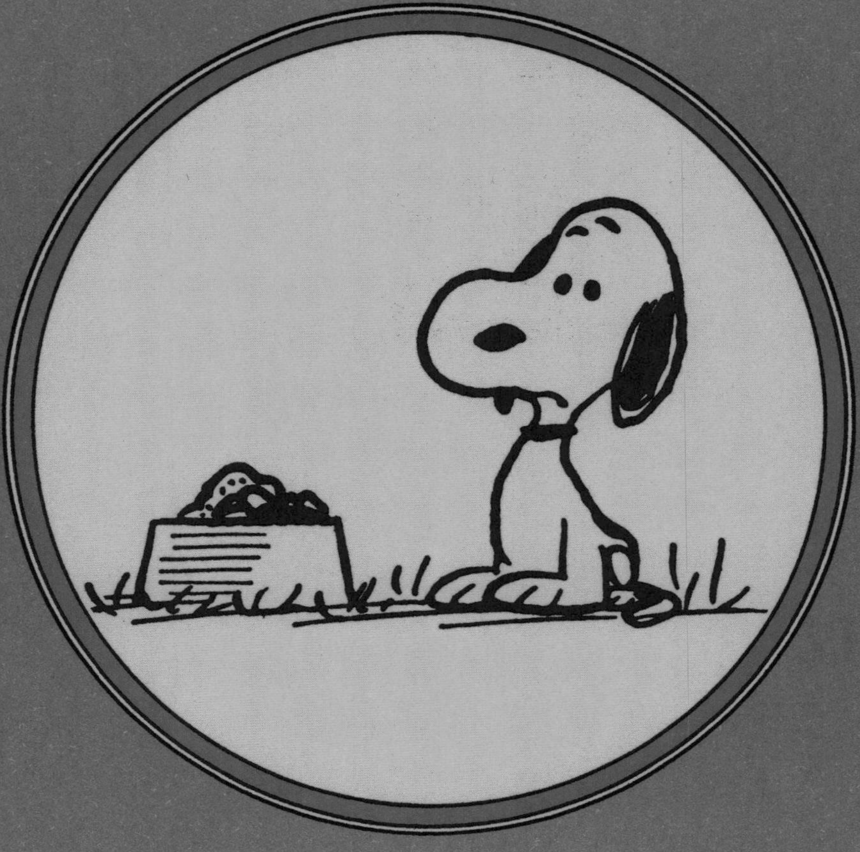

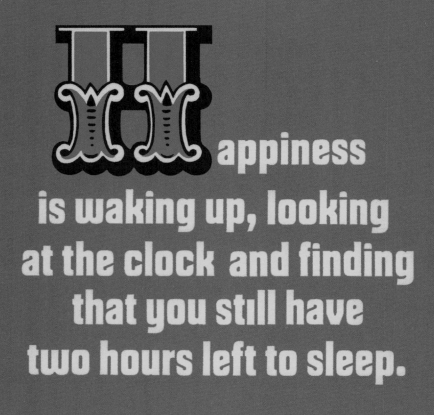

Happiness
is waking up, looking
at the clock and finding
that you still have
two hours left to sleep.

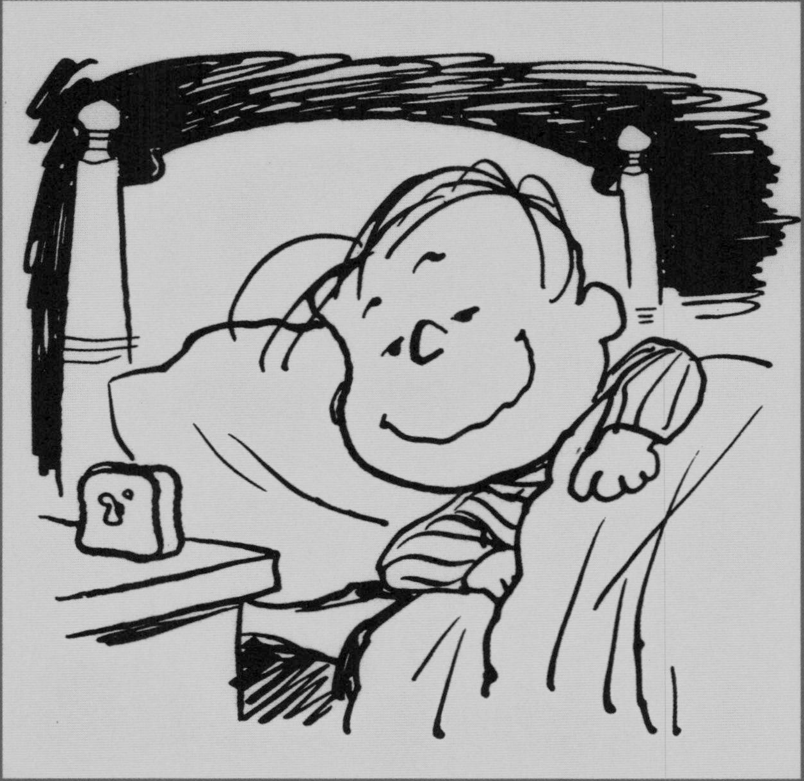

Happiness
is
a side dish
of
French-fries.

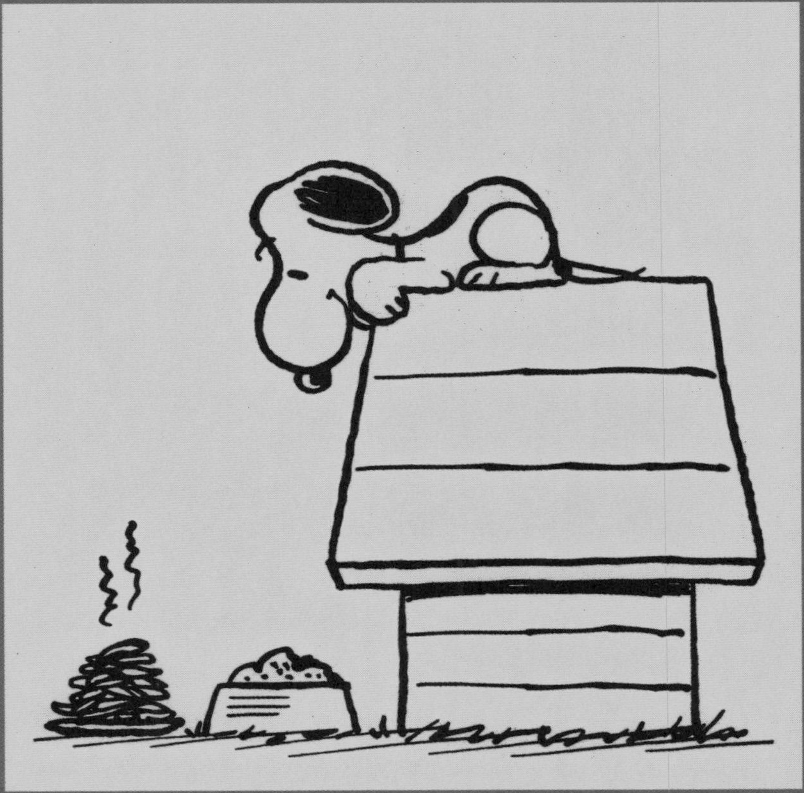

Happiness
is
a new sweatshirt
on a cold
Saturday morning.

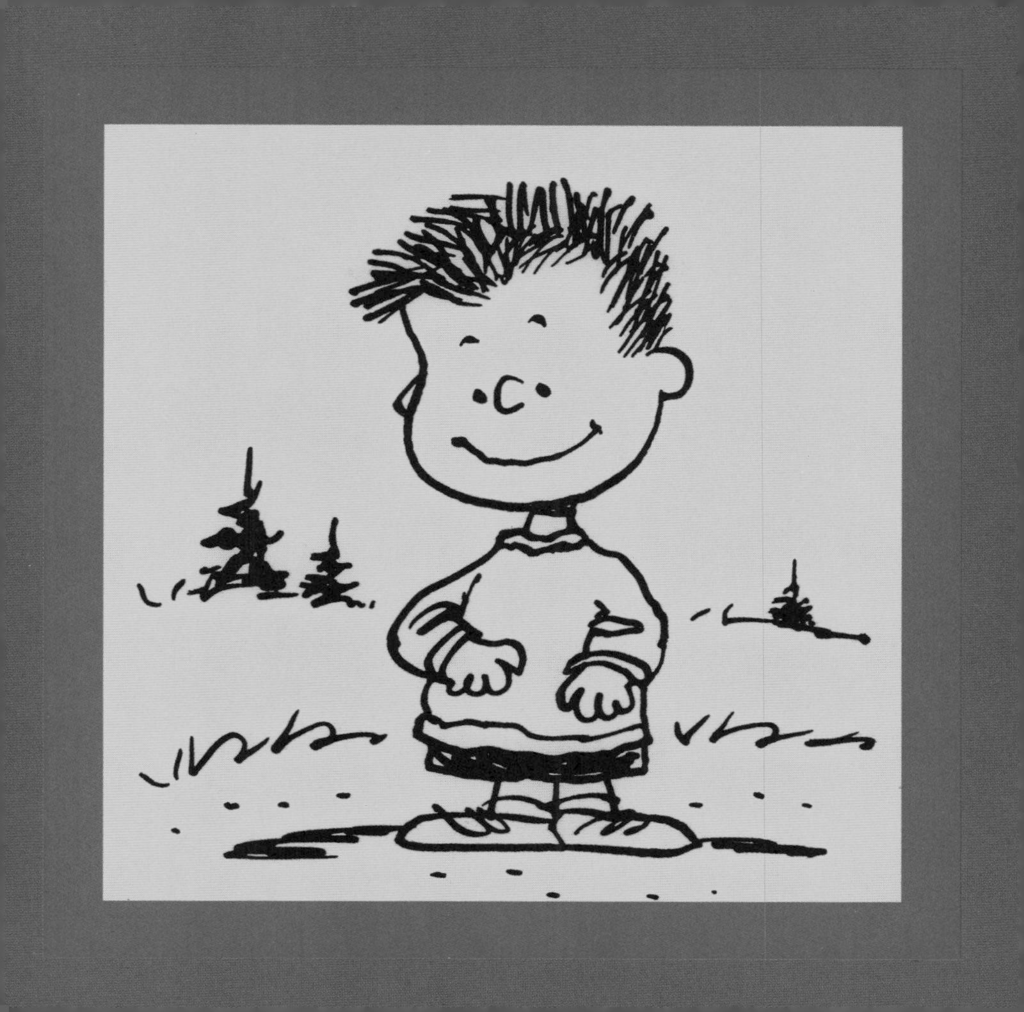

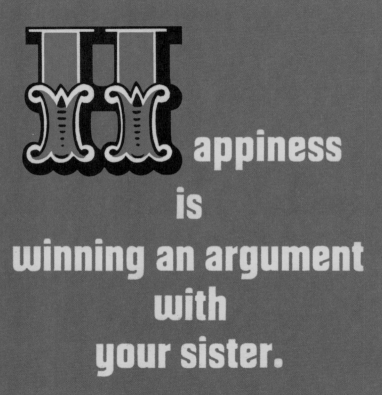

Happiness
is
winning an argument
with
your sister.

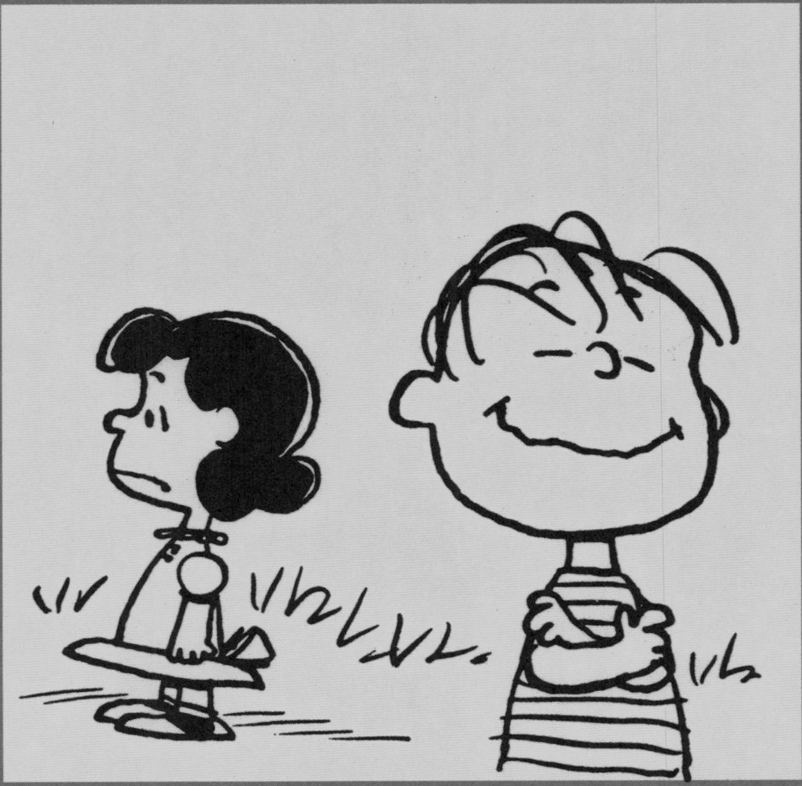

Happiness
is
having
something
to look forward to.

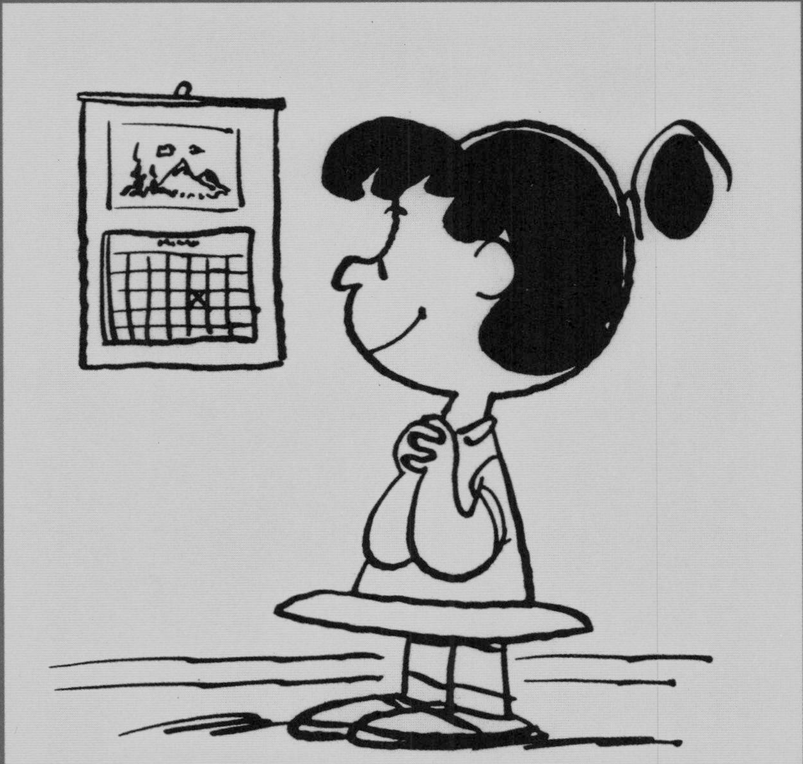

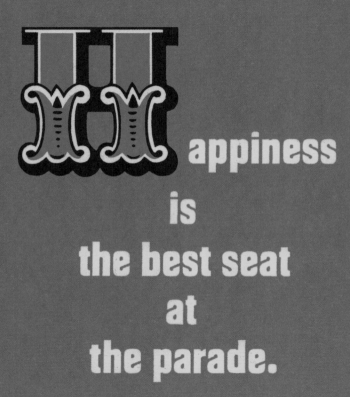

Happiness
is
the best seat
at
the parade.

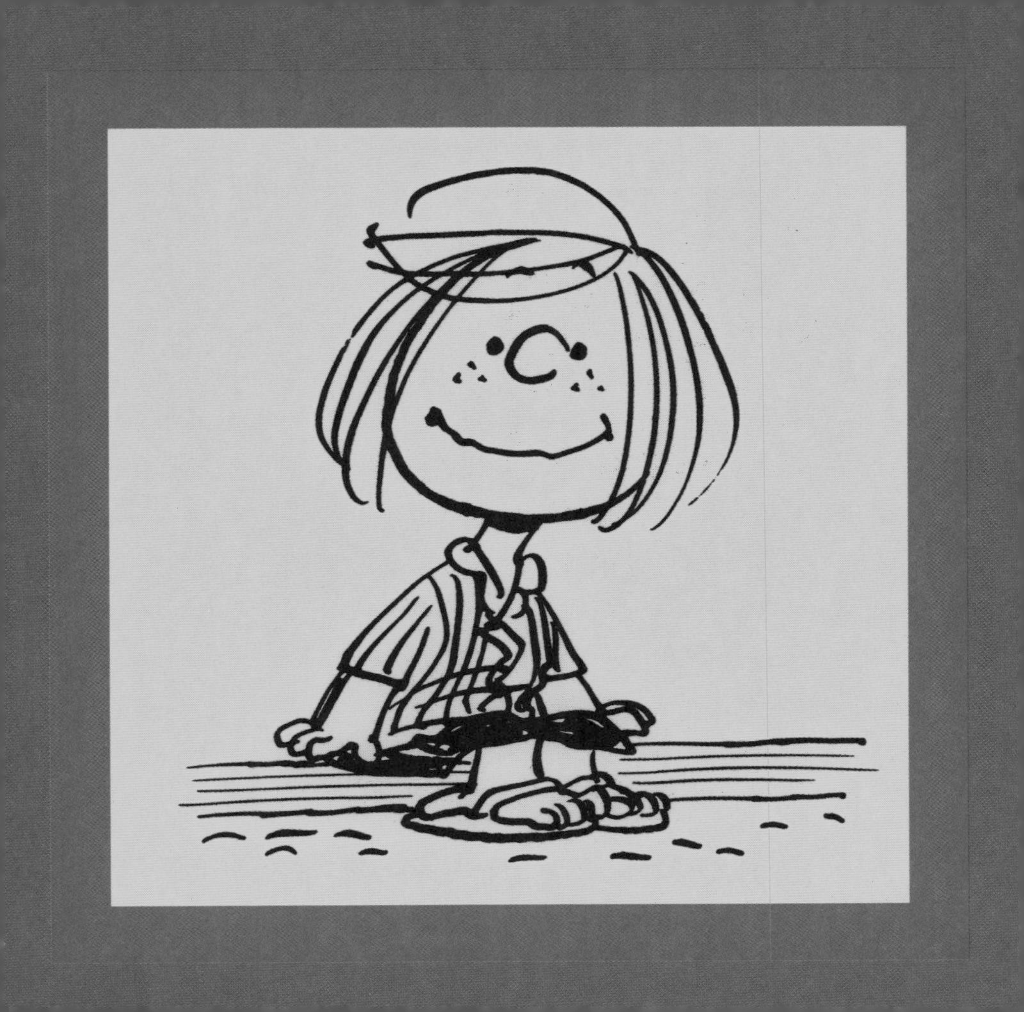

Happiness
is having
the bell ring
just as you are
being called on to recite.

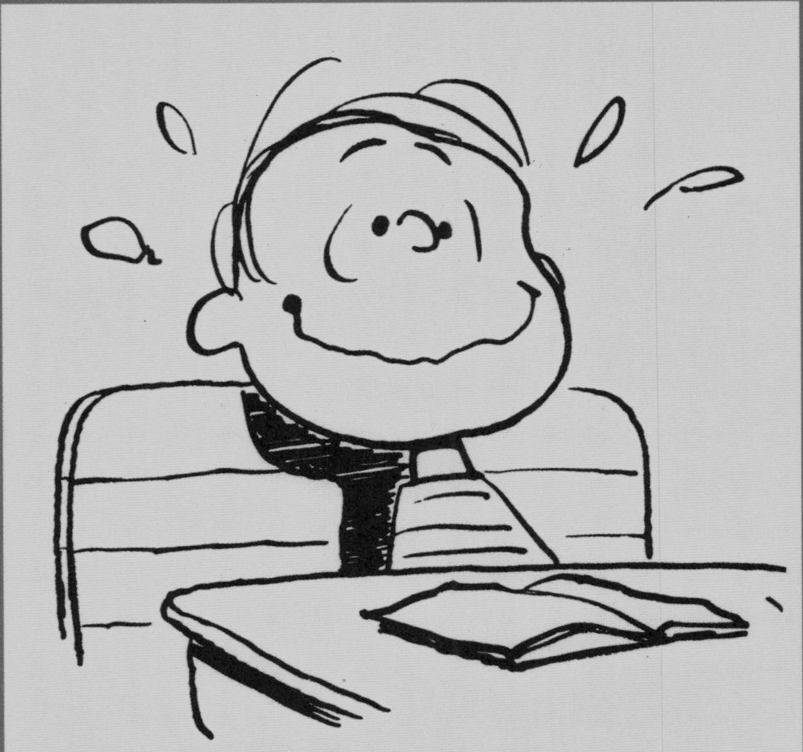

Happiness is a big muscle.

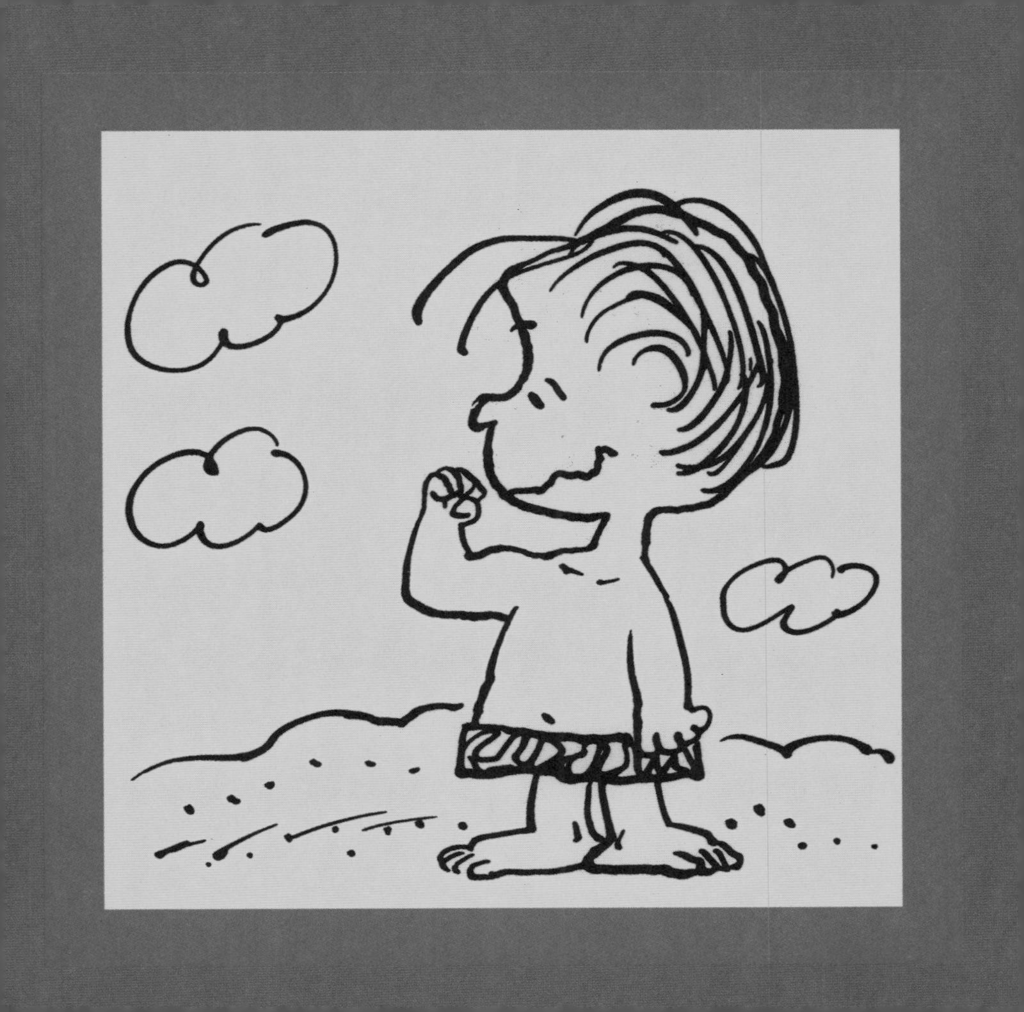

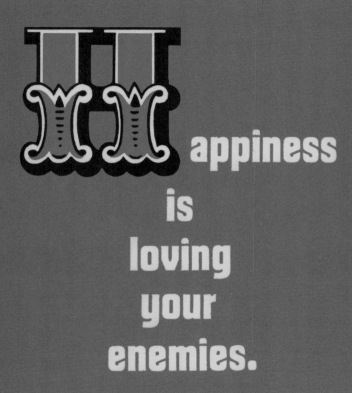

Happiness is loving your enemies.

Happiness
is hearing
the pediatrician say,
"No, I guess she won't
have to have a shot."

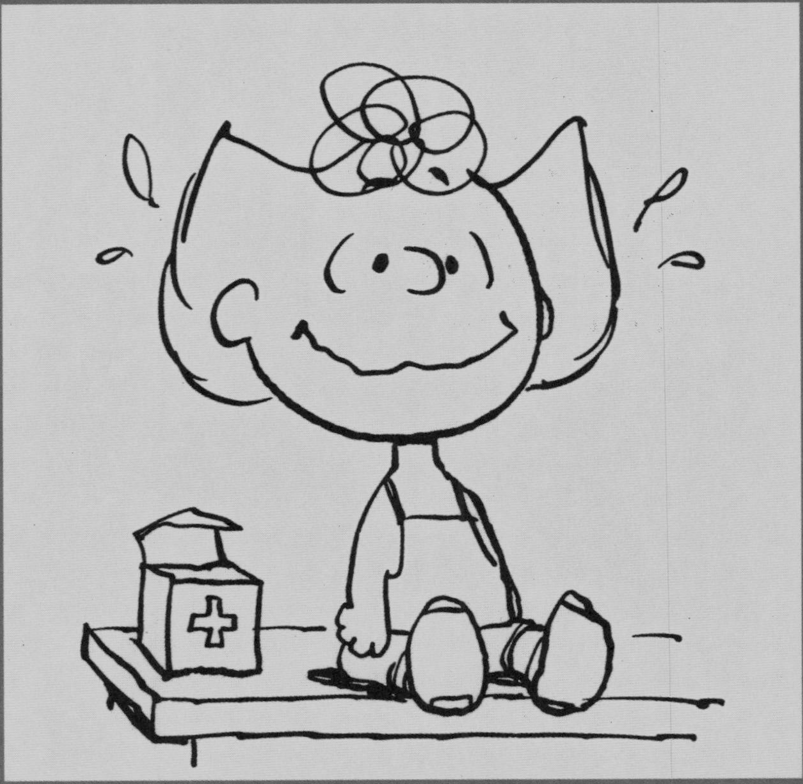

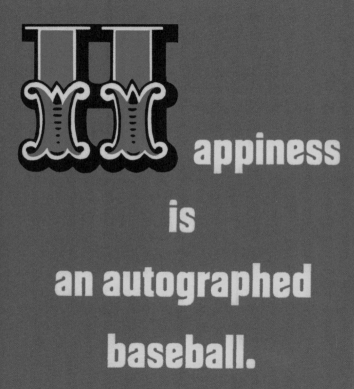

appiness

is

an autographed

baseball.

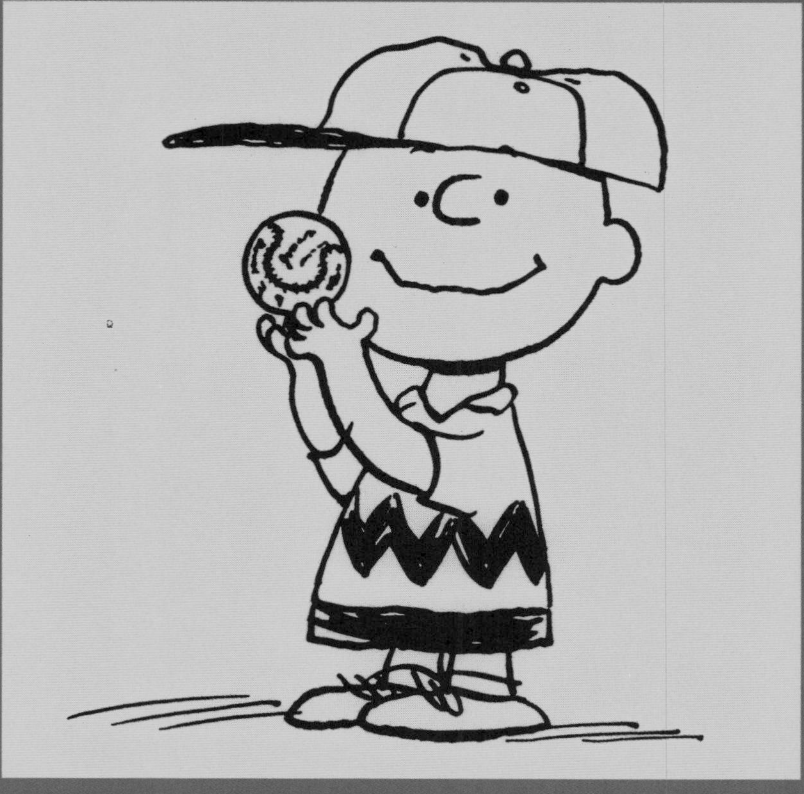

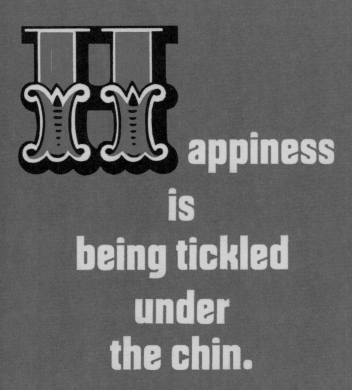

Happiness
is
being tickled
under
the chin.

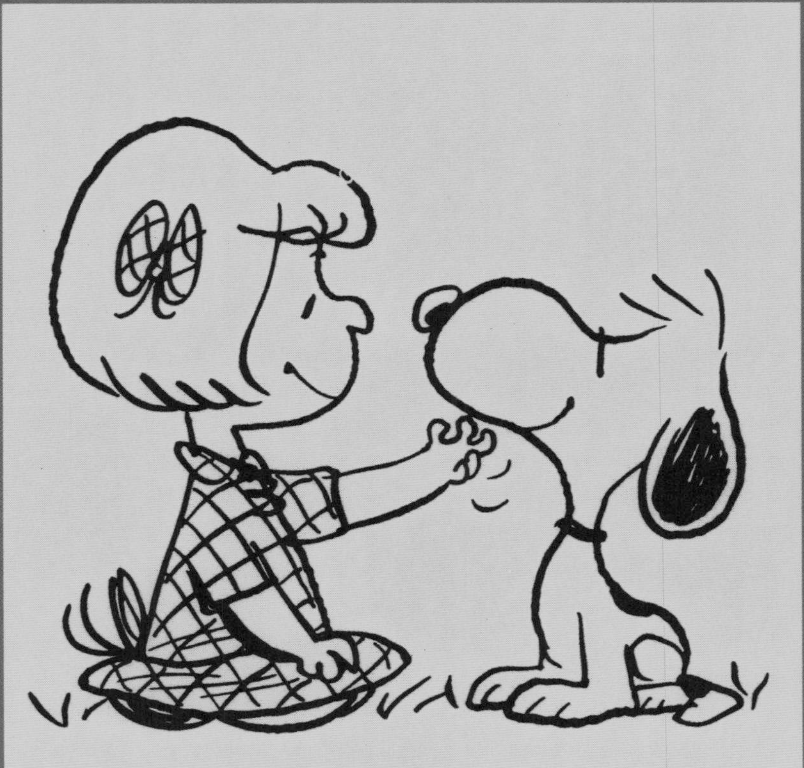

Happiness is coming home from the hospital.

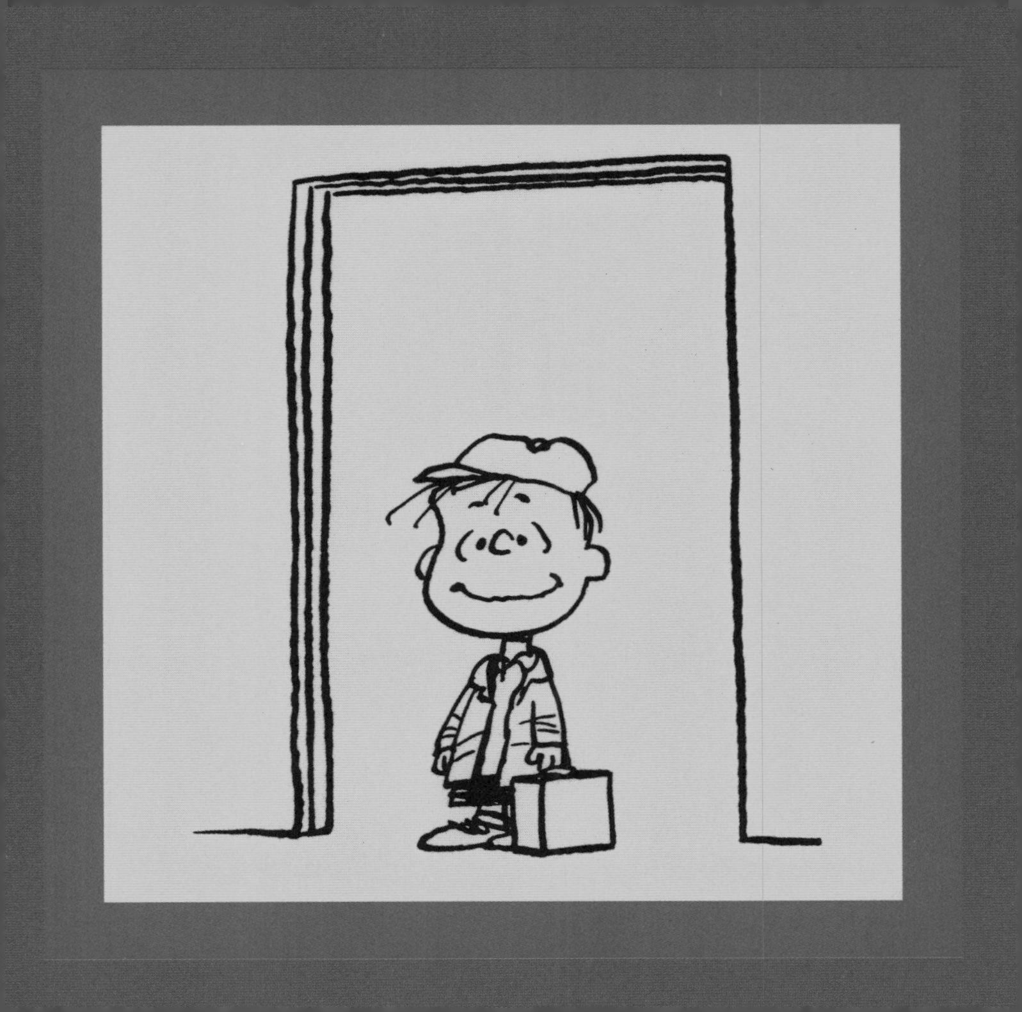

Happiness
is
a
circus
balloon.

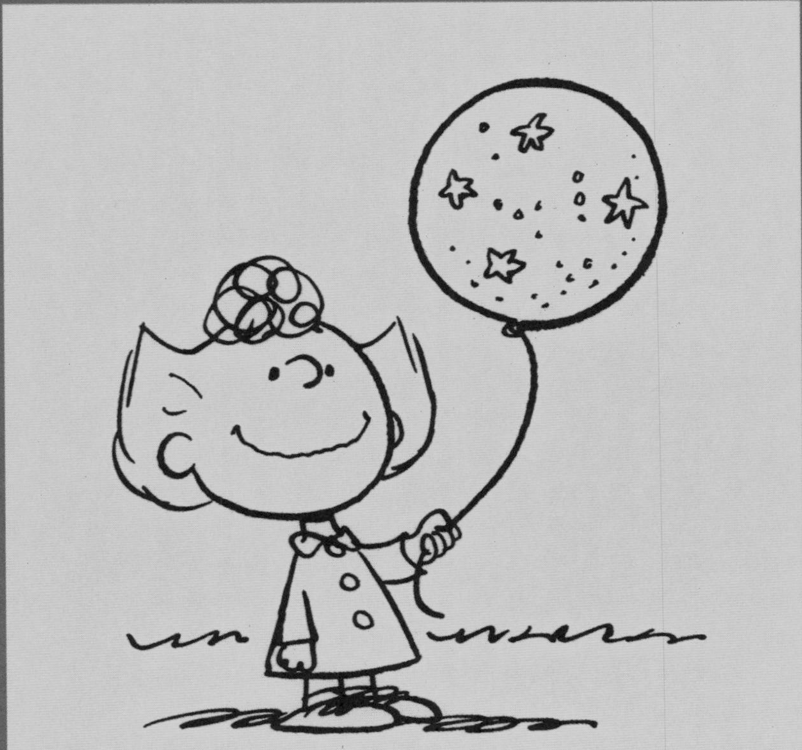

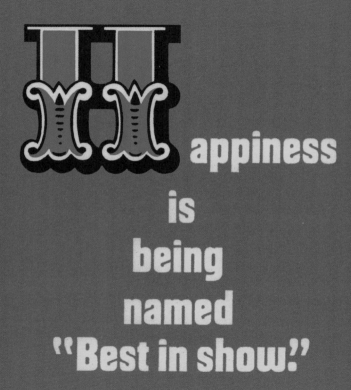

Happiness is being named "Best in show."

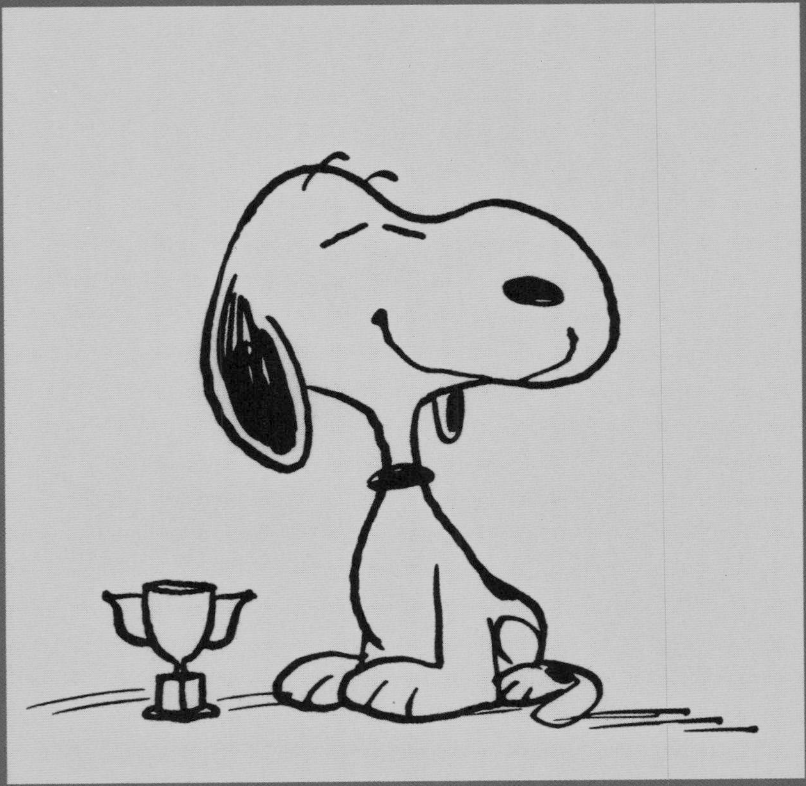

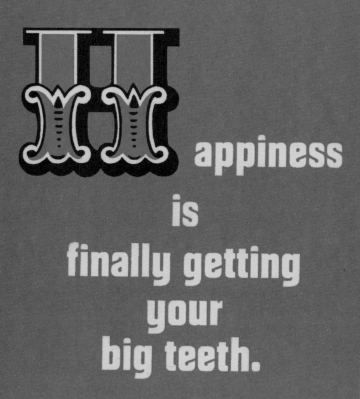

Happiness
is
finally getting
your
big teeth.

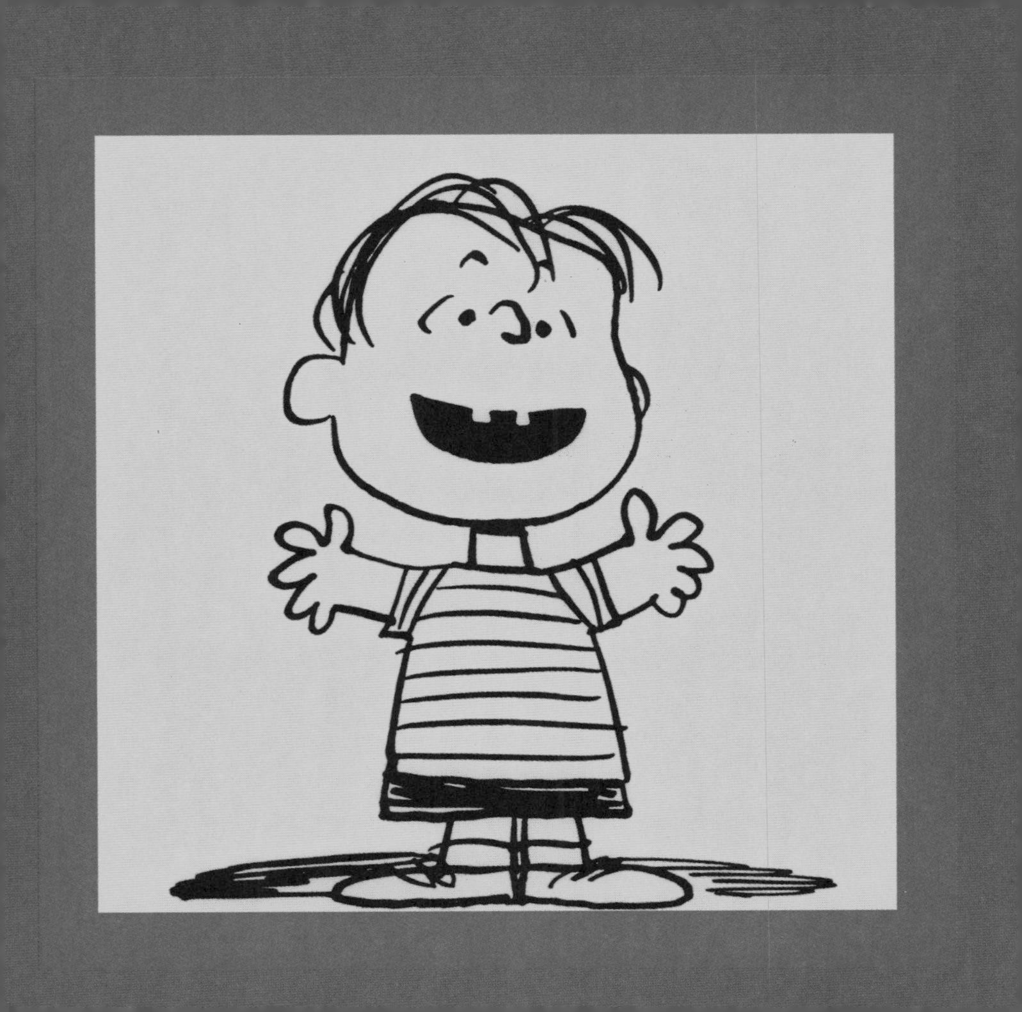

Happiness
is
a stack
of
old comic books.

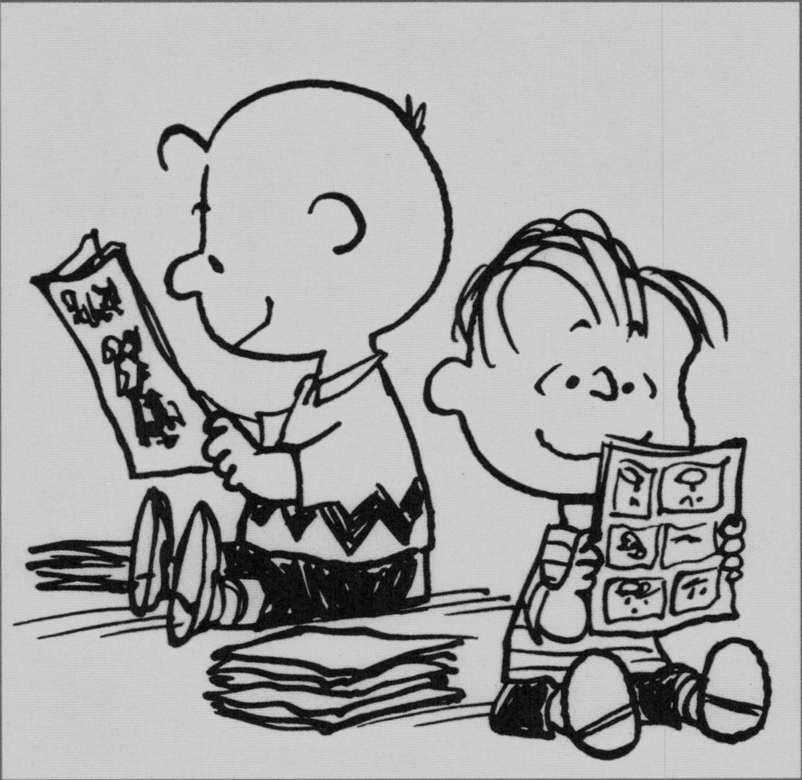

Happiness
is
a Christmas vacation
with
no book reports to write.

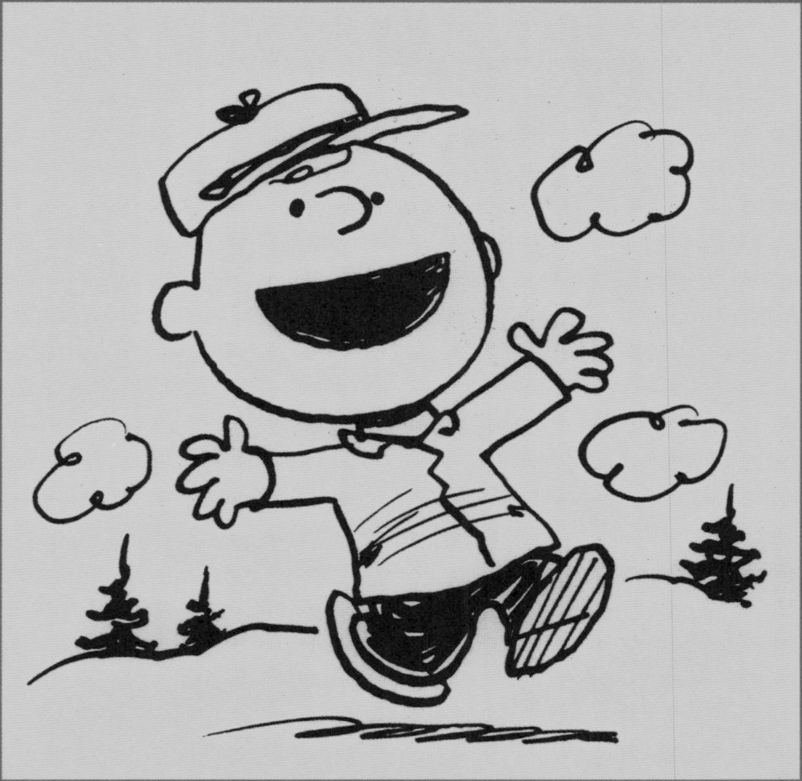

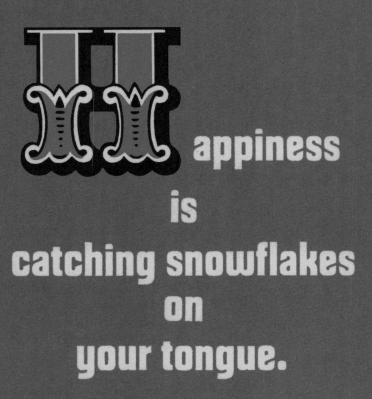

Happiness
is
catching snowflakes
on
your tongue.

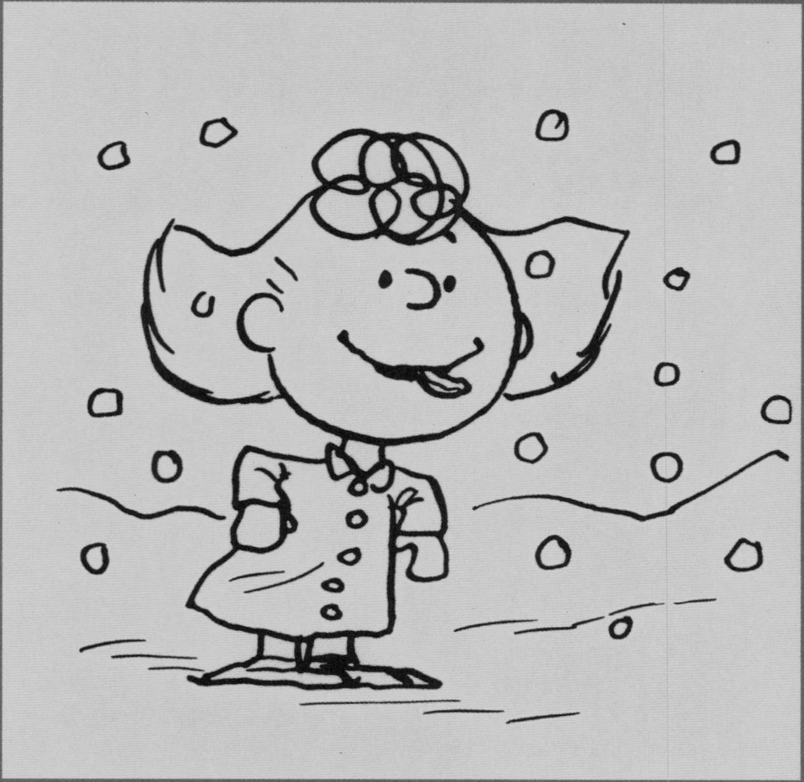

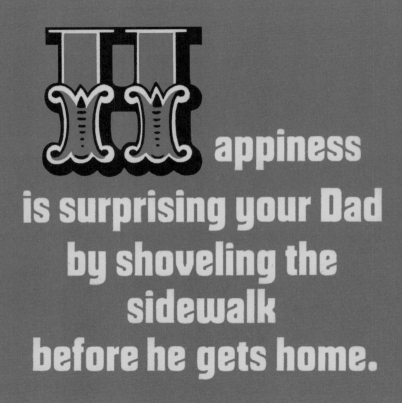appiness
is surprising your Dad
by shoveling the
sidewalk
before he gets home.

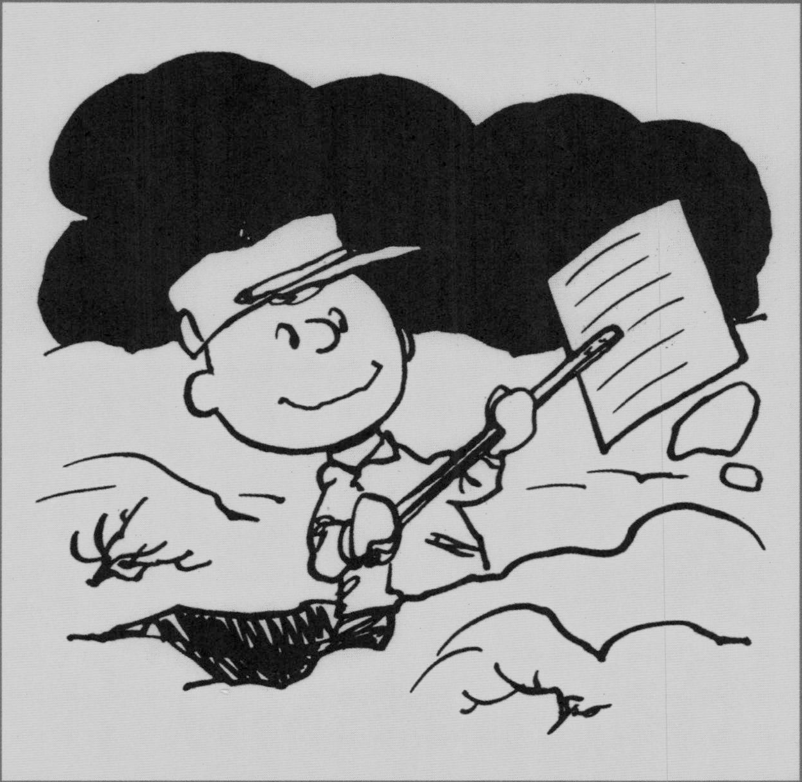

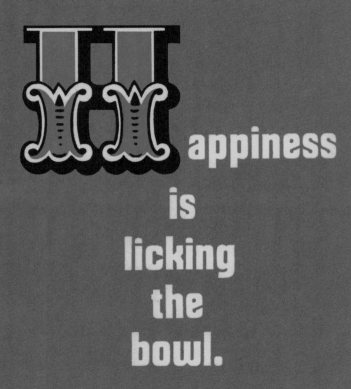

Happiness
is
licking
the
bowl.

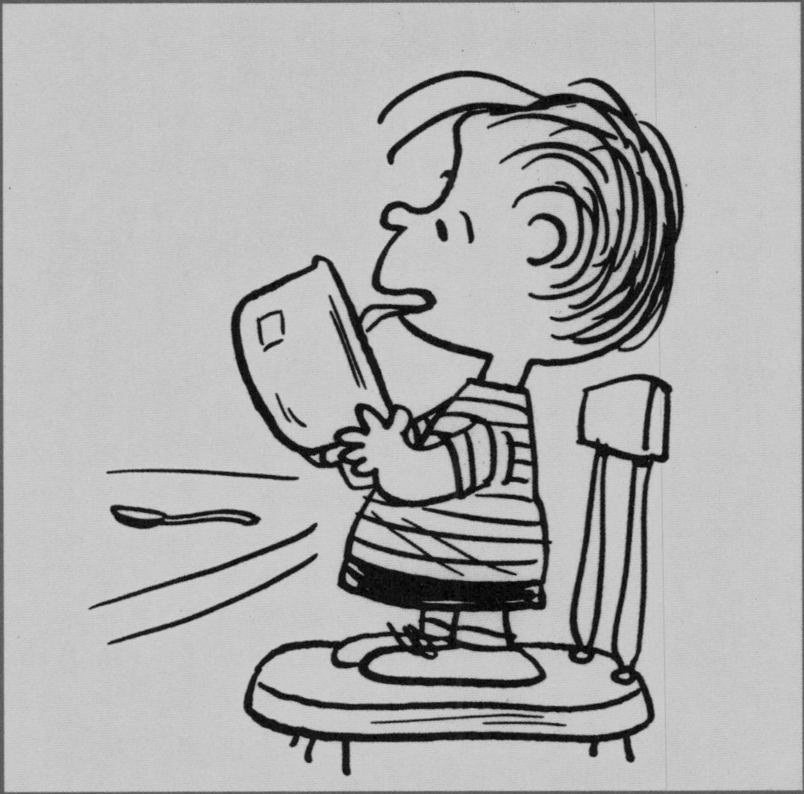

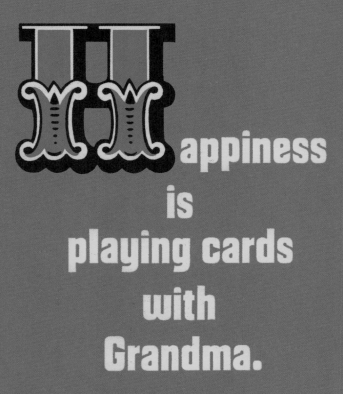

Happiness
is
playing cards
with
Grandma.

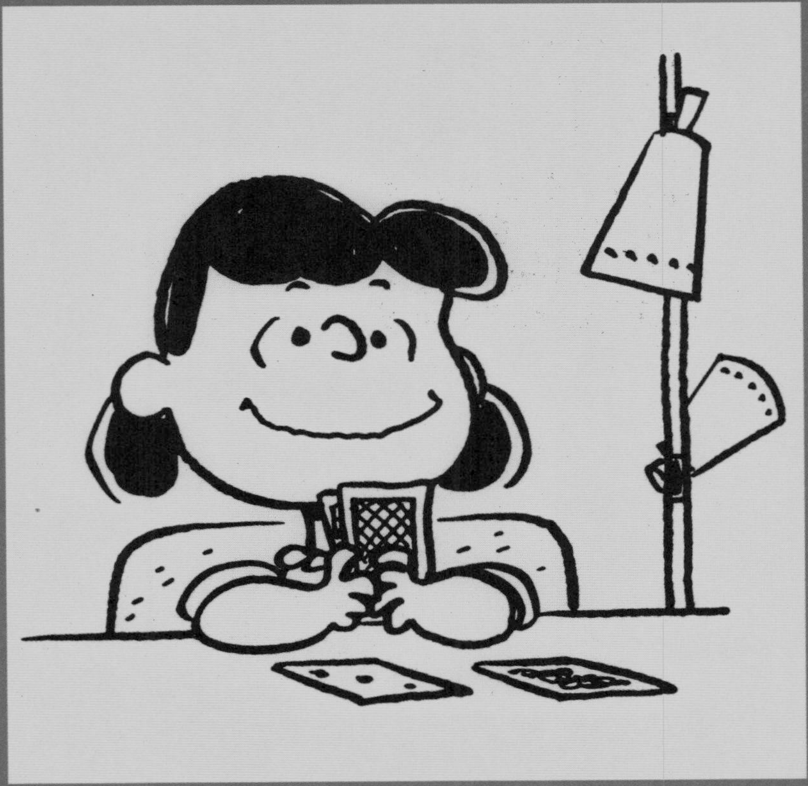

Happiness
is sleeping
in the back seat
on
the way home.

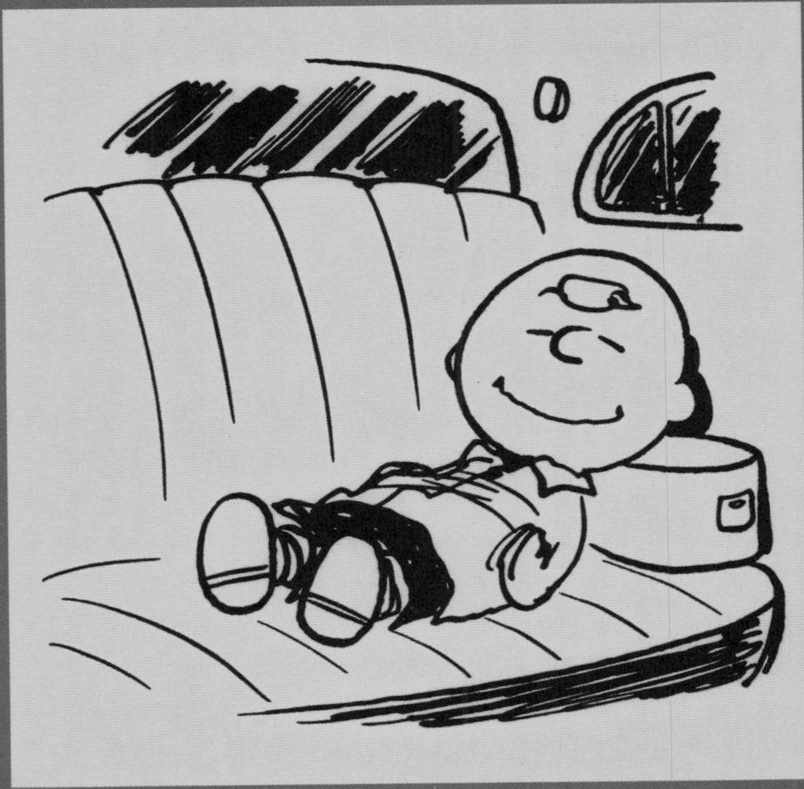

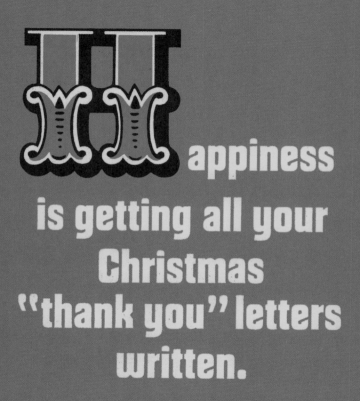

Happiness is getting all your Christmas "thank you" letters written.

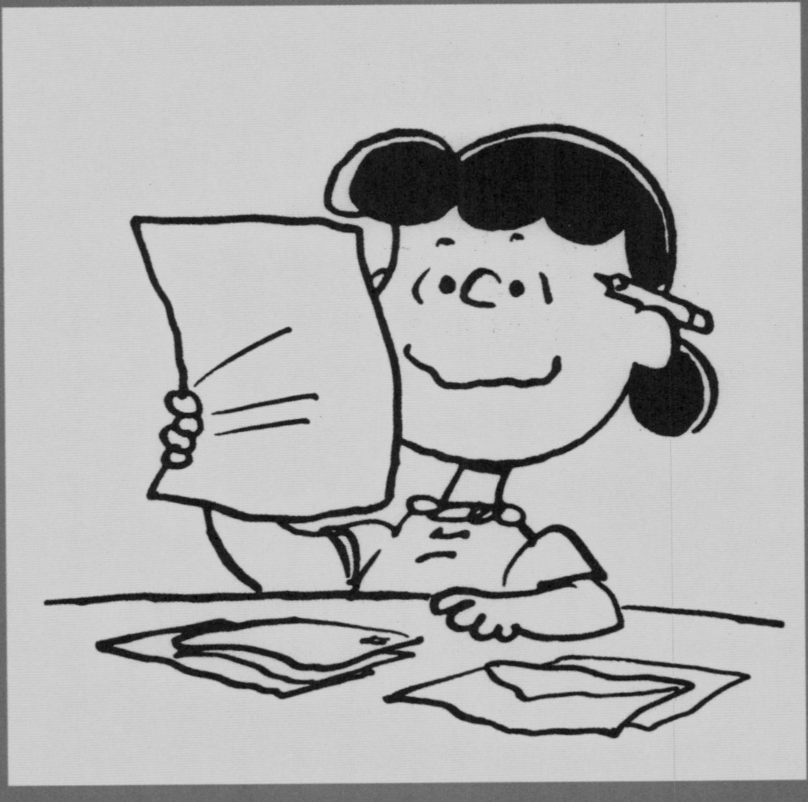

Happiness
is singing
"Blessed Assurance"
at
Camp Meeting.

Happiness is wearing the band from your Dad's cigar.

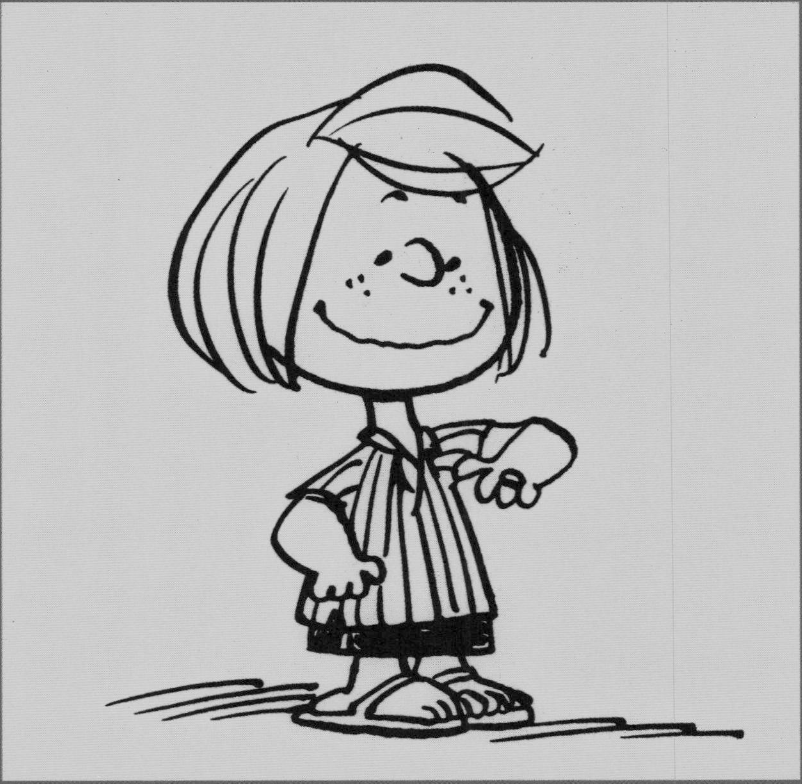

Happiness
is being
too sick to go to school,
but not too sick
to watch T.V.

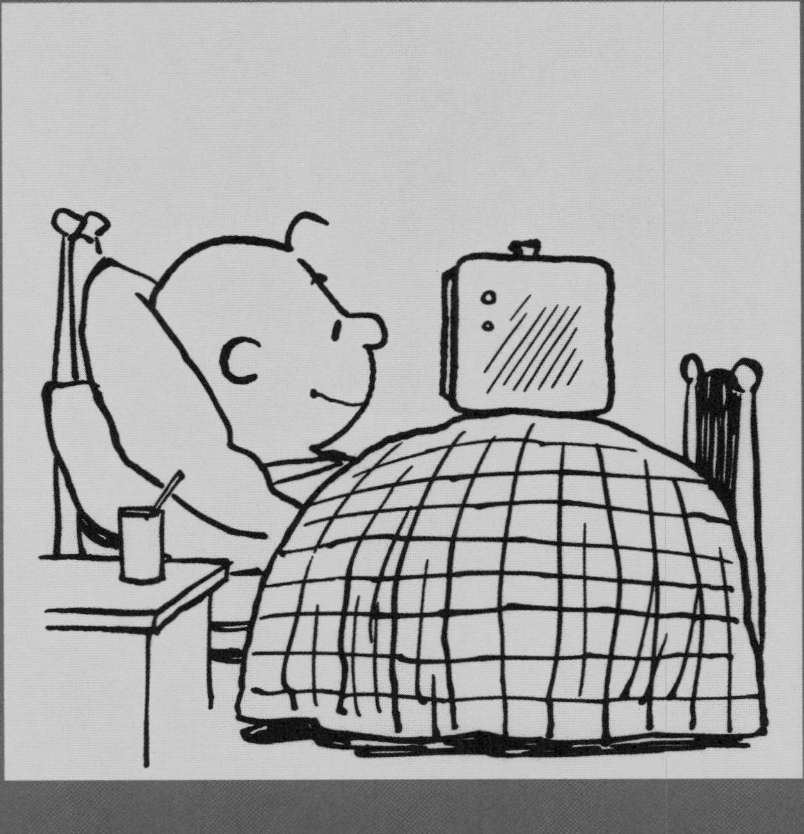

Happiness is being able to walk home from school without having to worry about getting beaten up.

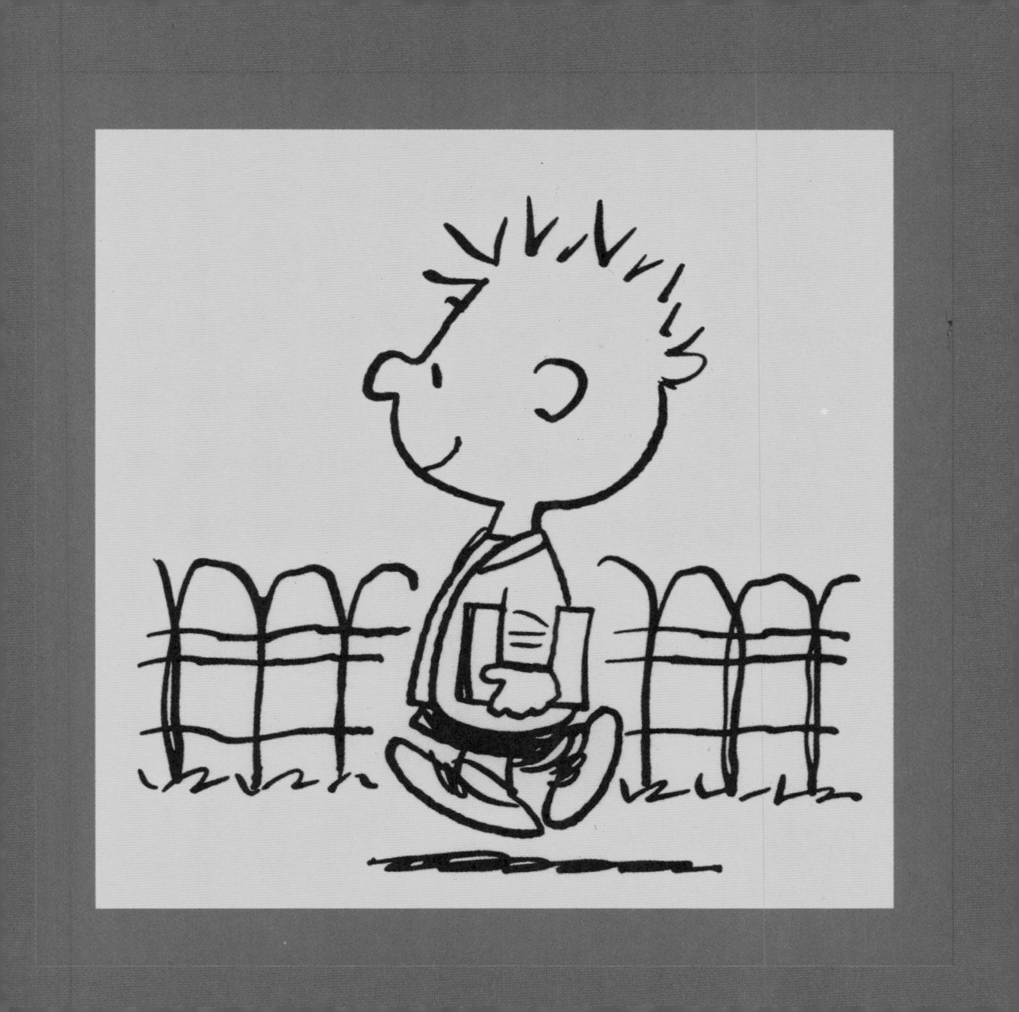

Happiness is a sad song.

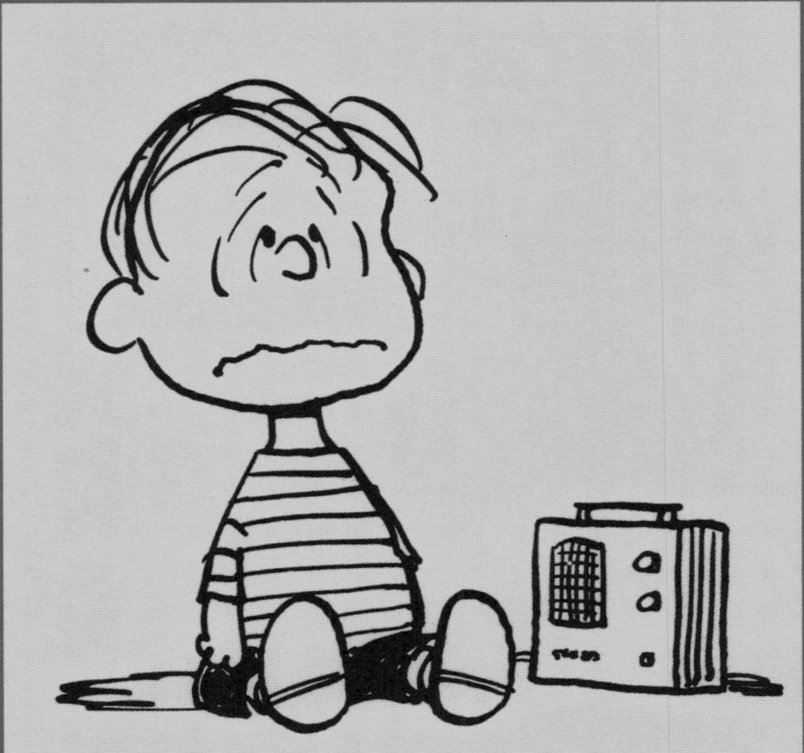

Happiness is knowing you've made it through one more day.

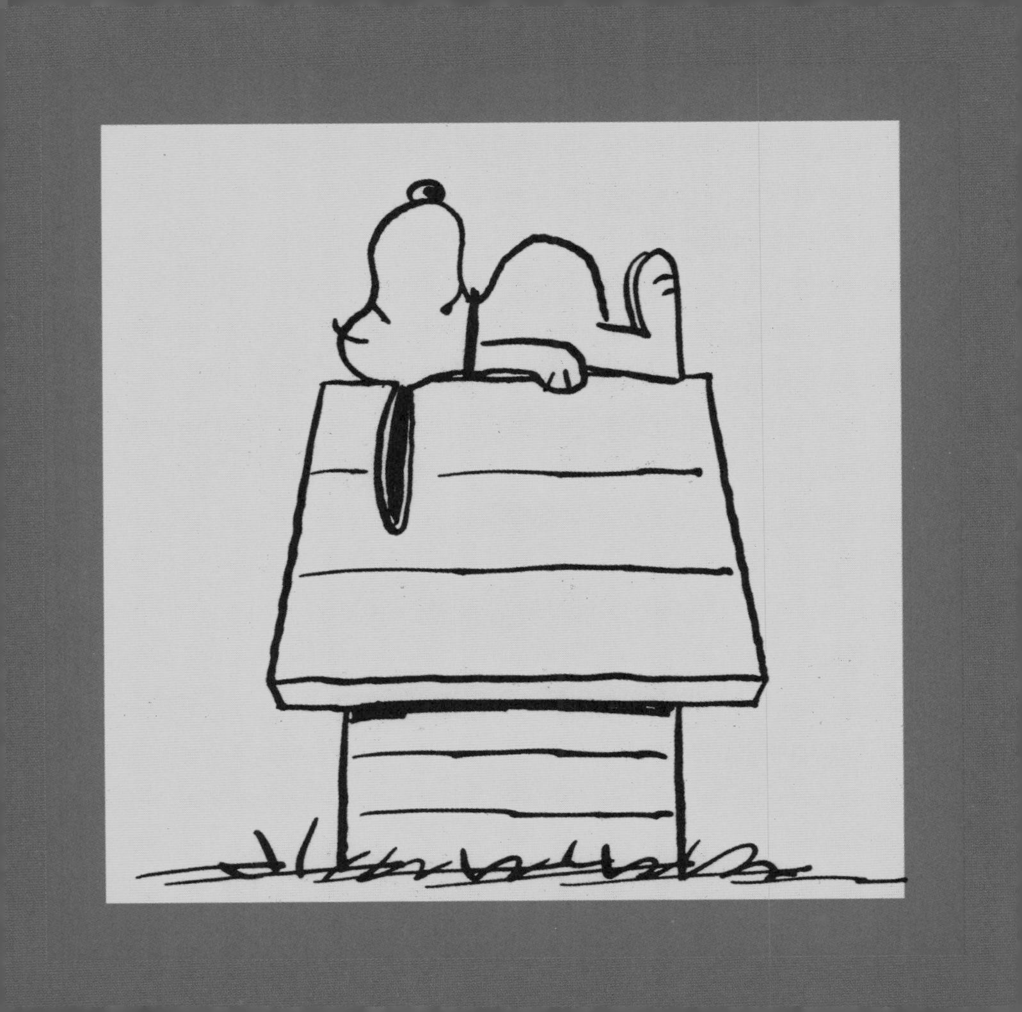

Outer space fascinates me.

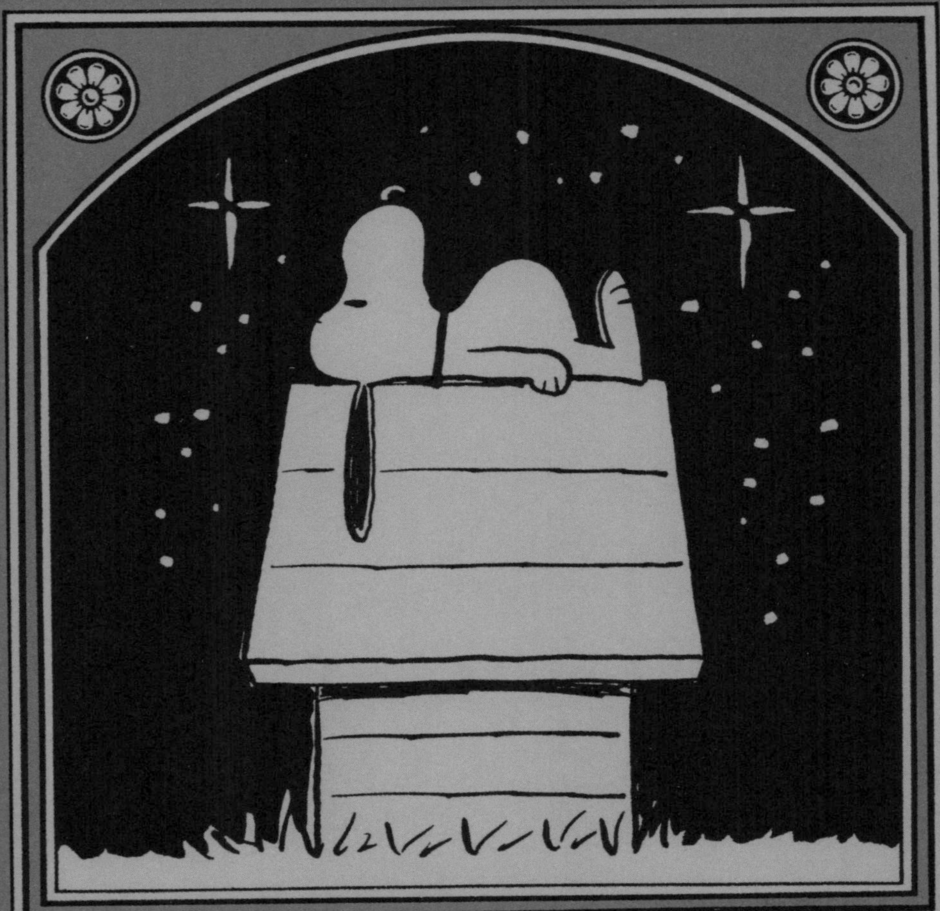

Show me a veterinarian, and I'll show you a man who loves to wield a needle!

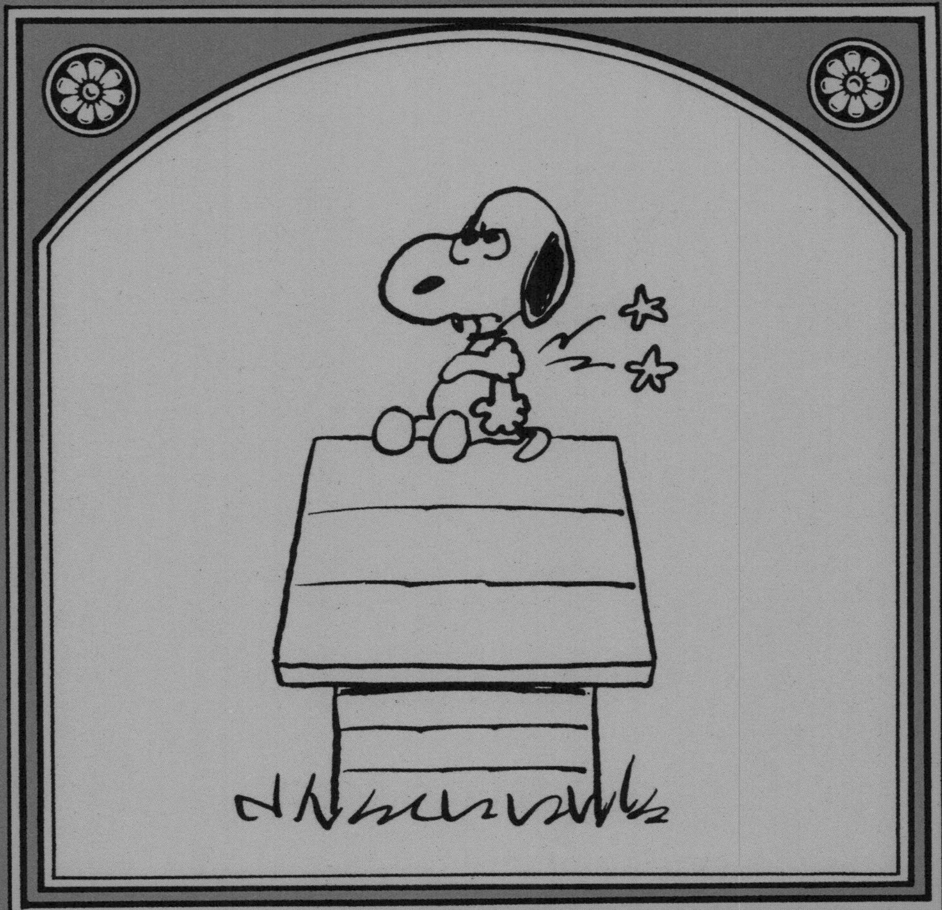

I love to hear the patter of rain on the roof while I'm sleeping.

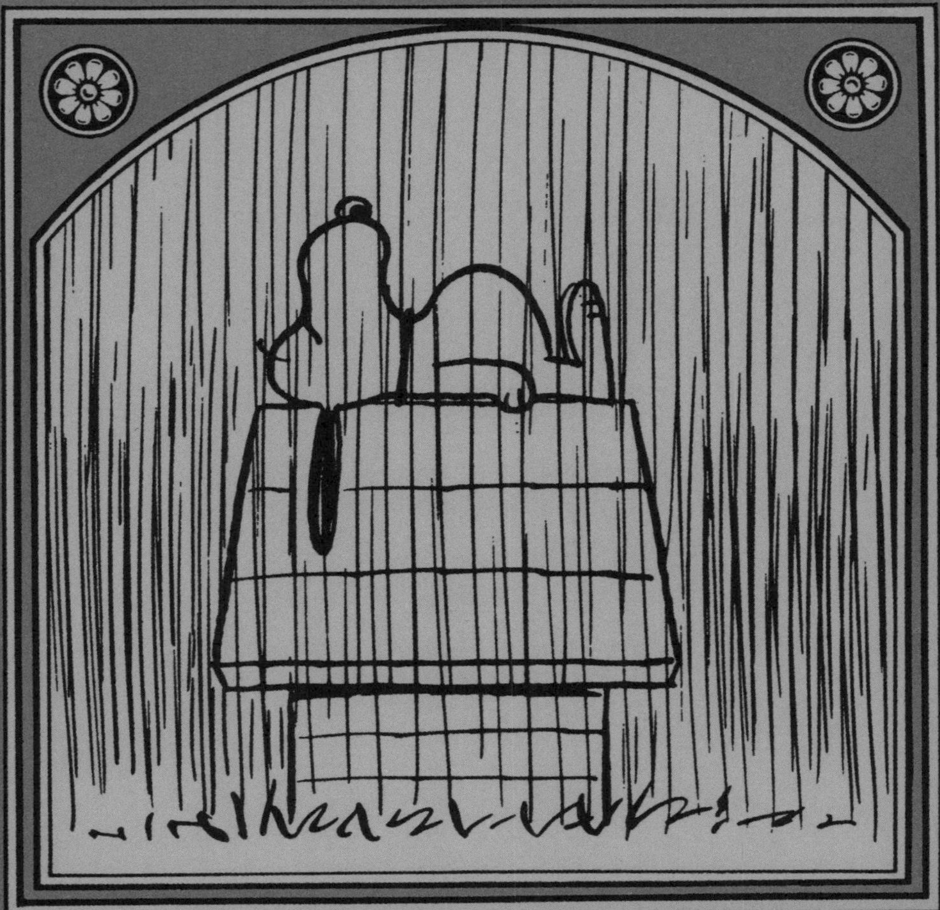

Snow is nice too.

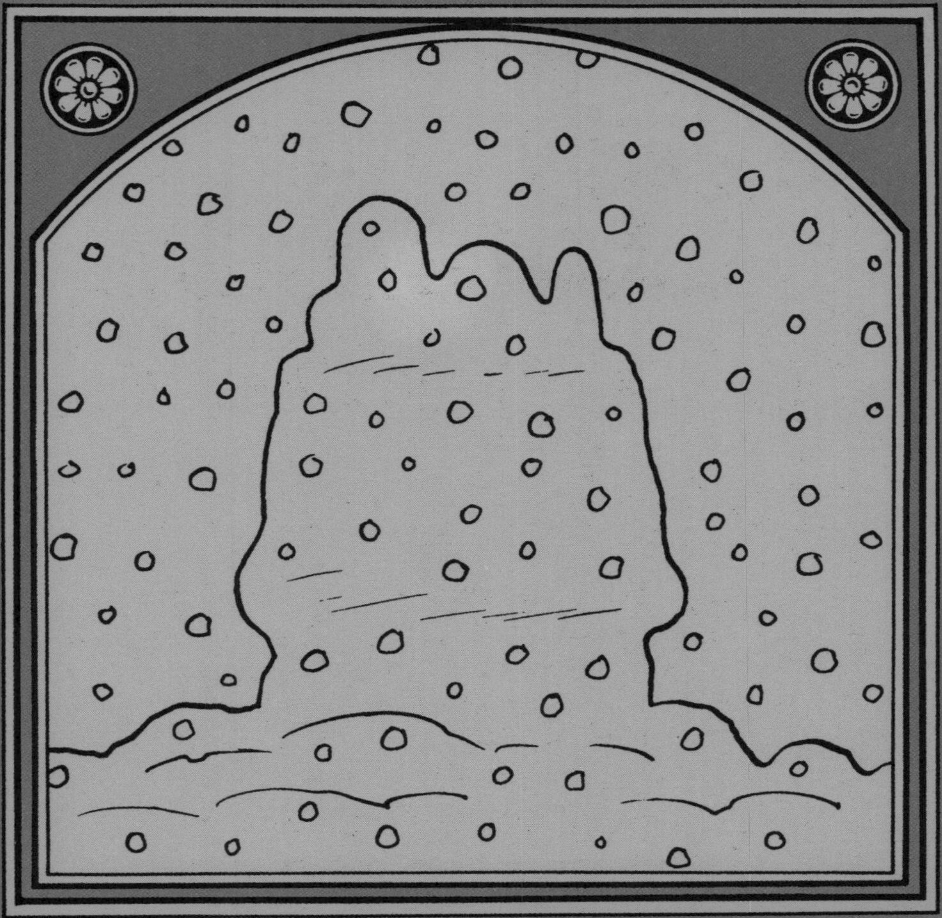

There's the ugliest sight in the world...an empty dog dish!

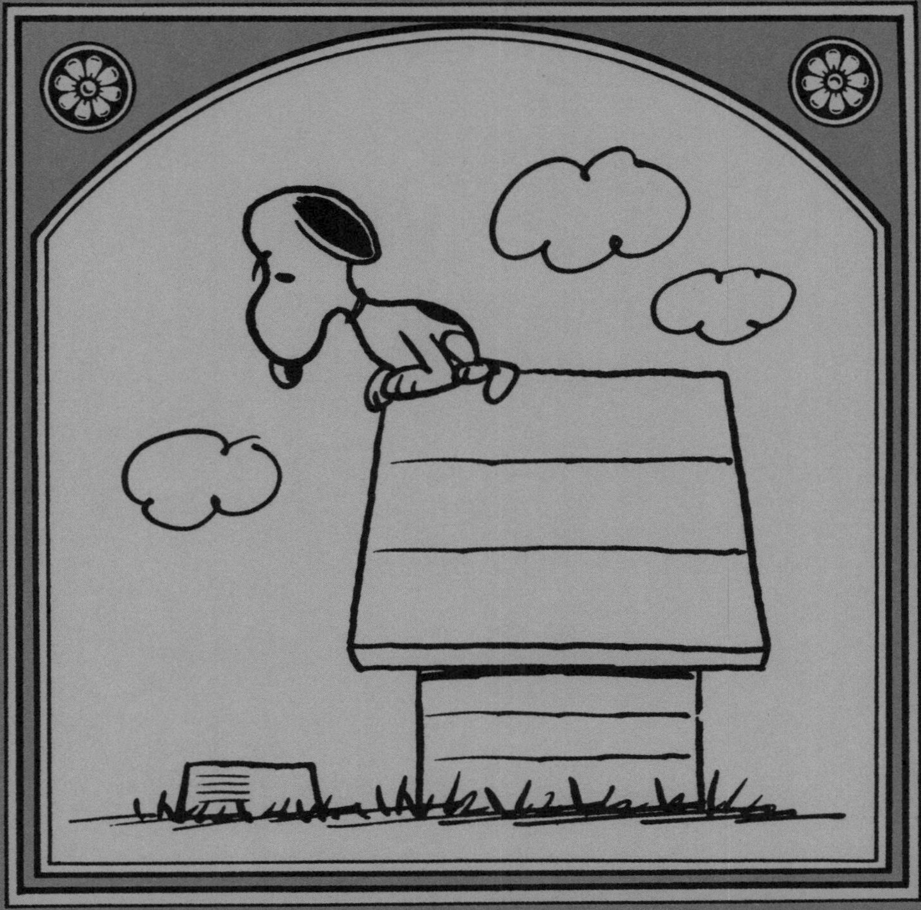

On a clear night I can get Mexico City.

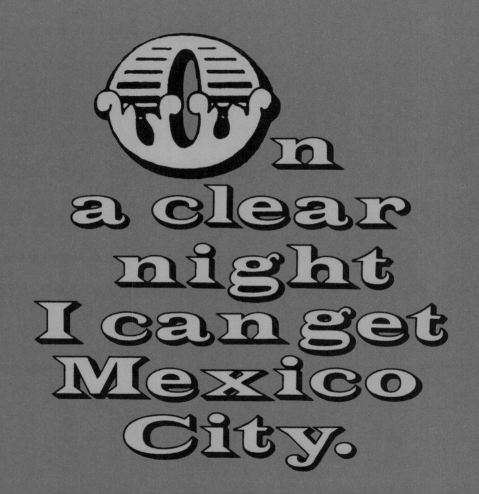

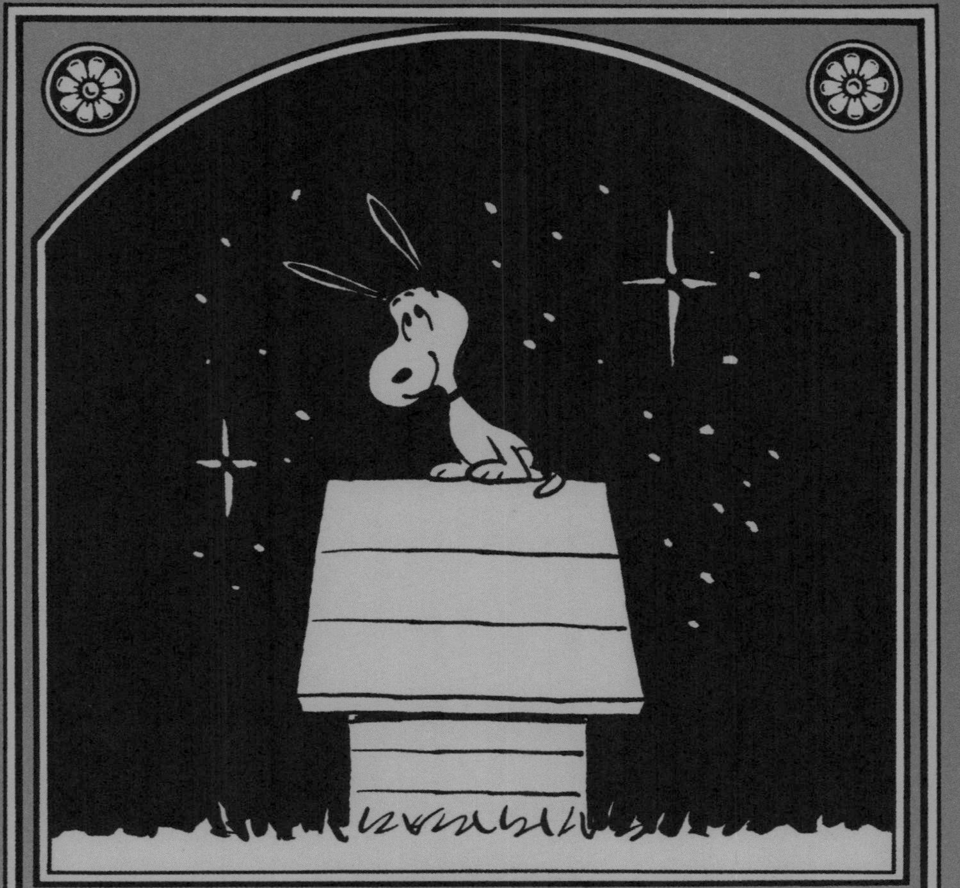

I miss Mr. Peepers.

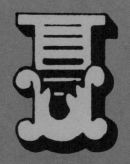

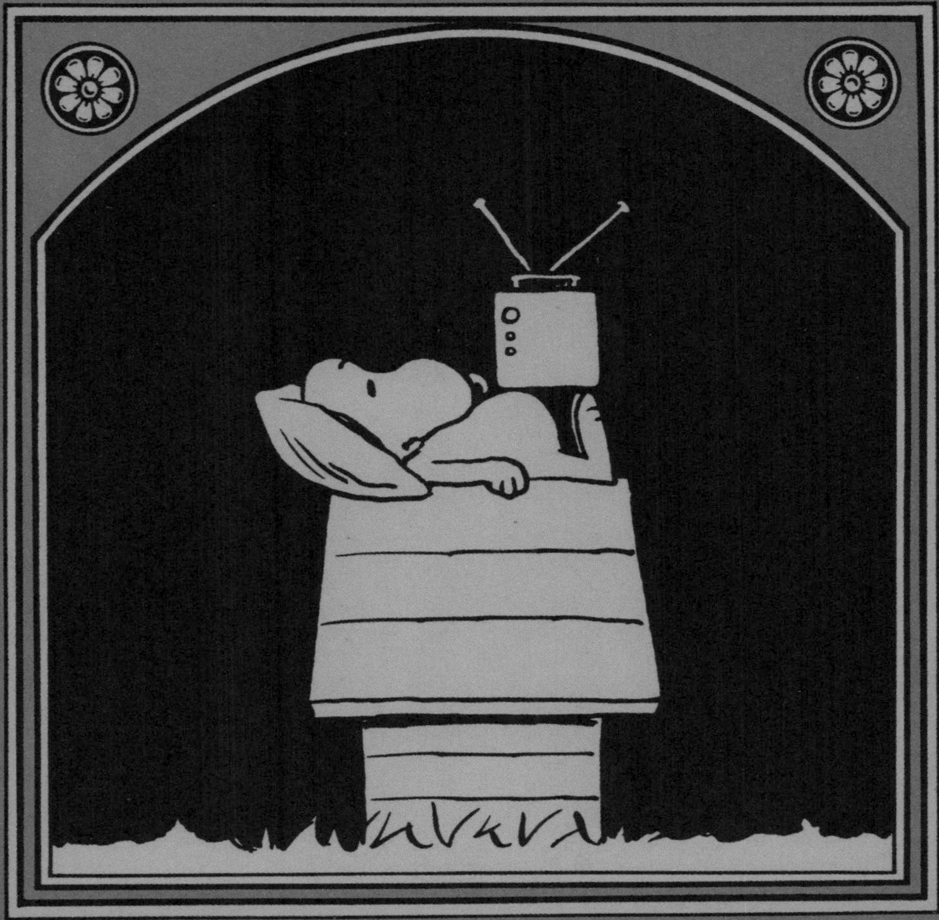

Some
guys
never really
learn
to do
anything.

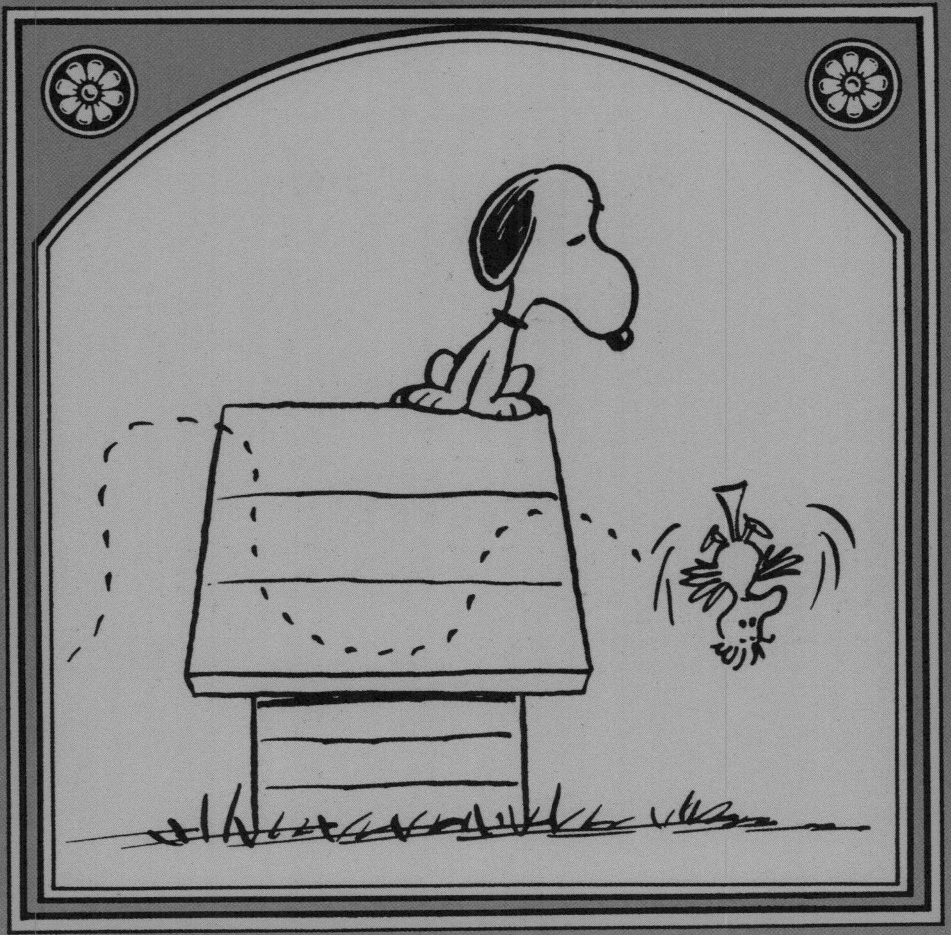

It is my humble opinion that a night's sleep dreaming of cats is no night's sleep at all.

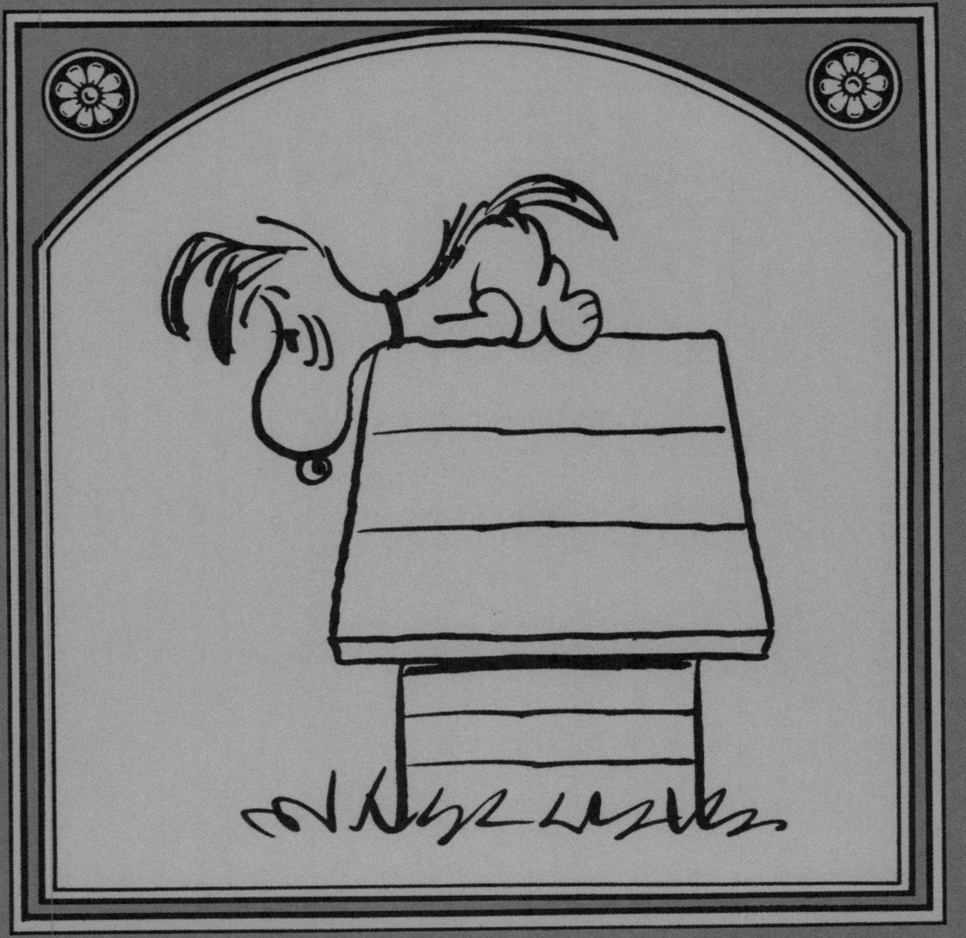

he
only time I hear
from the
Daisy Hill
Puppy Farm
Alumni Association
is when they
want another
donation!

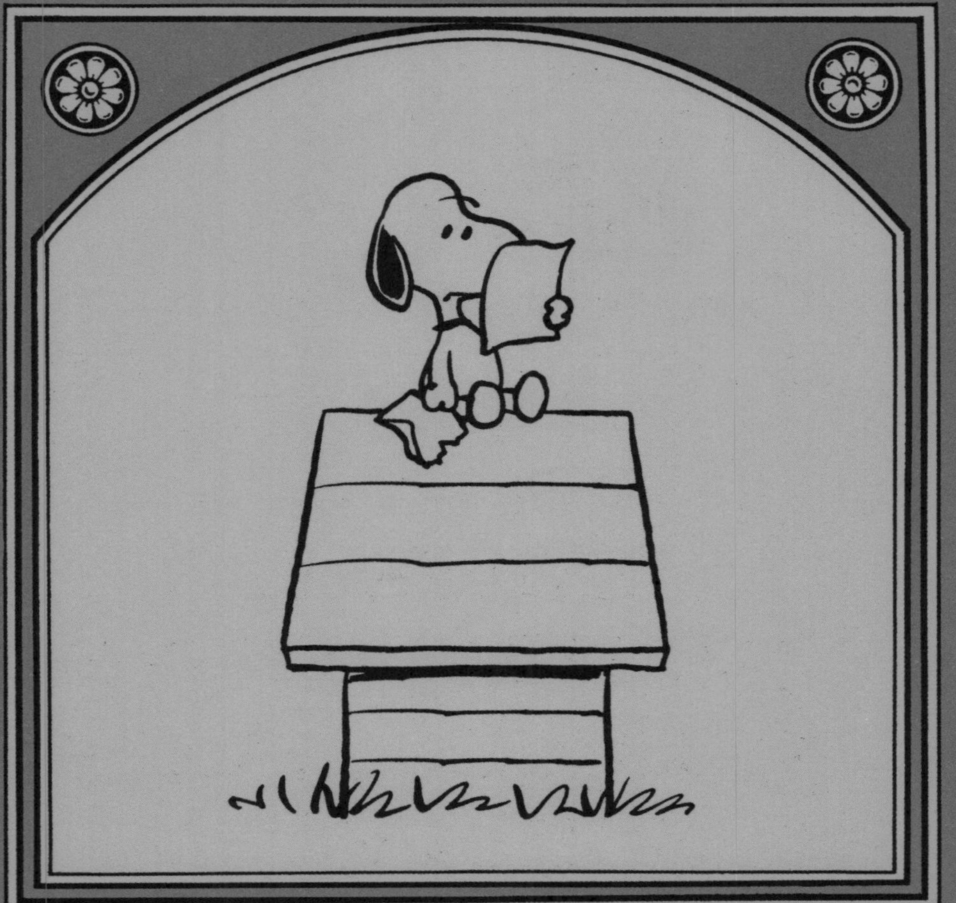

How can you do push-ups when your nose gets in the way?

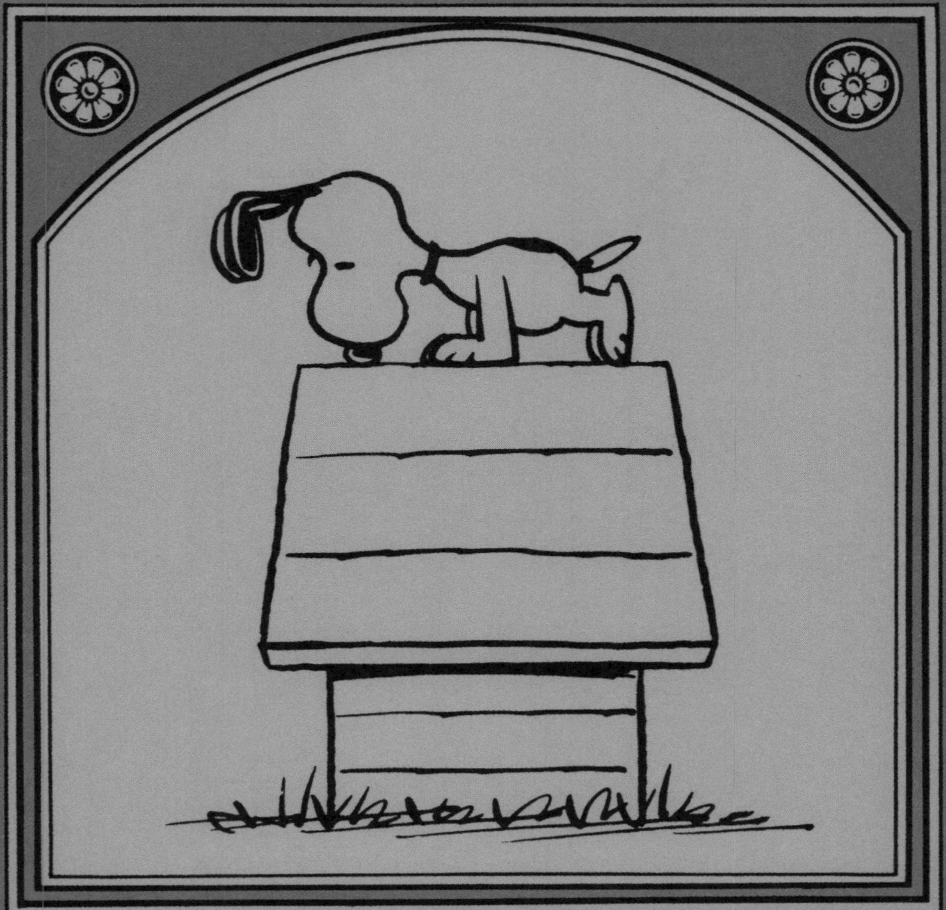

I always have a few friends over for Bridge on Thursdays.

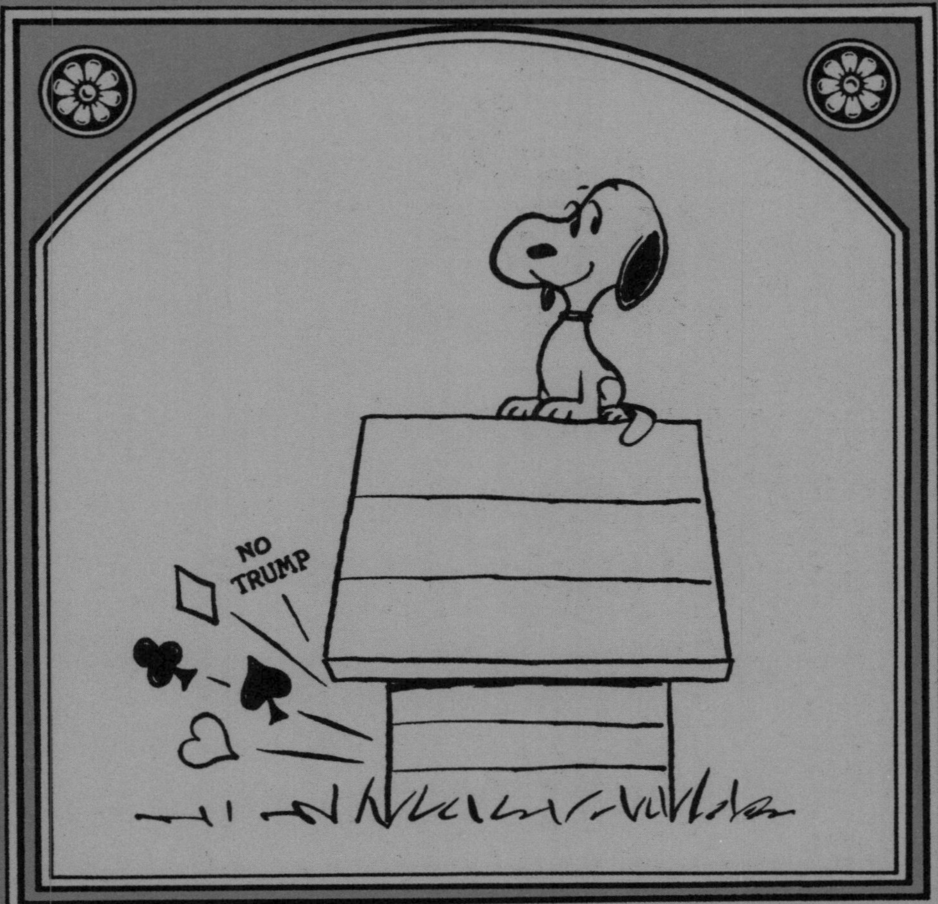
NO TRUMP

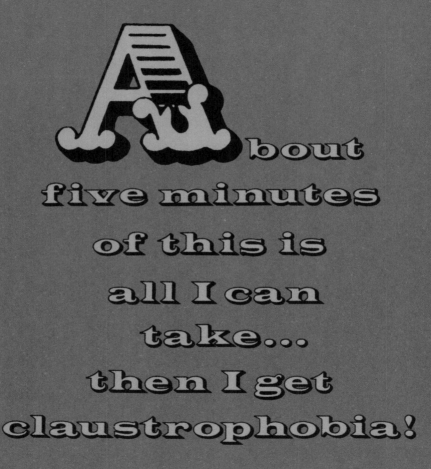

About five minutes of this is all I can take... then I get claustrophobia!

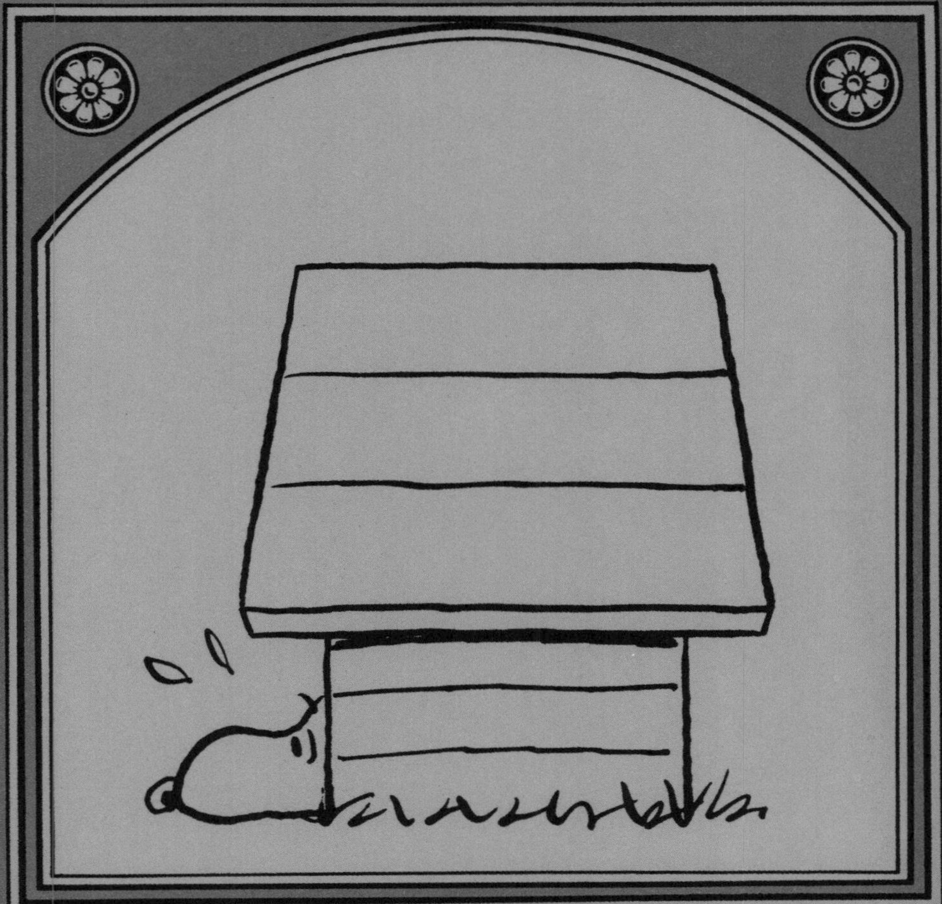

Commuter!

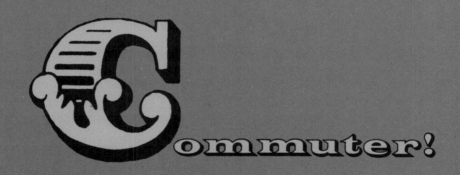

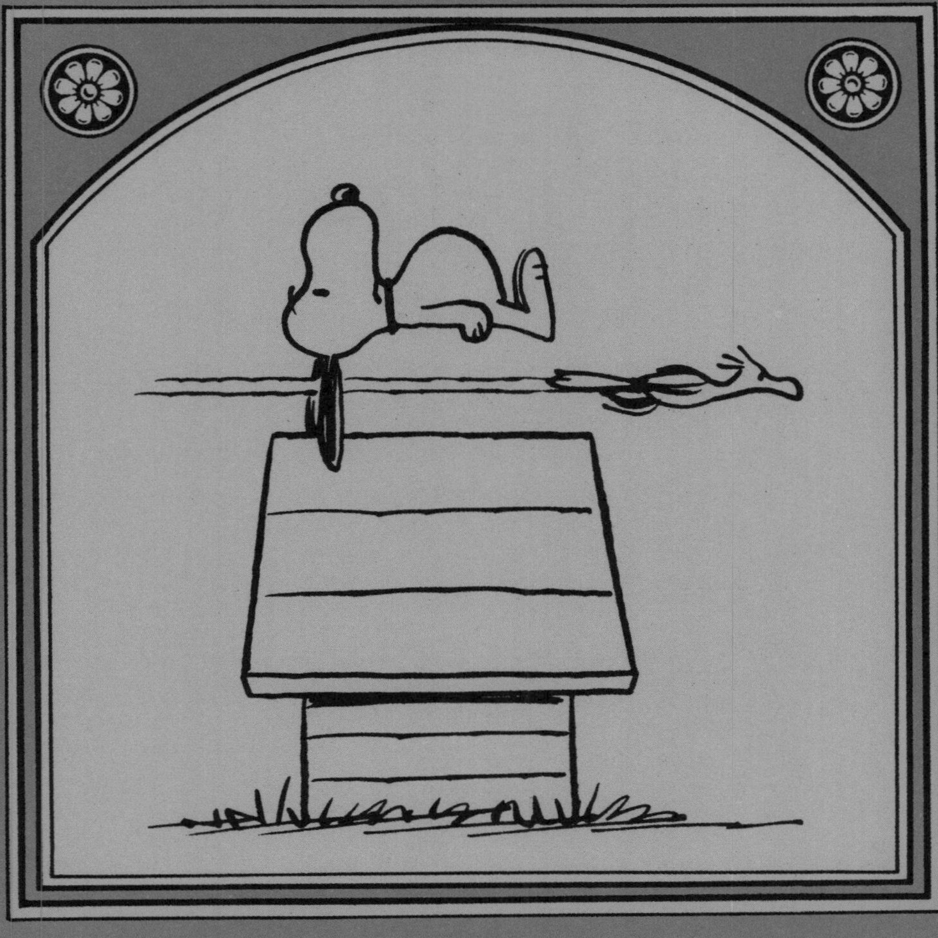

What do you do when your National Geographics begin to overflow?

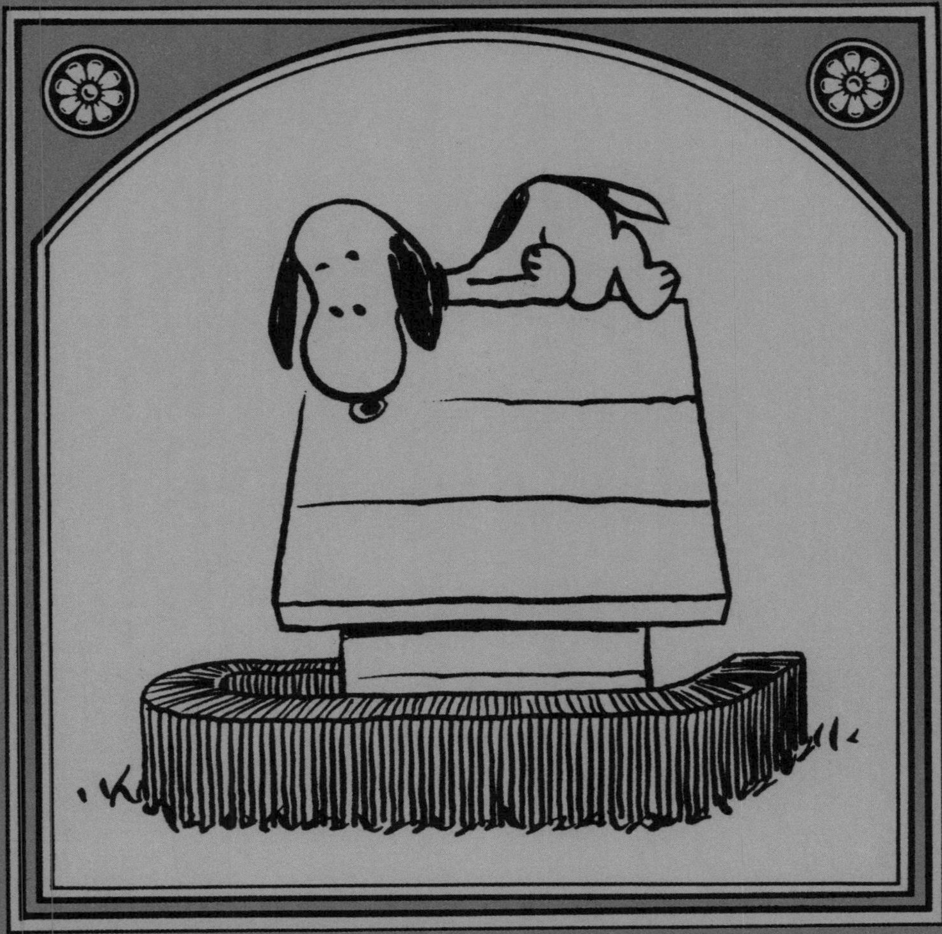

Is it fall already?

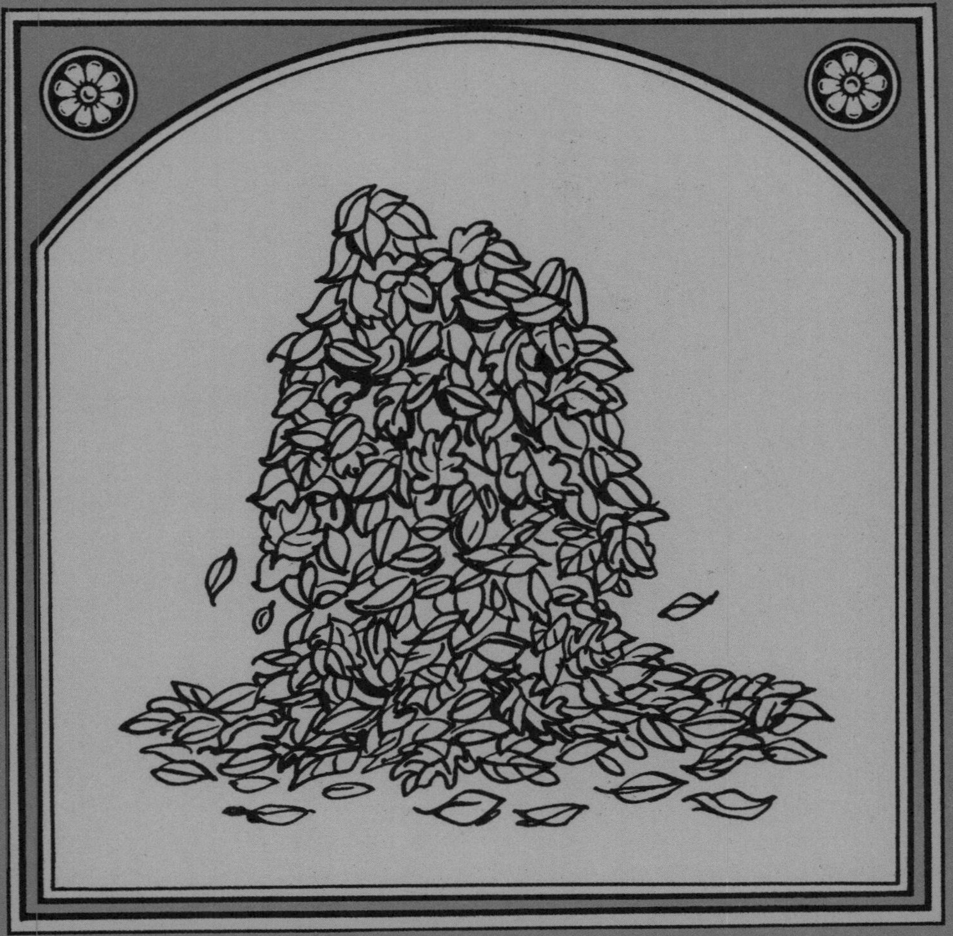

 live
in constant fear
that someone
will break in
and
steal all of my
Hank Williams
records.

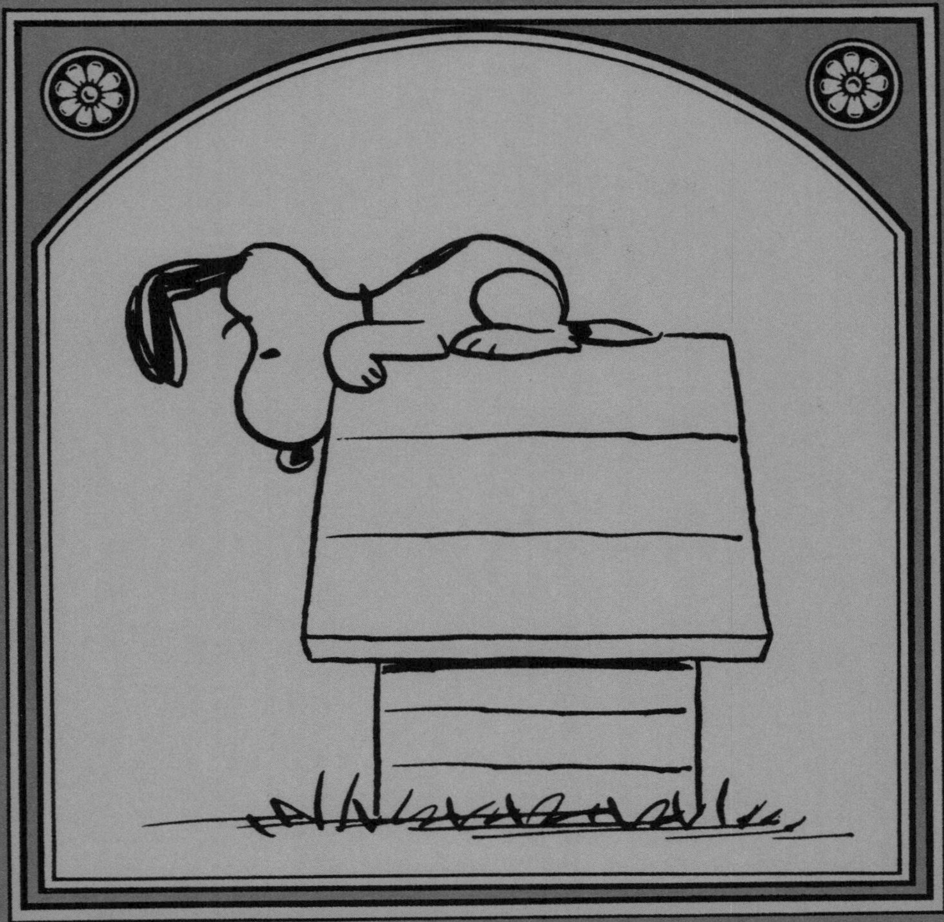

So what's wrong with having a night light?

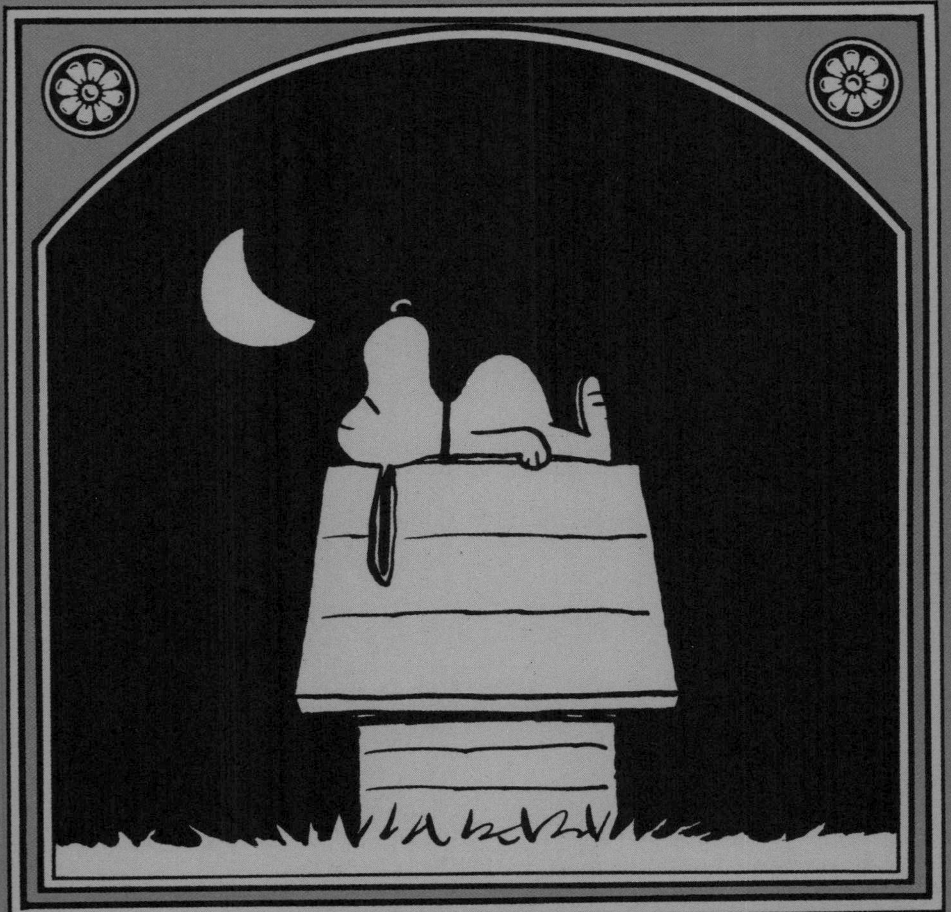

What terrible luck... I plan a picnic for today, and what happens? A locust plague!

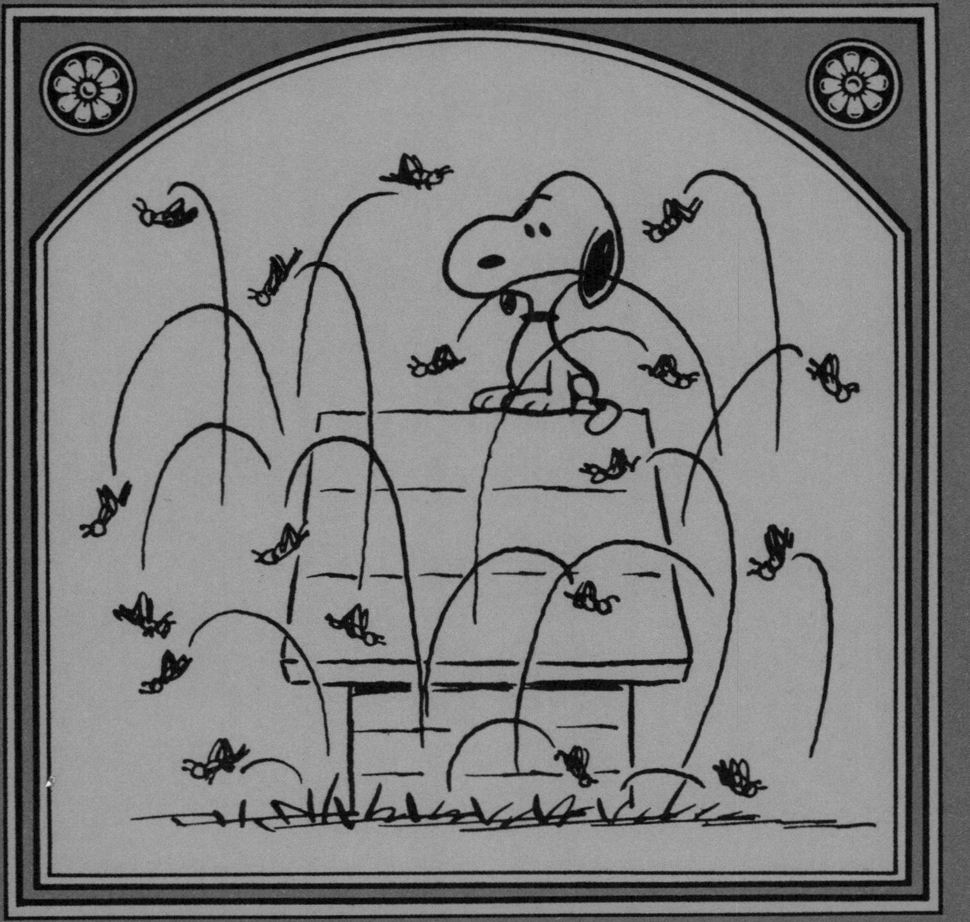

There's nothing like having a friend at the Army Surplus store.

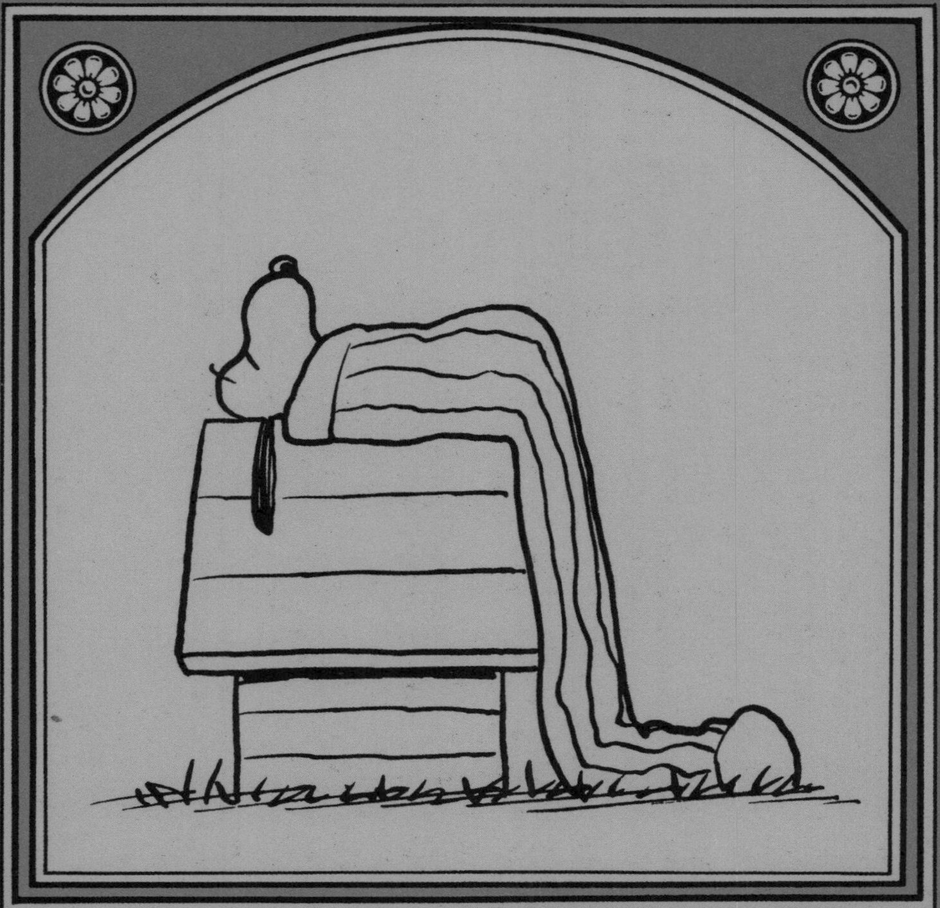

Rats!
Someone left
the
light on
over
the
pool table!

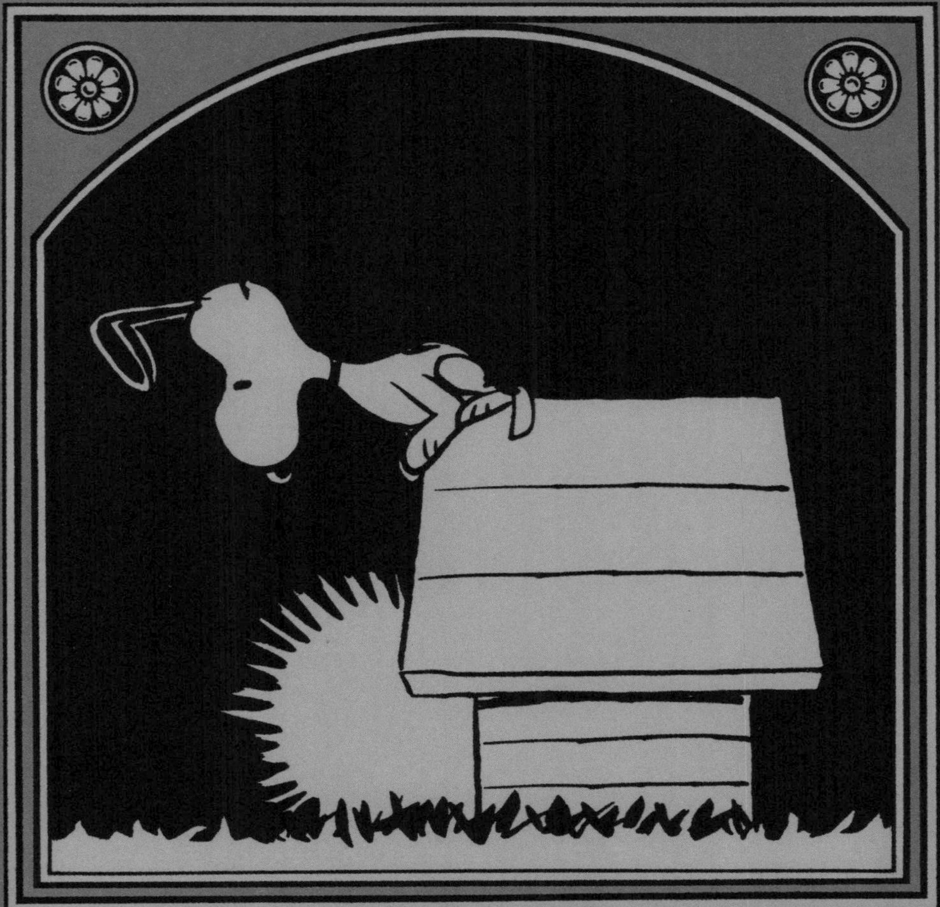

think
I'm
allergic
to
morning.

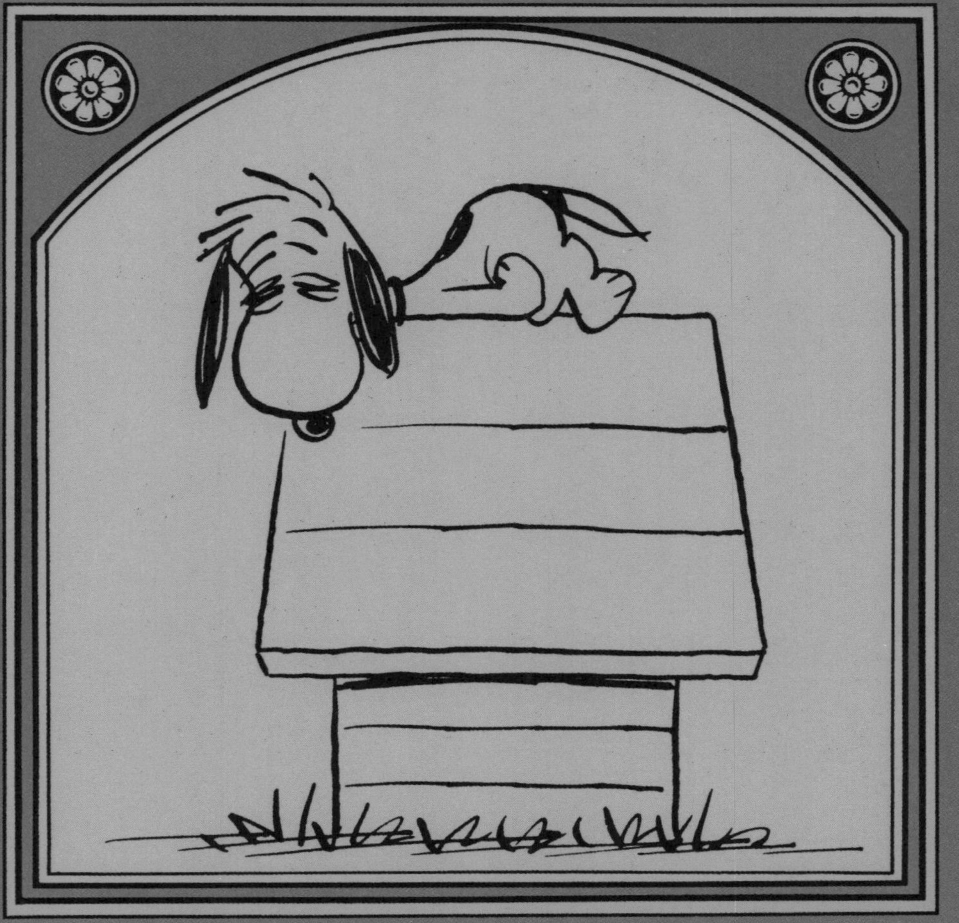

"Pigeons in the grass alas. Beagle on the roof aloof!"

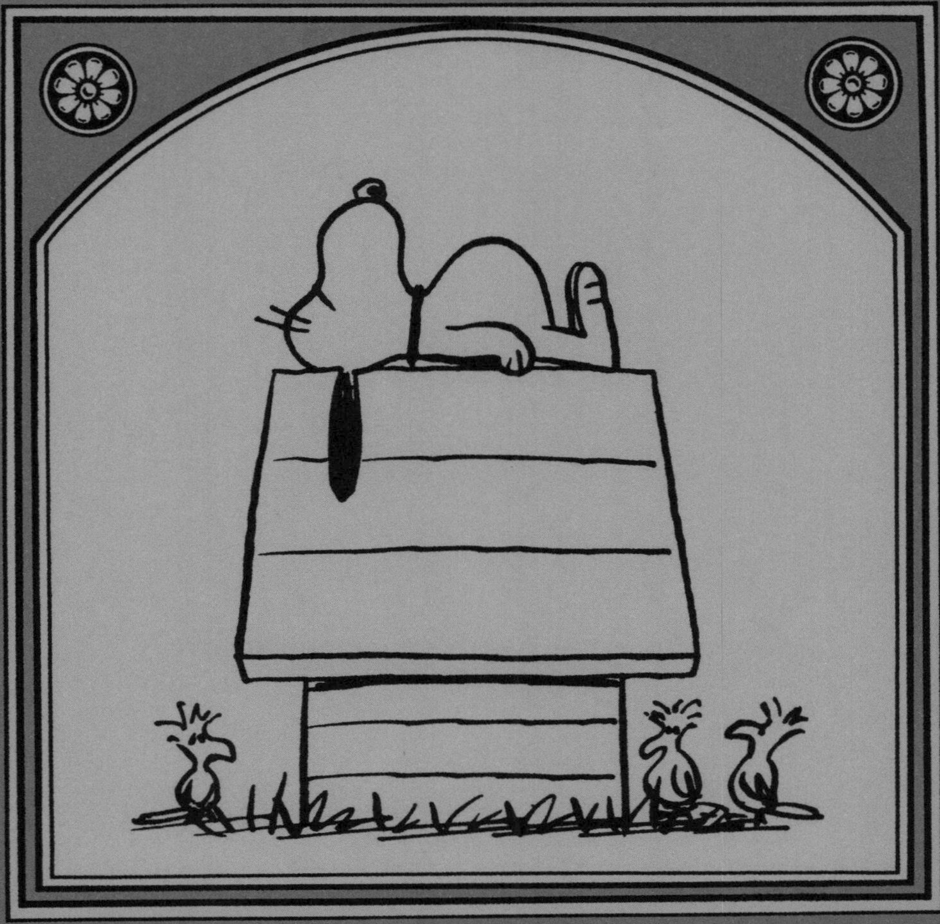

I hate windy days.

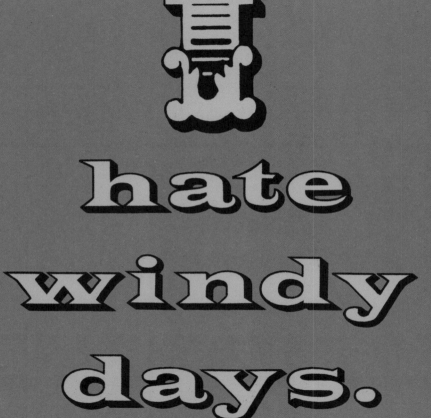

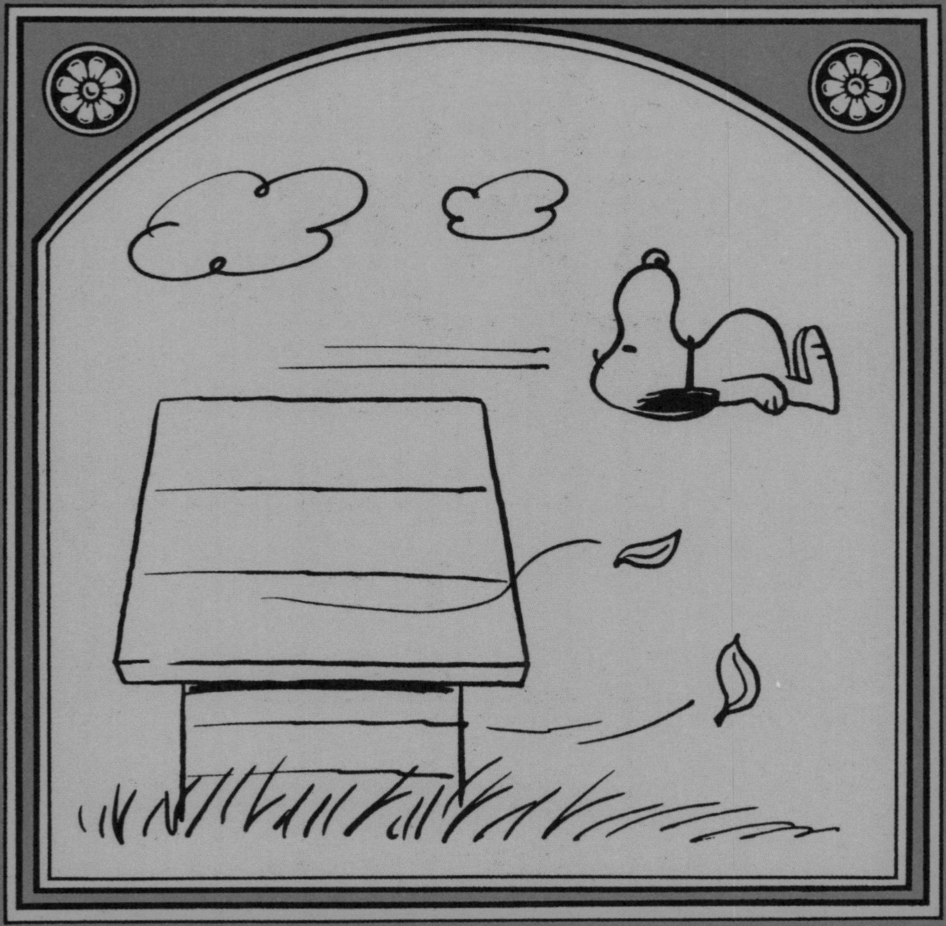

Who
else
do you know
who
can do
the
"Beagle"?

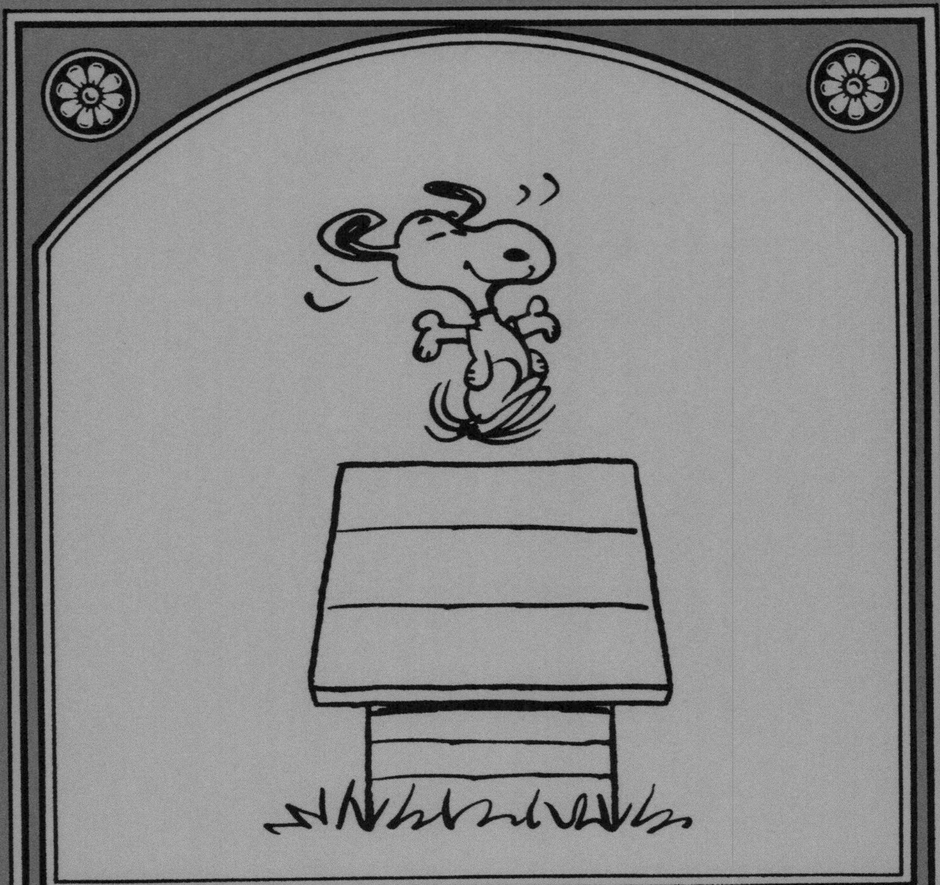

Actually, all I did was put this sweet potato in a jar of water, see... and... well...

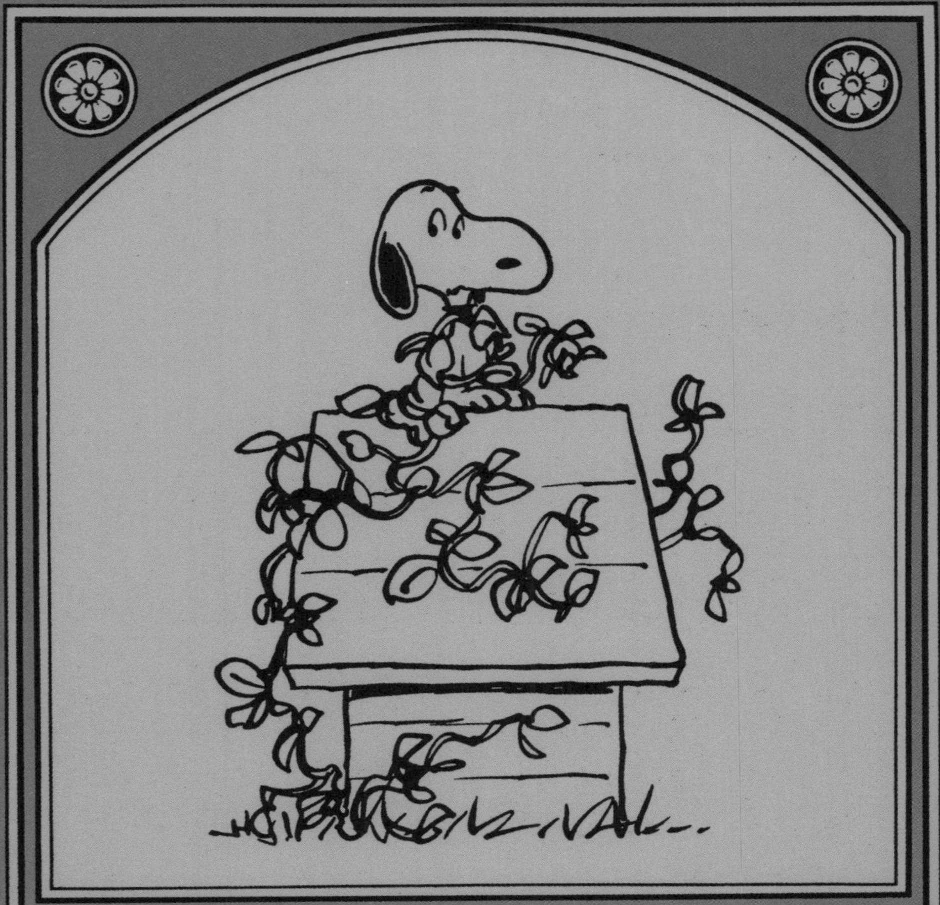

Everyone should spend at least one night during the summer camping out.

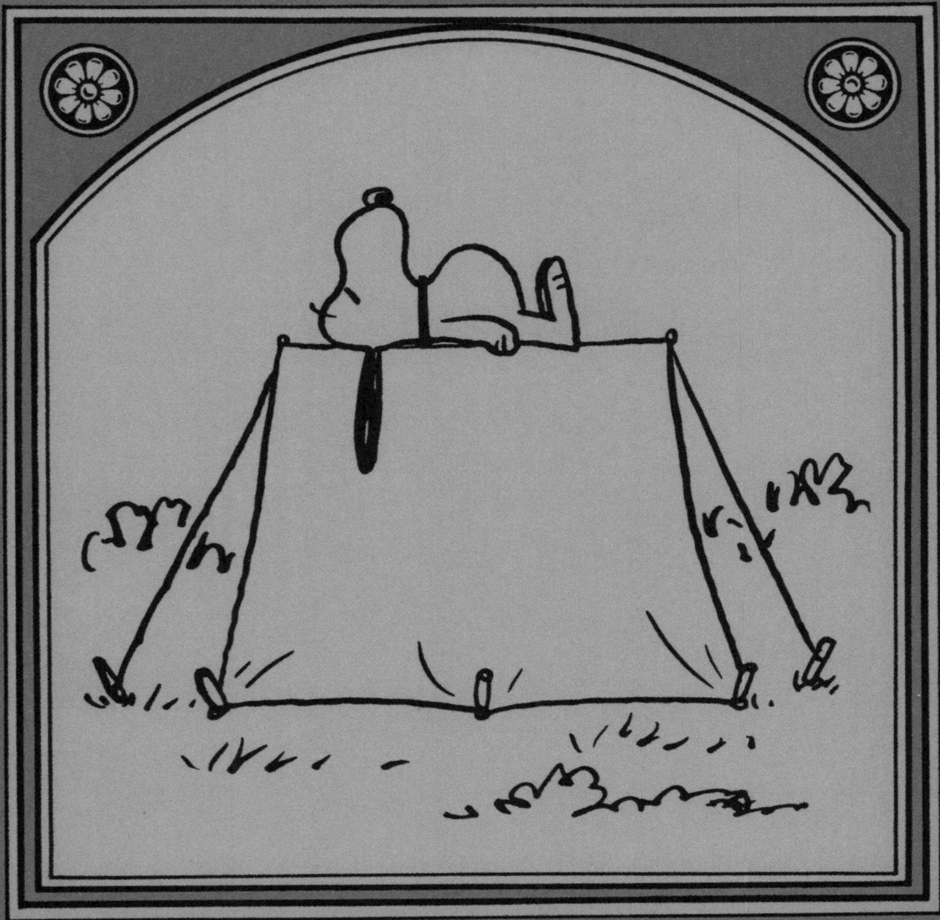

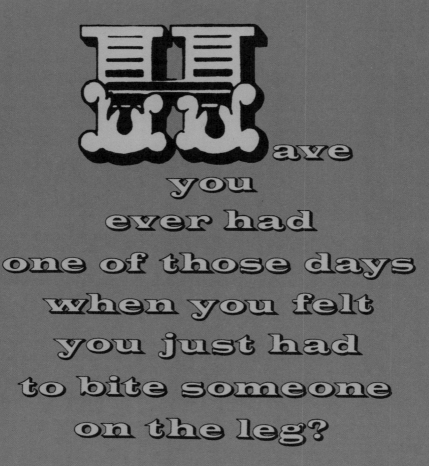

Have you ever had one of those days when you felt you just had to bite someone on the leg?

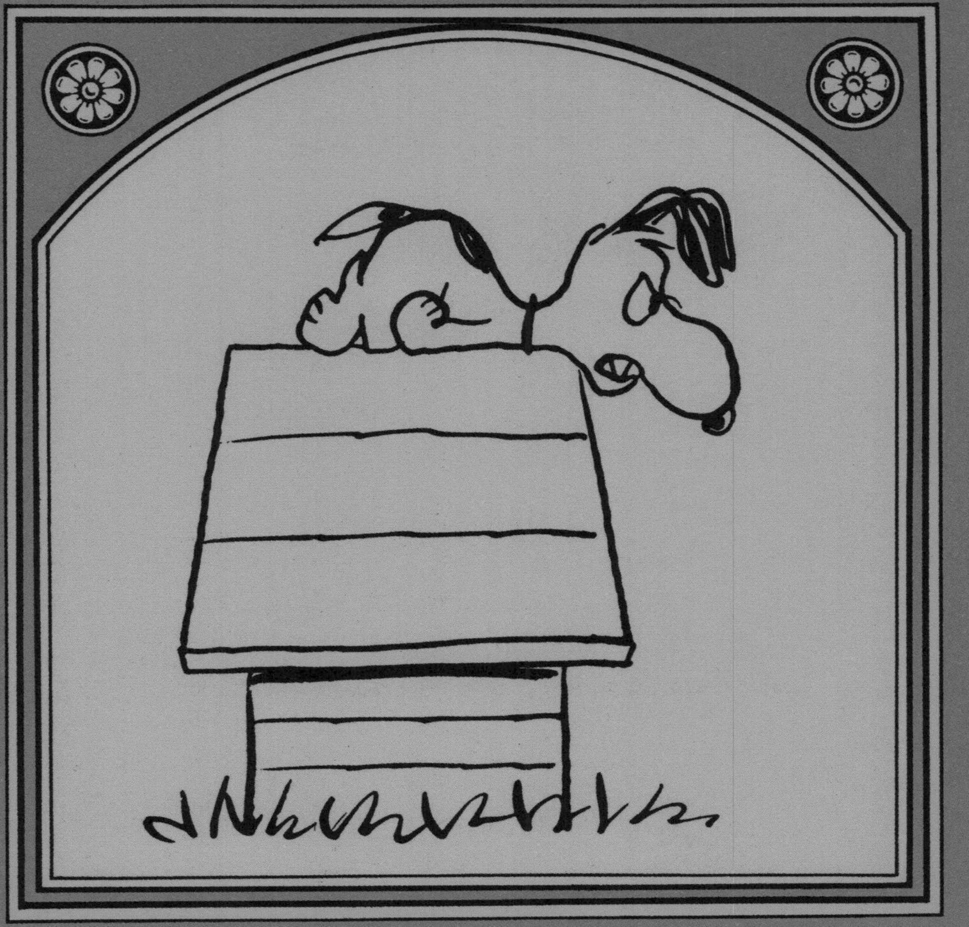

The worst part about living alone is not having someone to bring you tea and toast at bedtime.

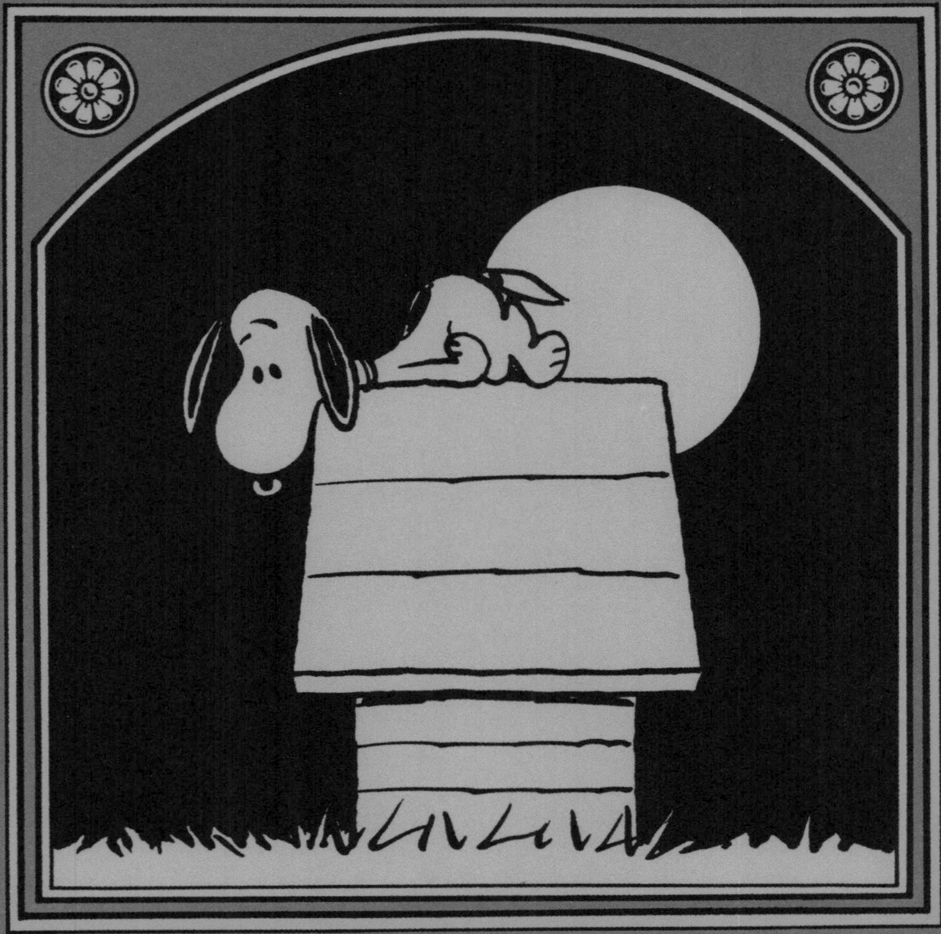

I do
a lot of
complaining,
but actually
I love
my
home!

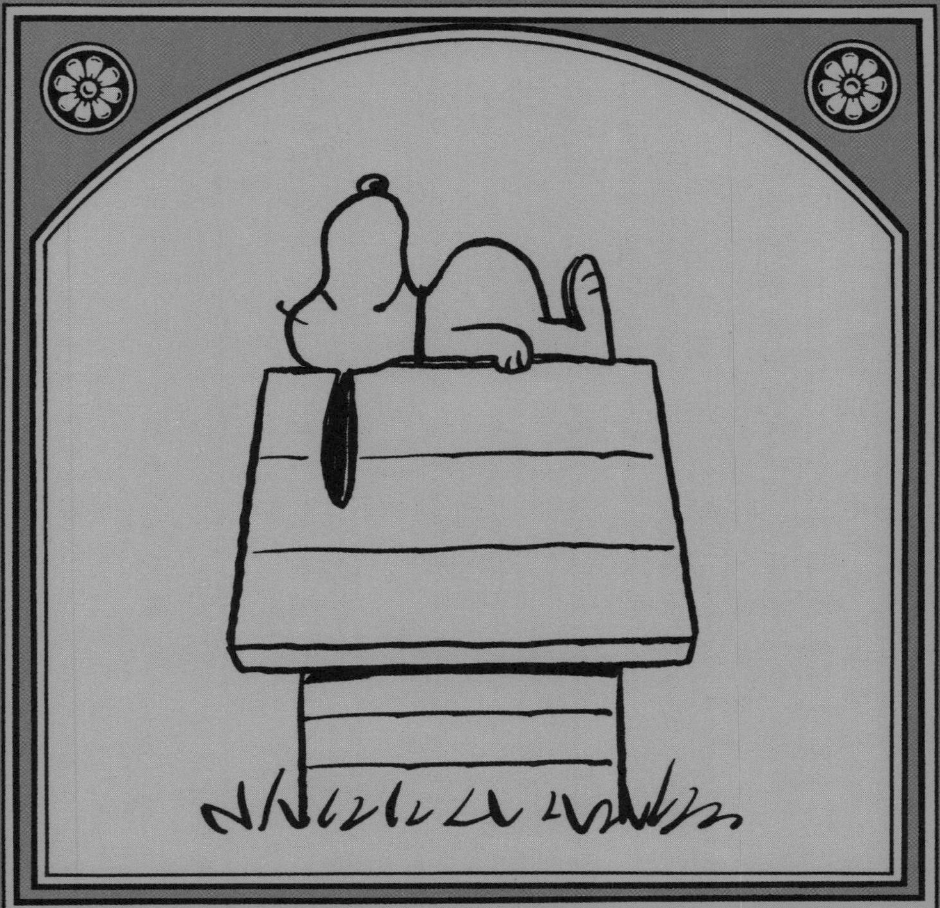

Christmas is the decorations that go up on the day after Halloween . . . and Thanksgiving isn't even here yet!

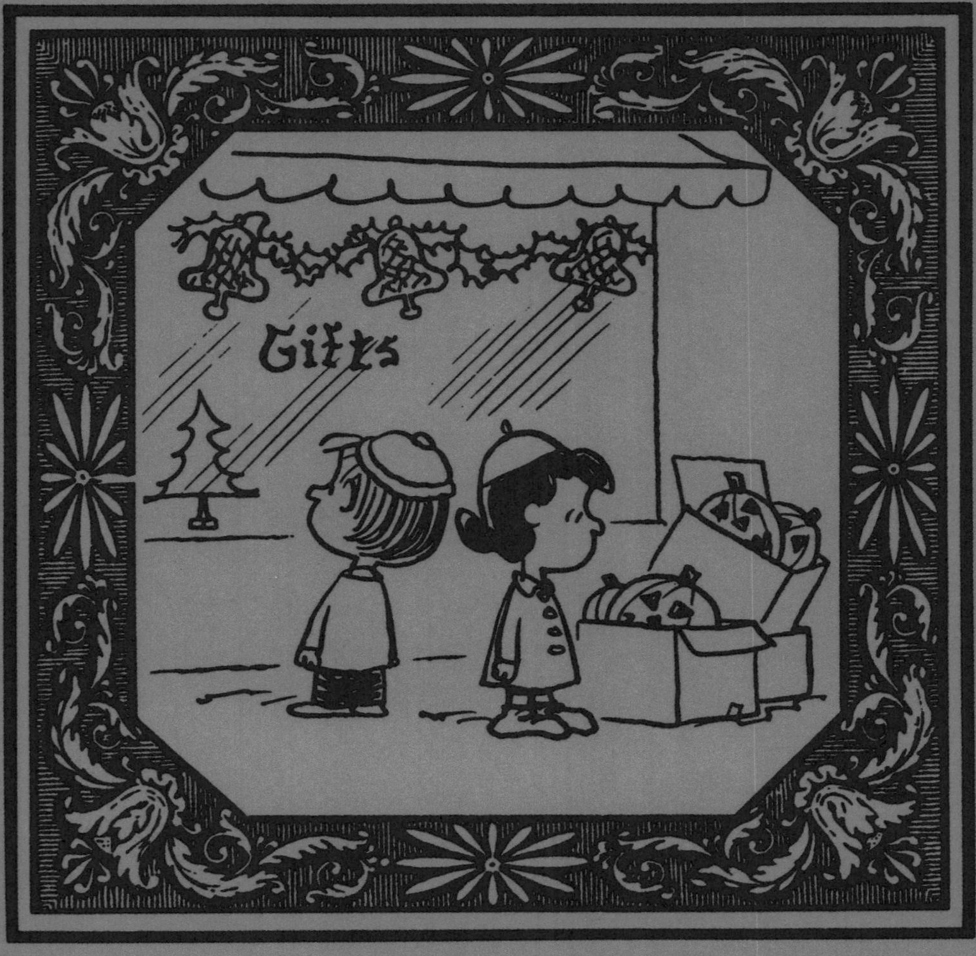
Gifts

Christmas is making a secret present for your dad at school, but it's always a calendar.

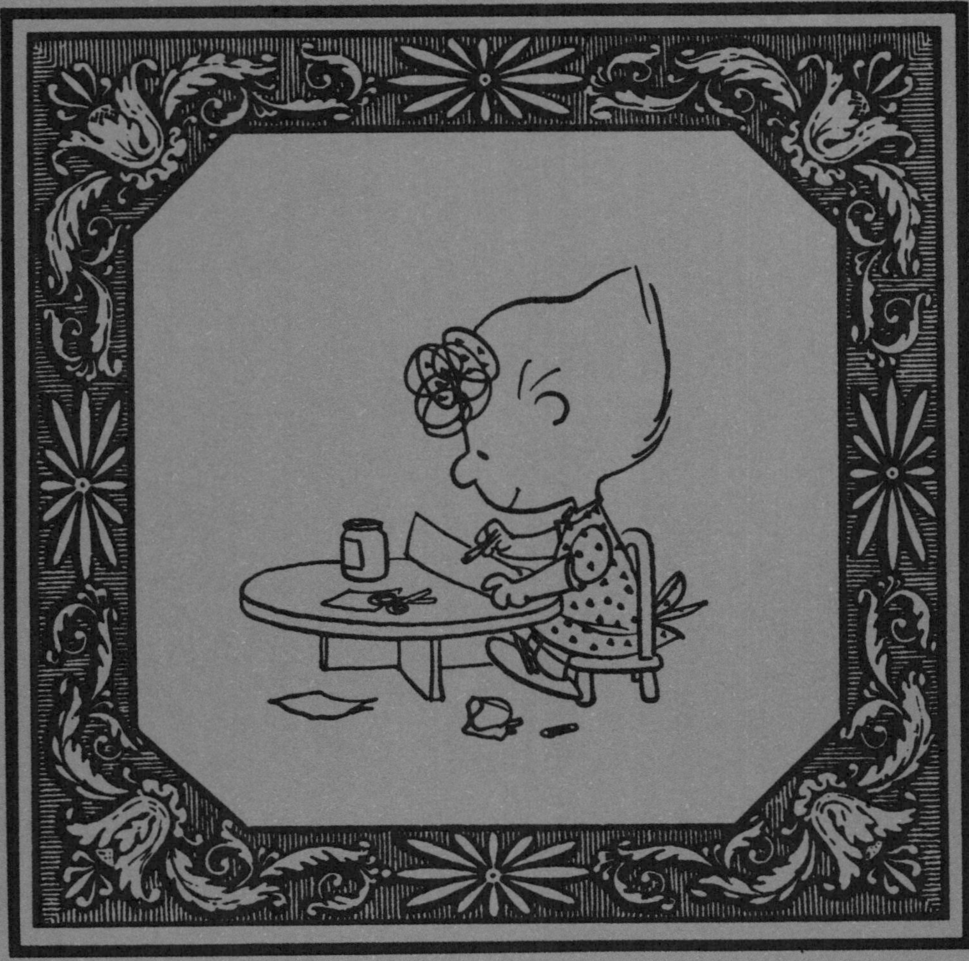

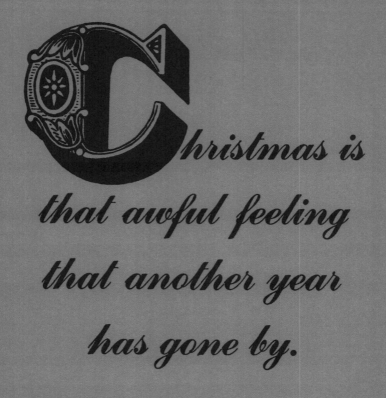

Christmas is
that awful feeling
that another year
has gone by.

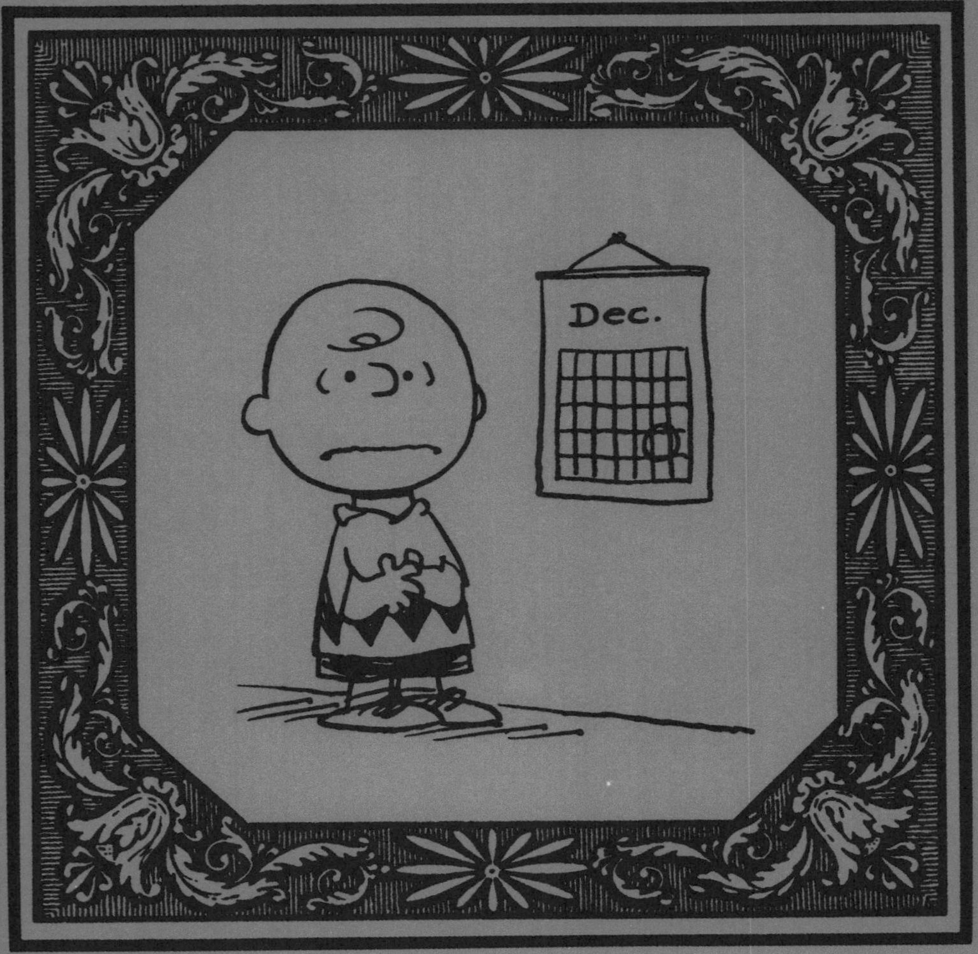
Dec.

Christmas is hearing about those partridges and pear trees until you're ready to lose your mind.

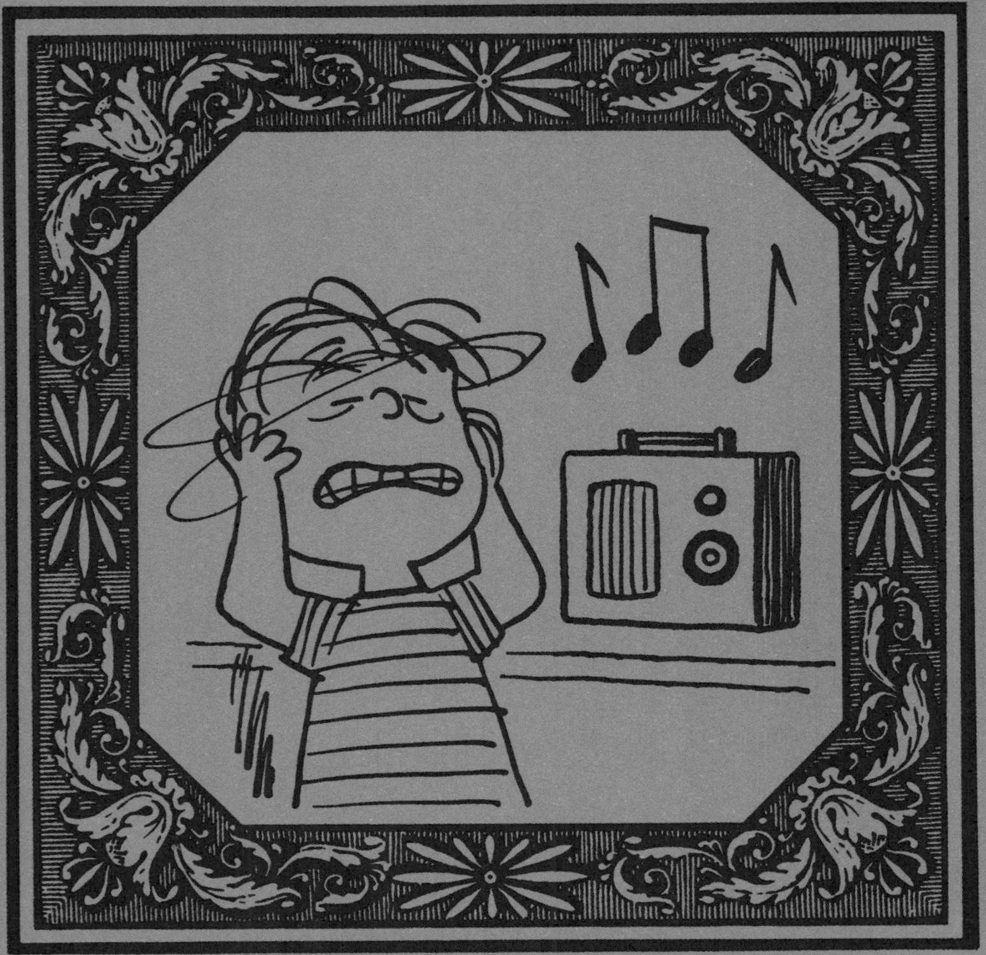

Christmas is
a bowl of hard candy...
that always sticks
together.

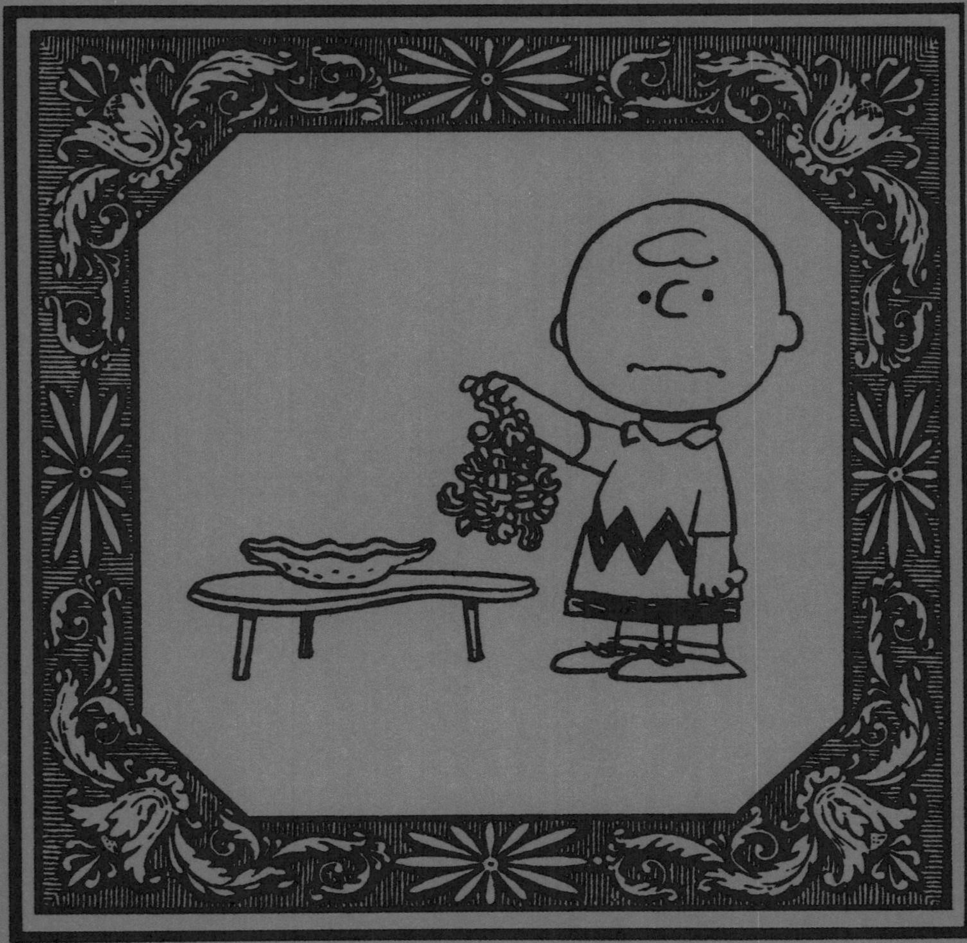

Christmas is not really understanding this business about the flying reindeer.

Christmas is when people say nice things to you who otherwise don't even know you're alive.

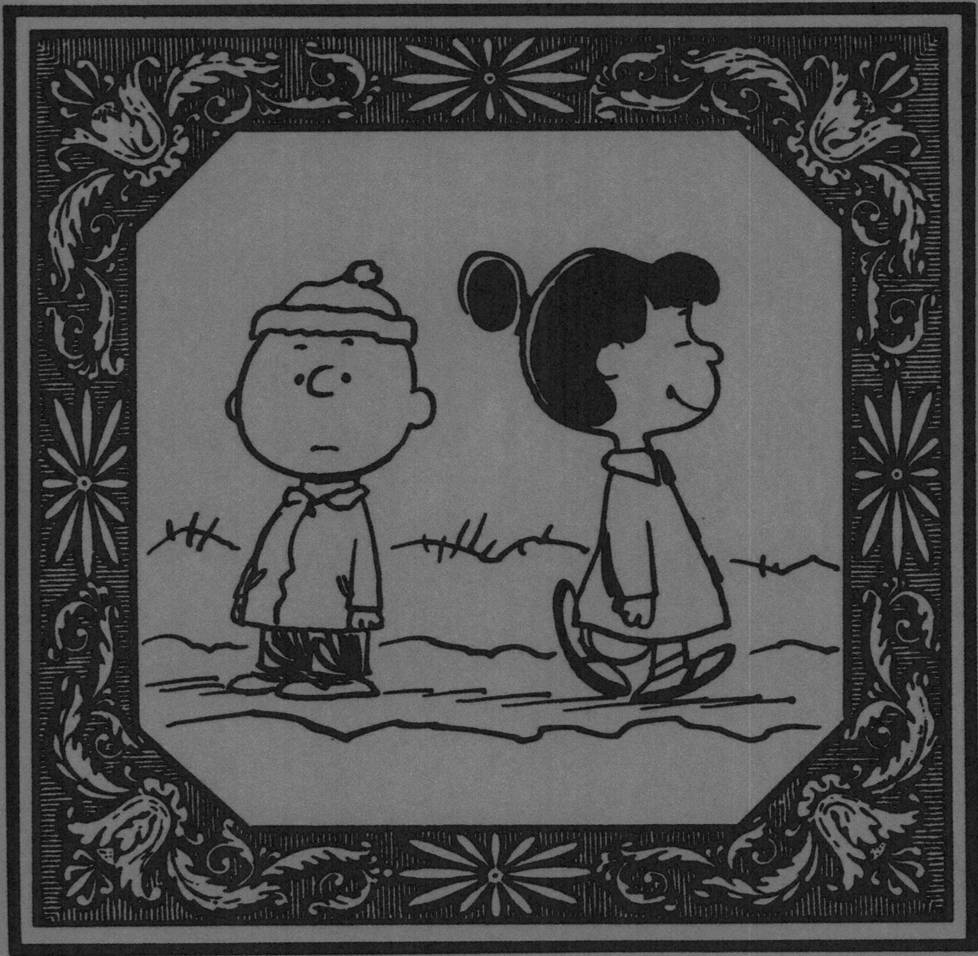

Christmas is when you hug your little brother.

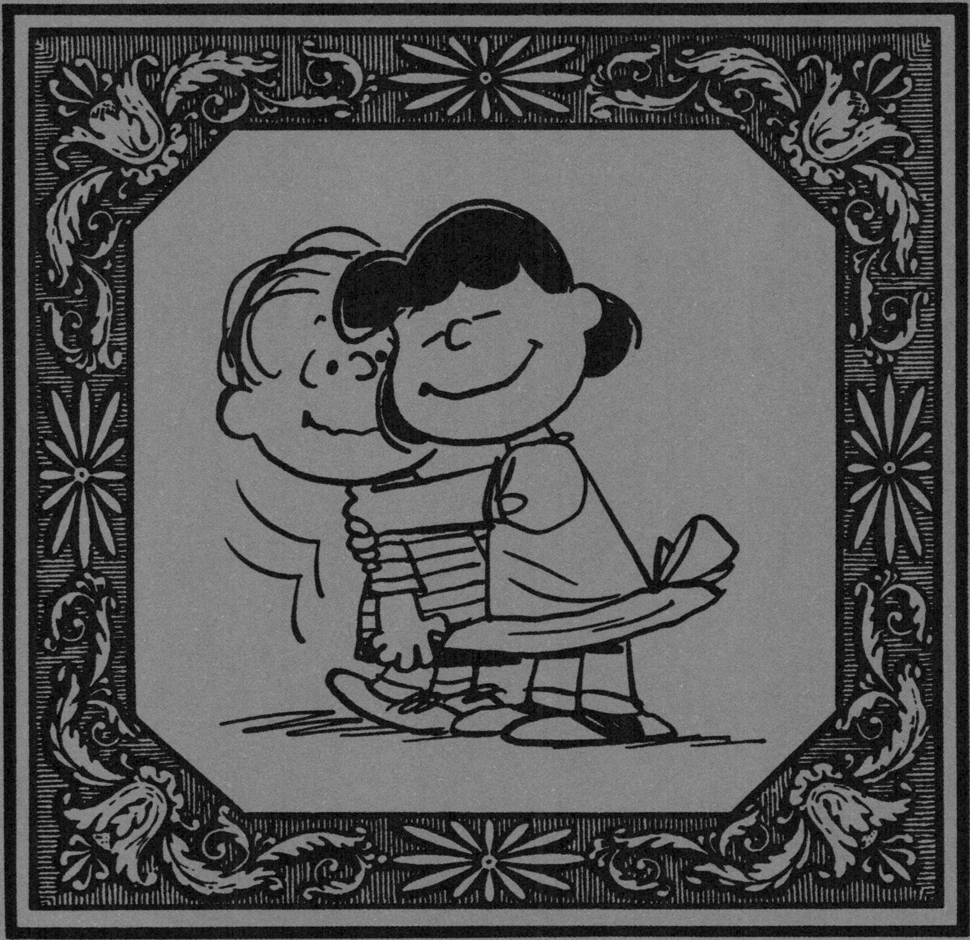

Christmas is giving your last two nickels to the Salvation Army... cheerfully.

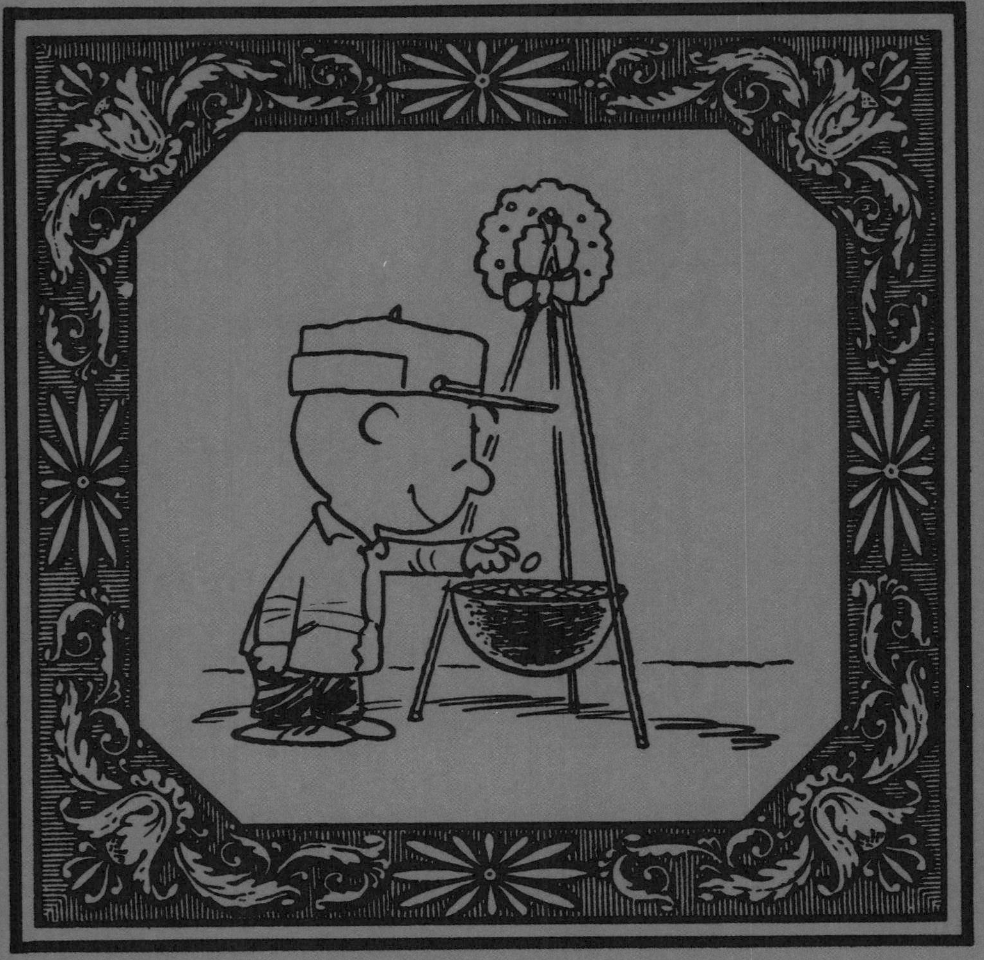

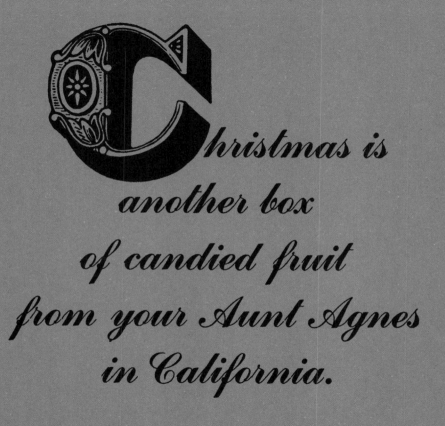

Christmas is another box of candied fruit from your Aunt Agnes in California.

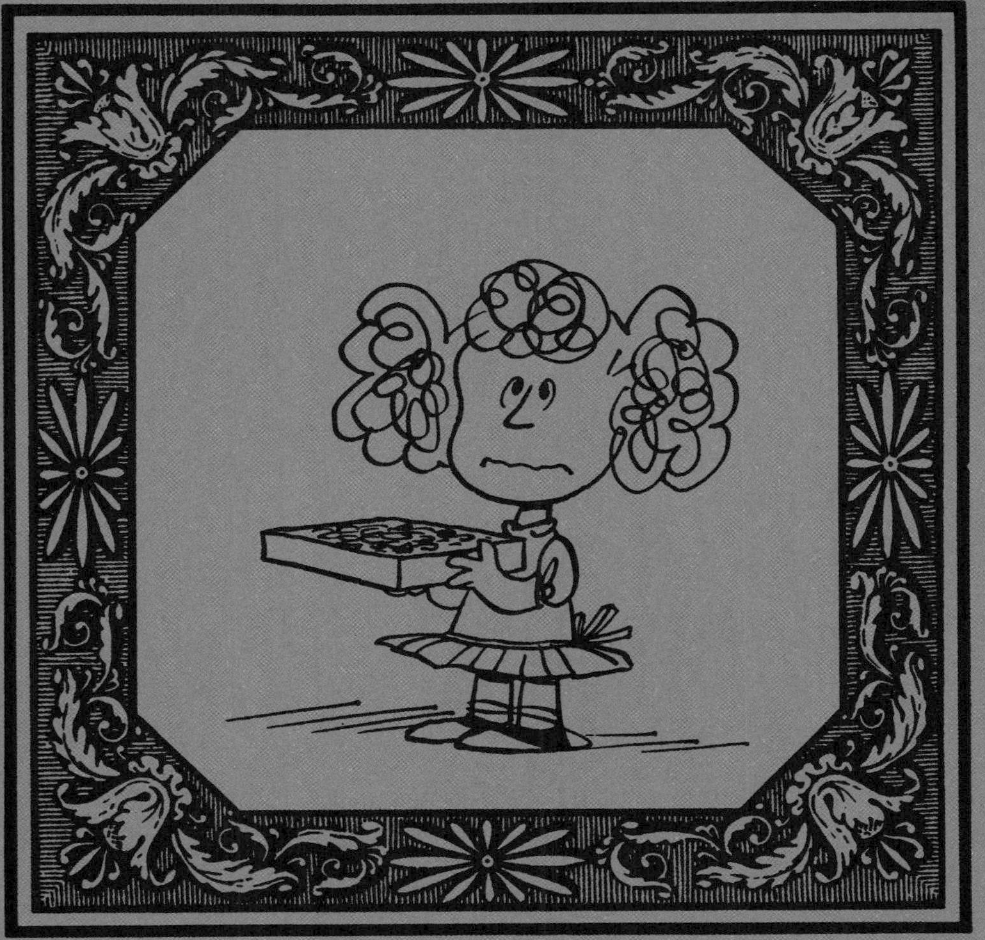

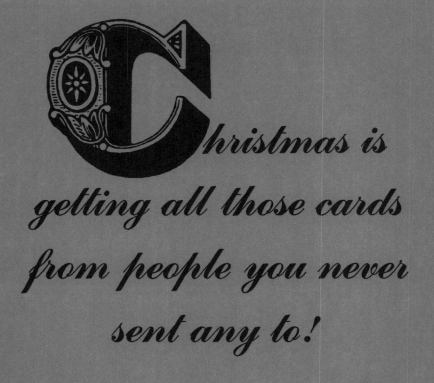

Christmas is getting all those cards from people you never sent any to!

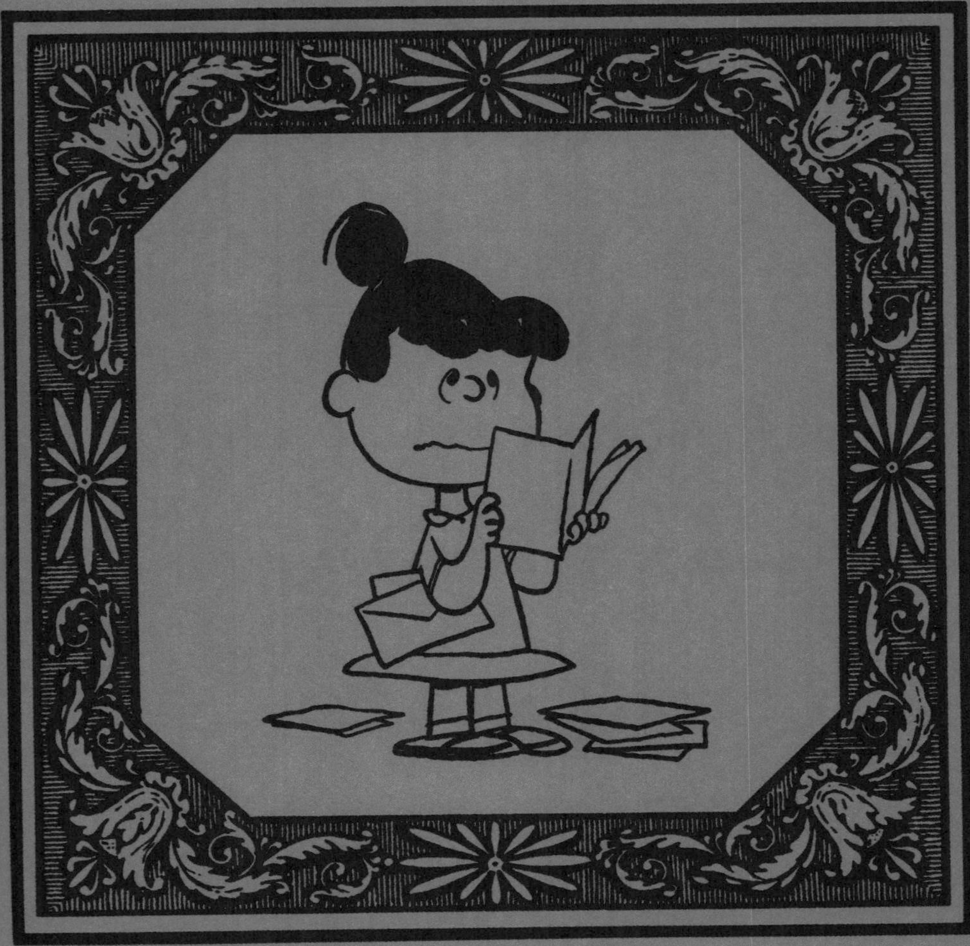

Christmas is the church play...
But why do I always have to be the shepherd?

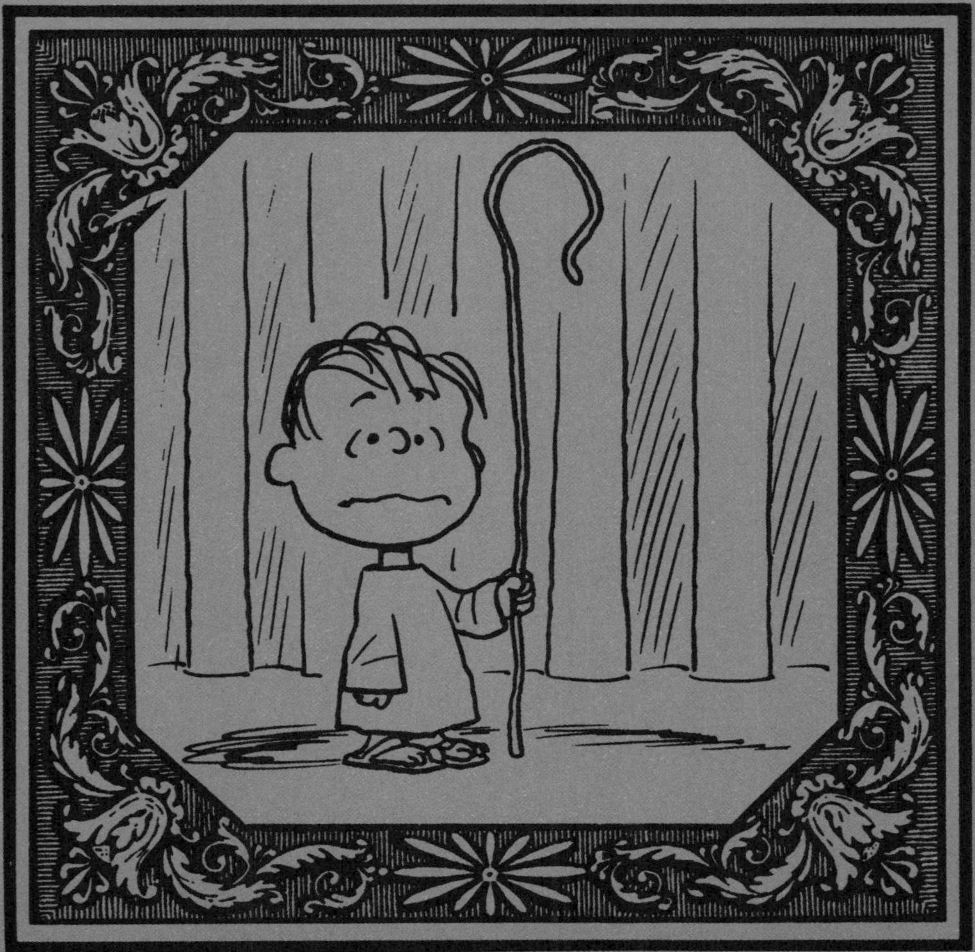

Christmas is losing your mother downtown in a crowded store.

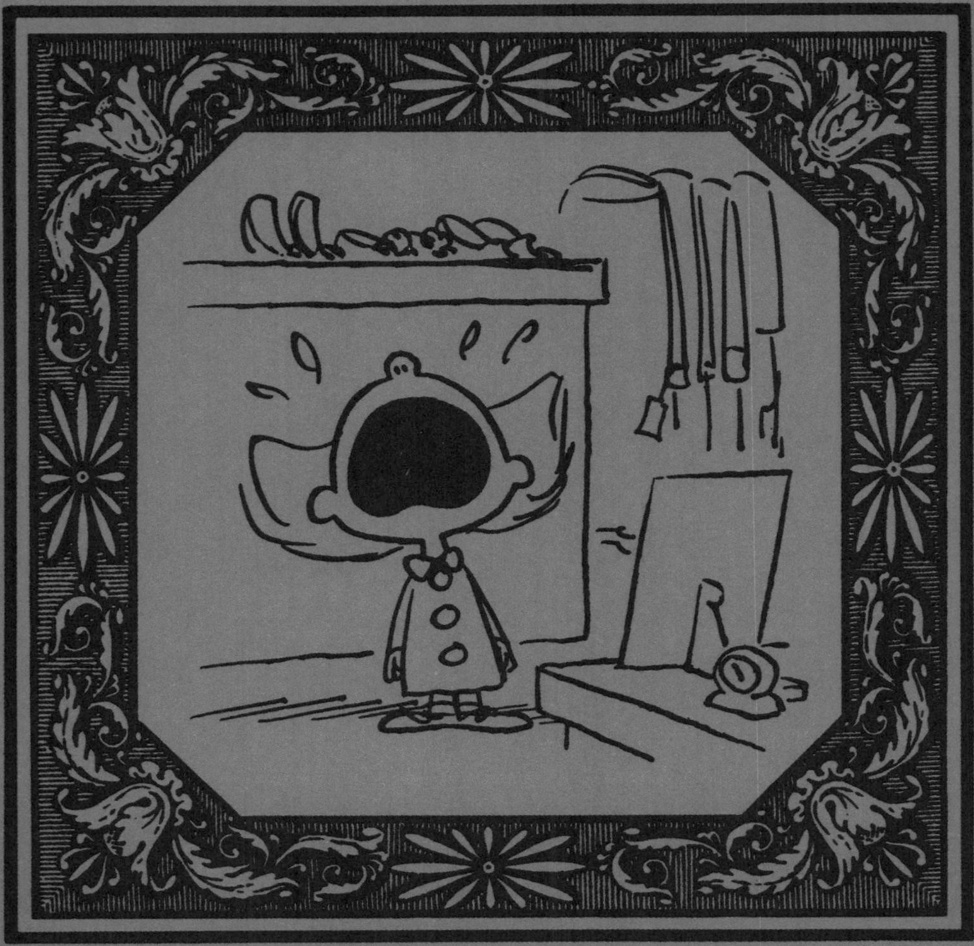

Christmas is buying your Mom something she's always wanted... a forty=nine cent bottle of bath salts.

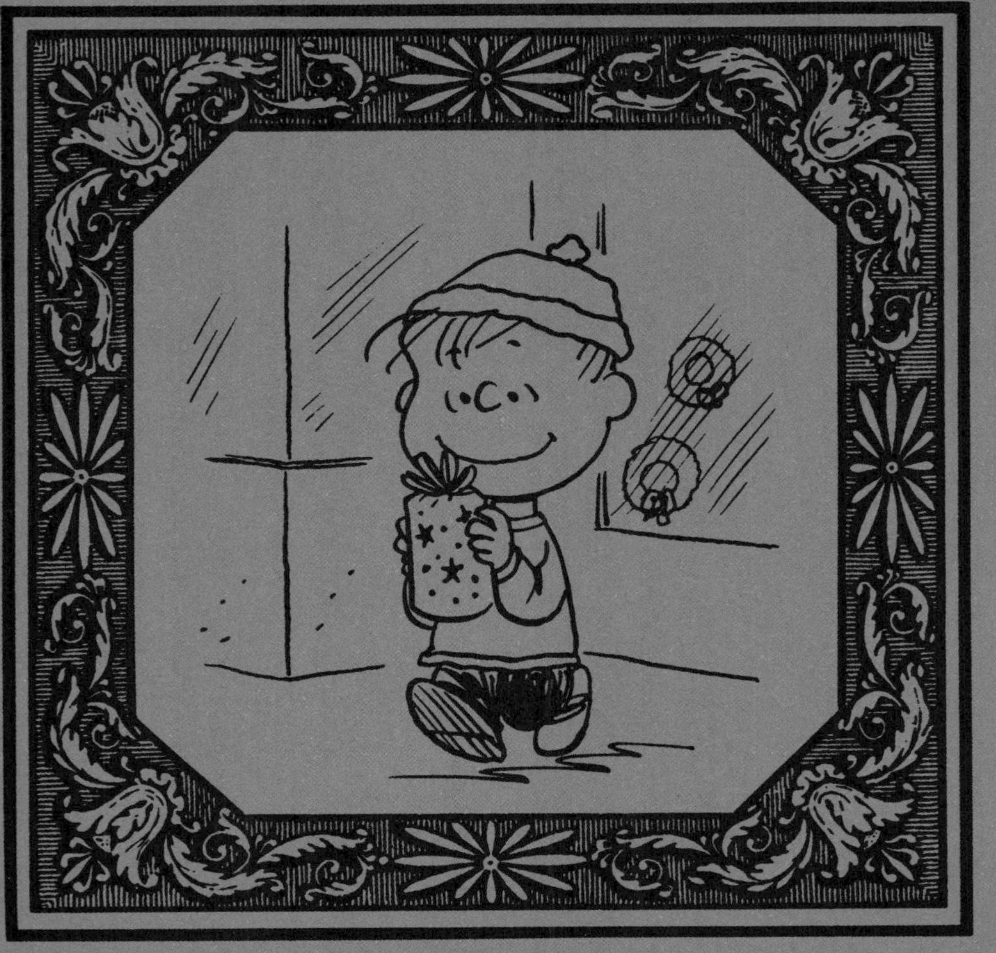

Christmas is when you realize how little you can buy with fifty cents.

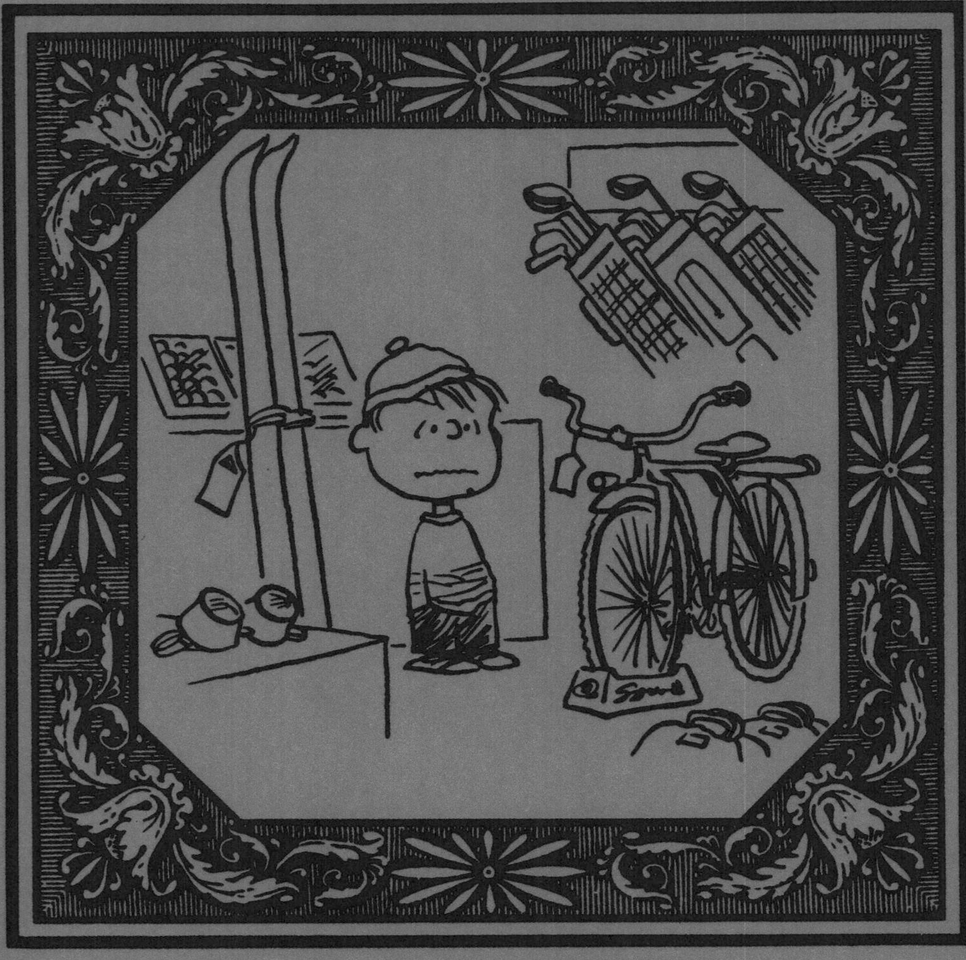

Christmas is wishing you had gotten this stupid present gift=wrapped.

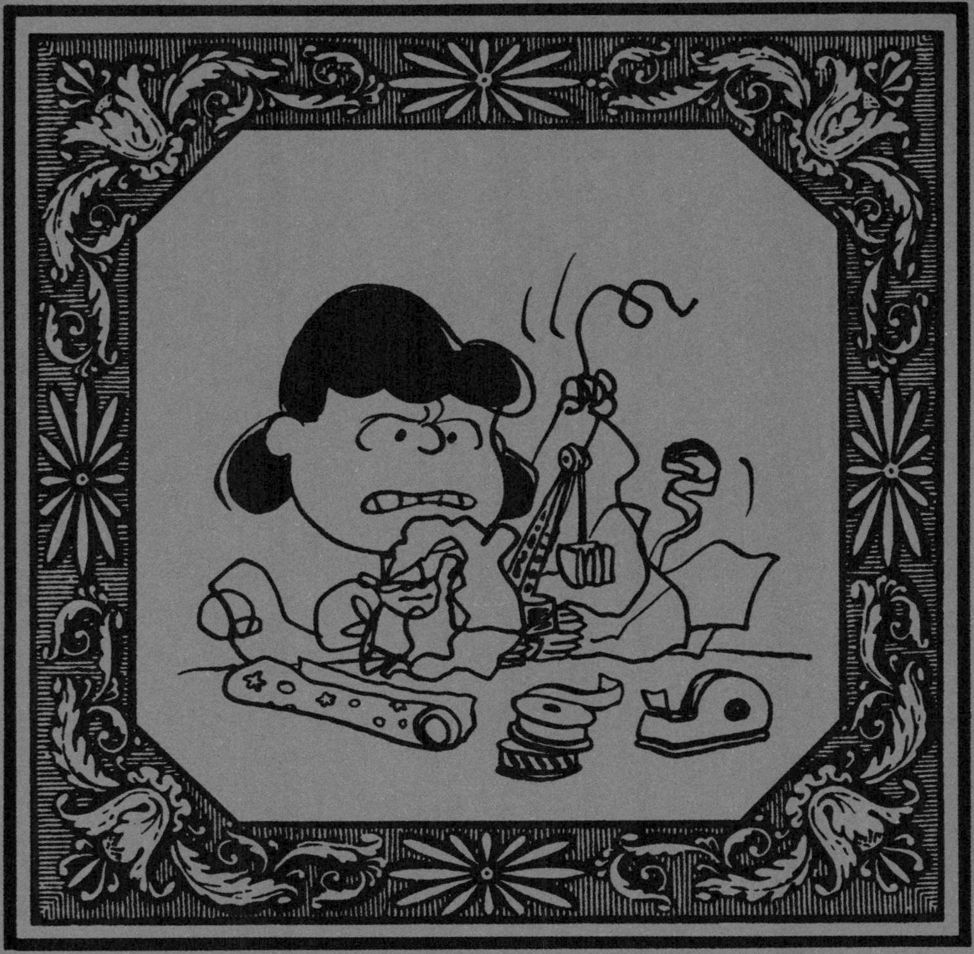

Christmas is a box of tree ornaments that have become part of the family.

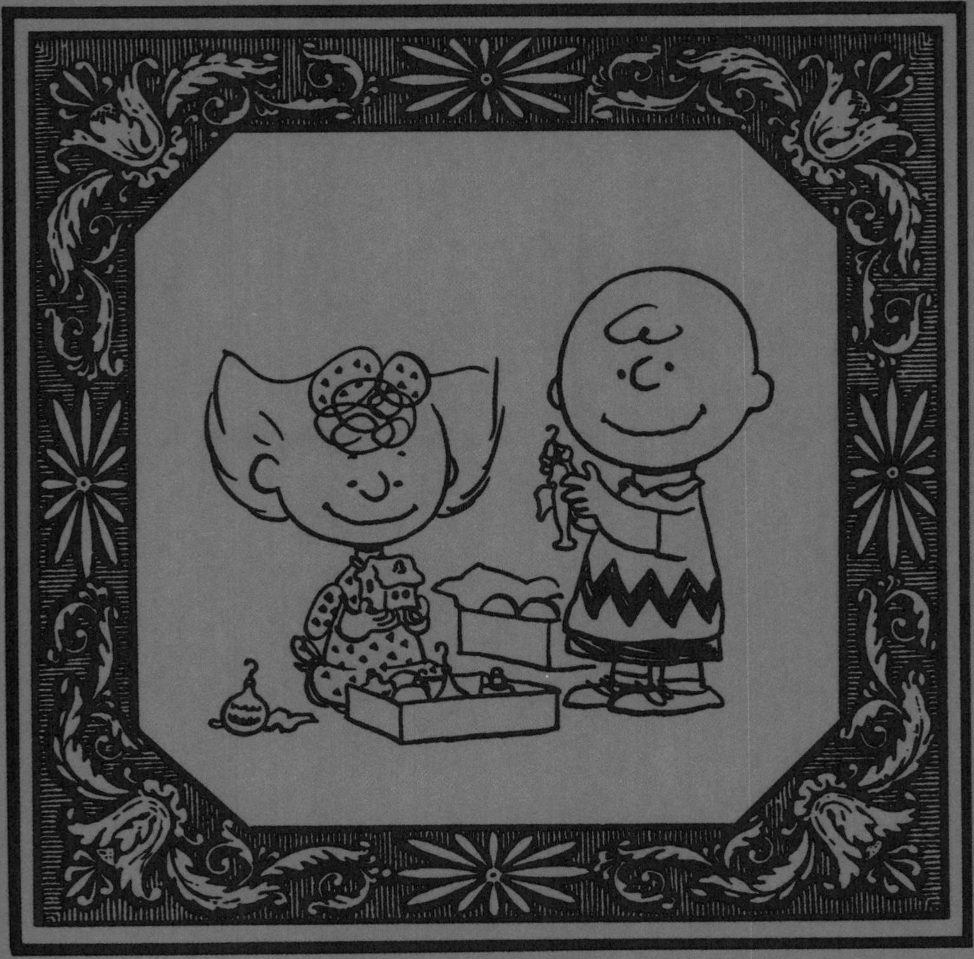

Christmas is suggesting we decorate the tree with strings of popcorn and cranberries like in the old days, but we never do it.

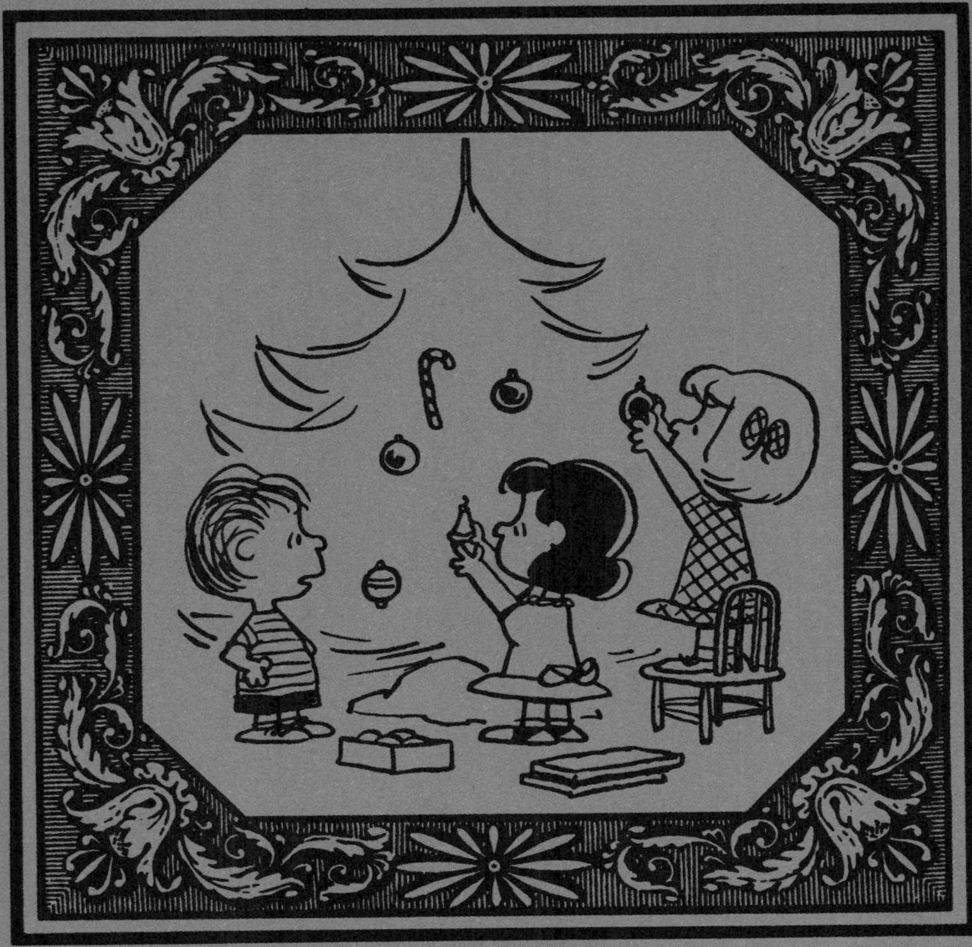

Christmas is wishing there really was such a thing as an old=fashioned Christmas.

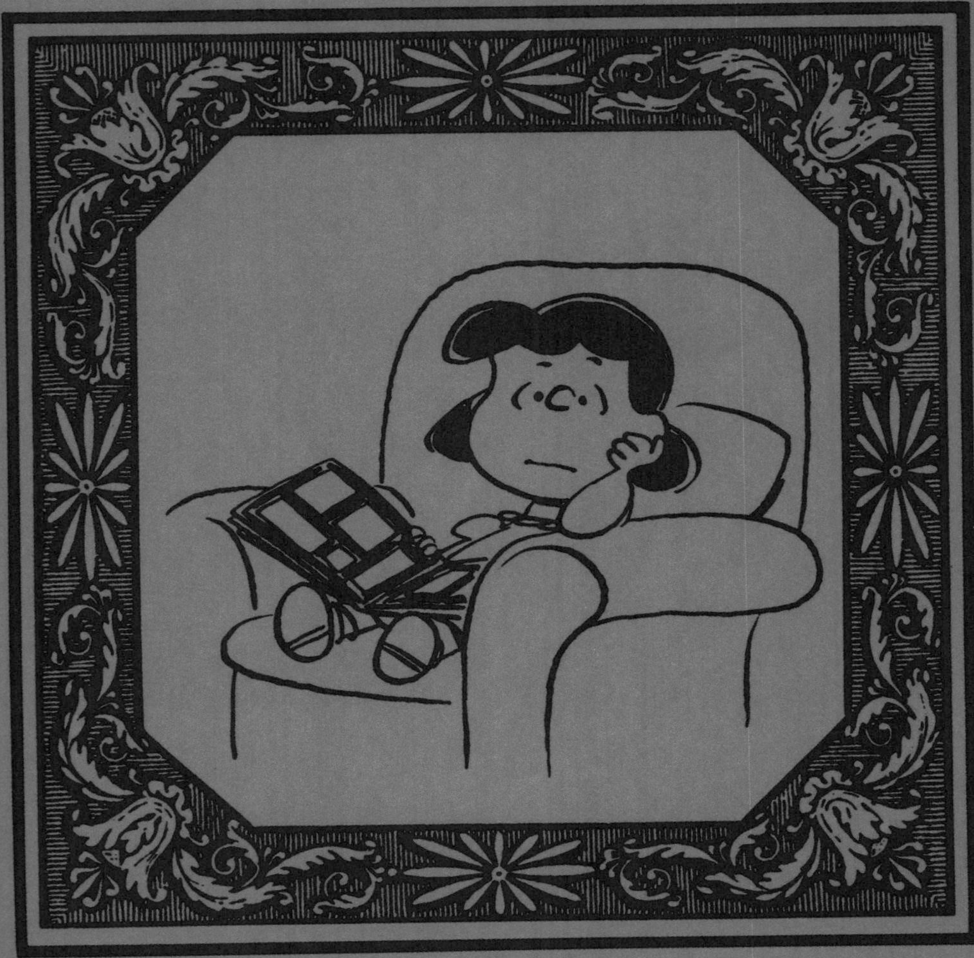

Christmas is
doing
a little something extra
for someone.

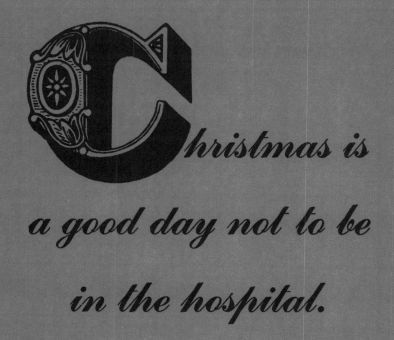

Christmas is a good day not to be in the hospital.

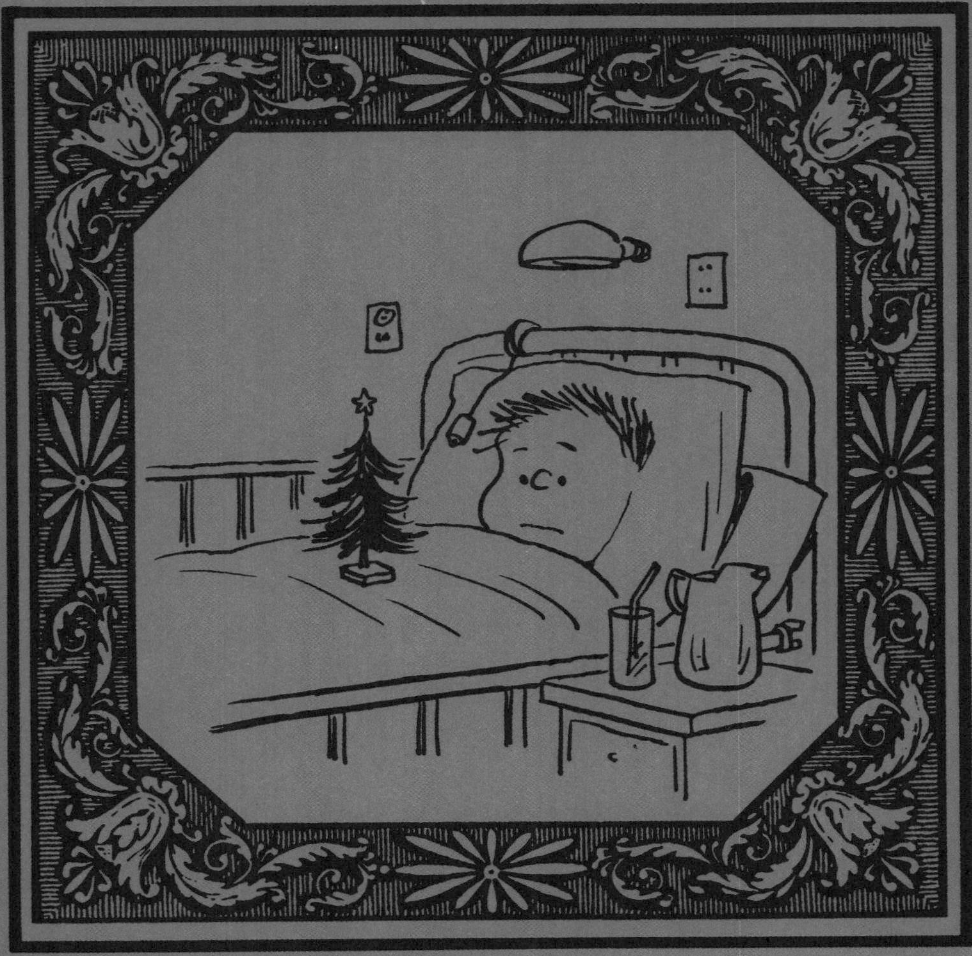

Christmas is going over the hills and through the woods to grandmother's house ...except she's moved to an apartment.

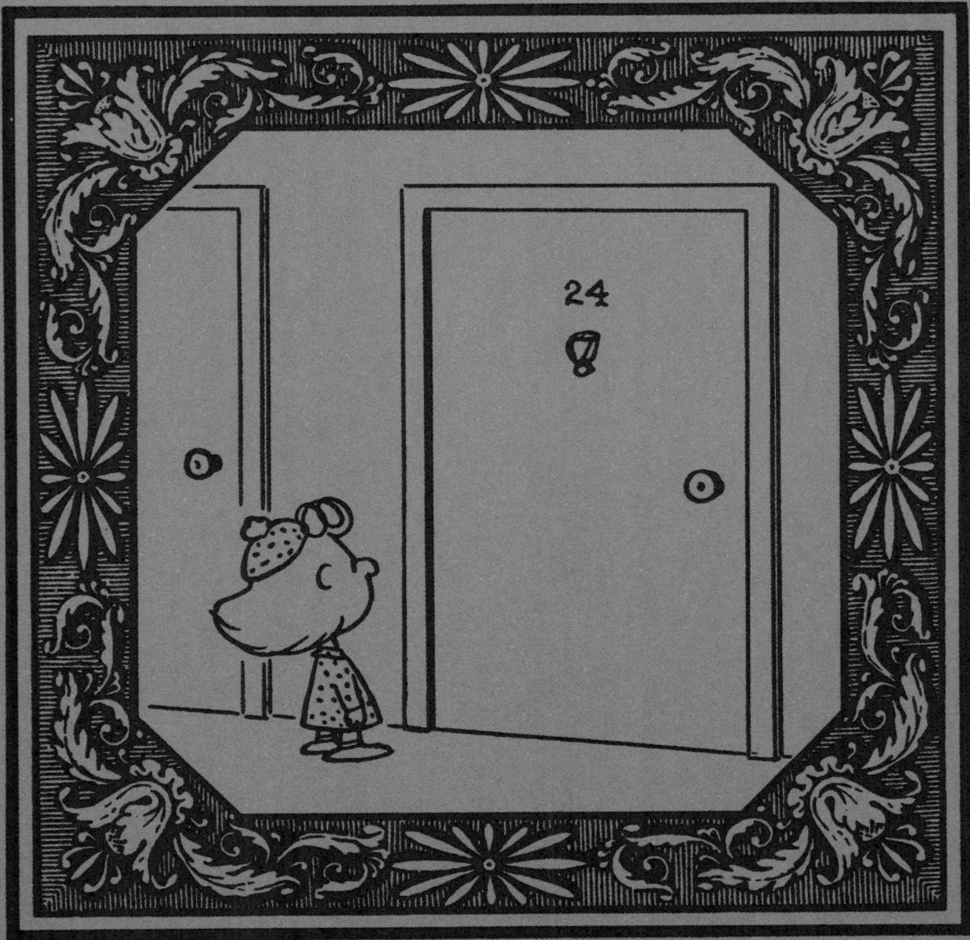
24

Christmas is candy canes and can't I eat just one?

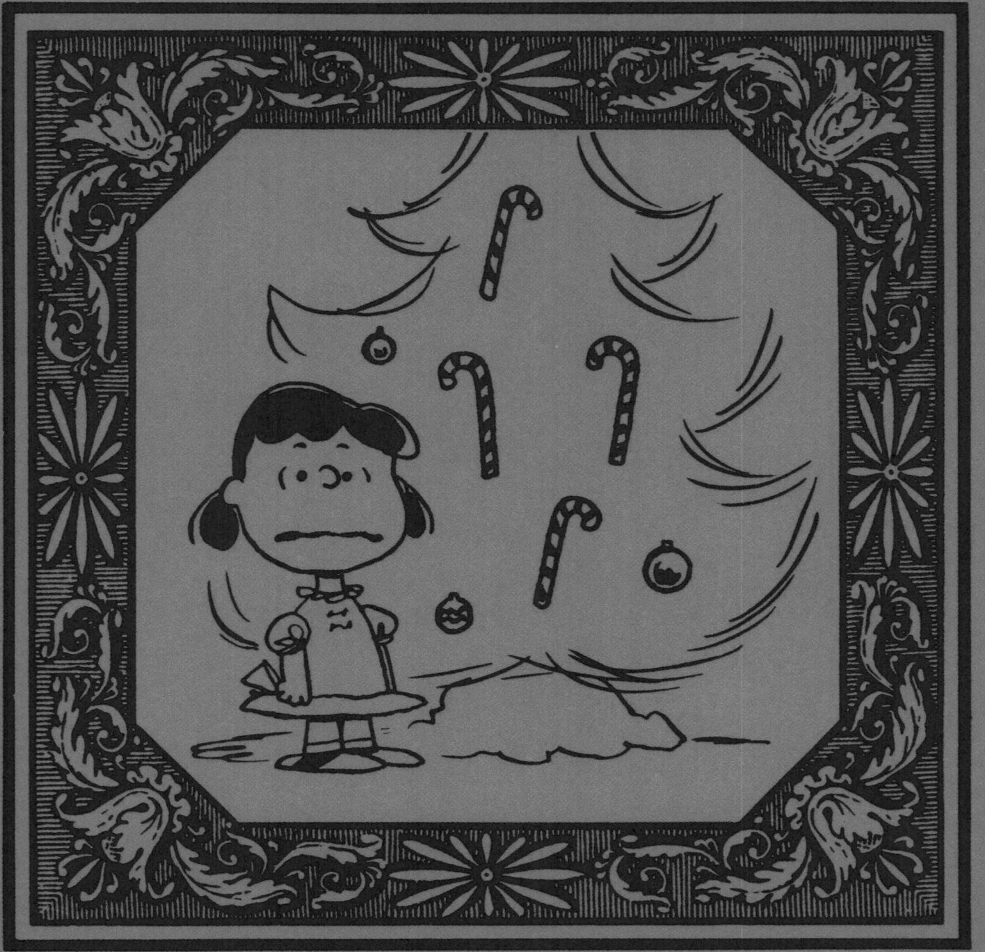

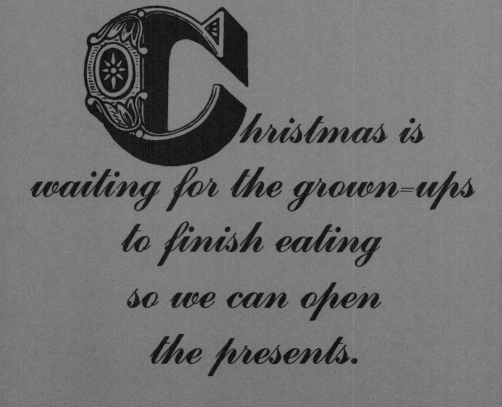

Christmas is
waiting for the grown=ups
to finish eating
so we can open
the presents.

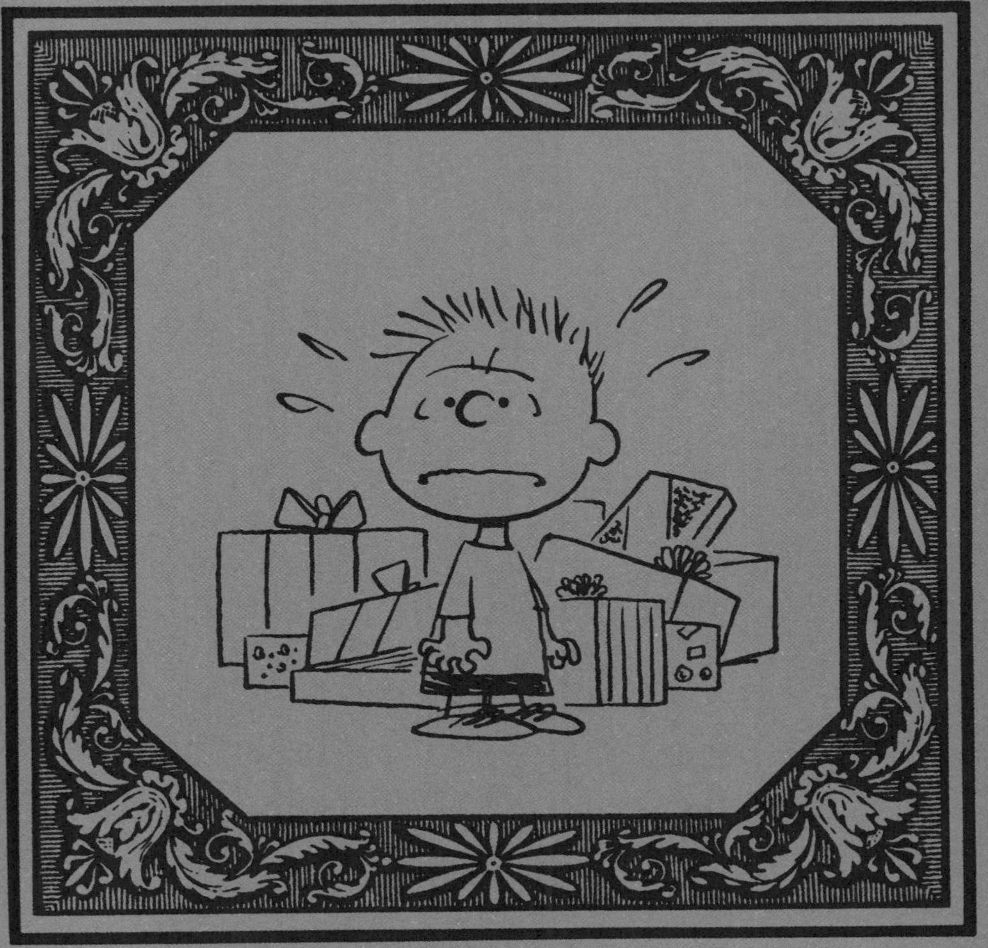

Christmas is
the joy of giving,
but getting
is pretty good too.

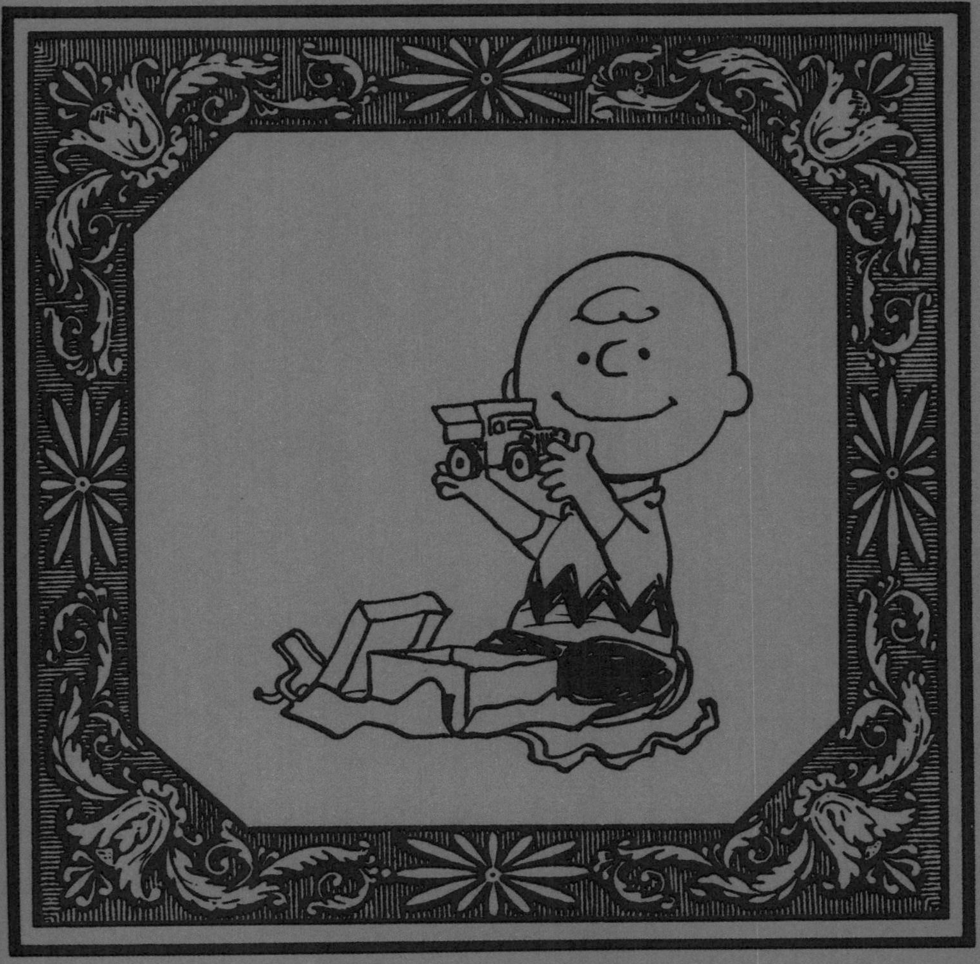

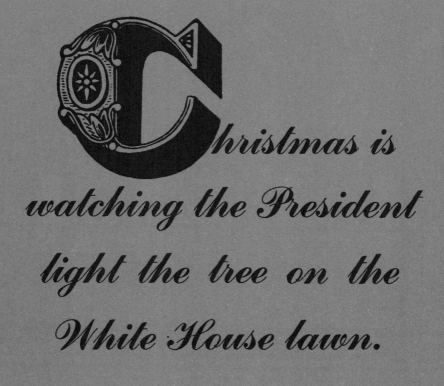

Christmas is watching the President light the tree on the White House lawn.

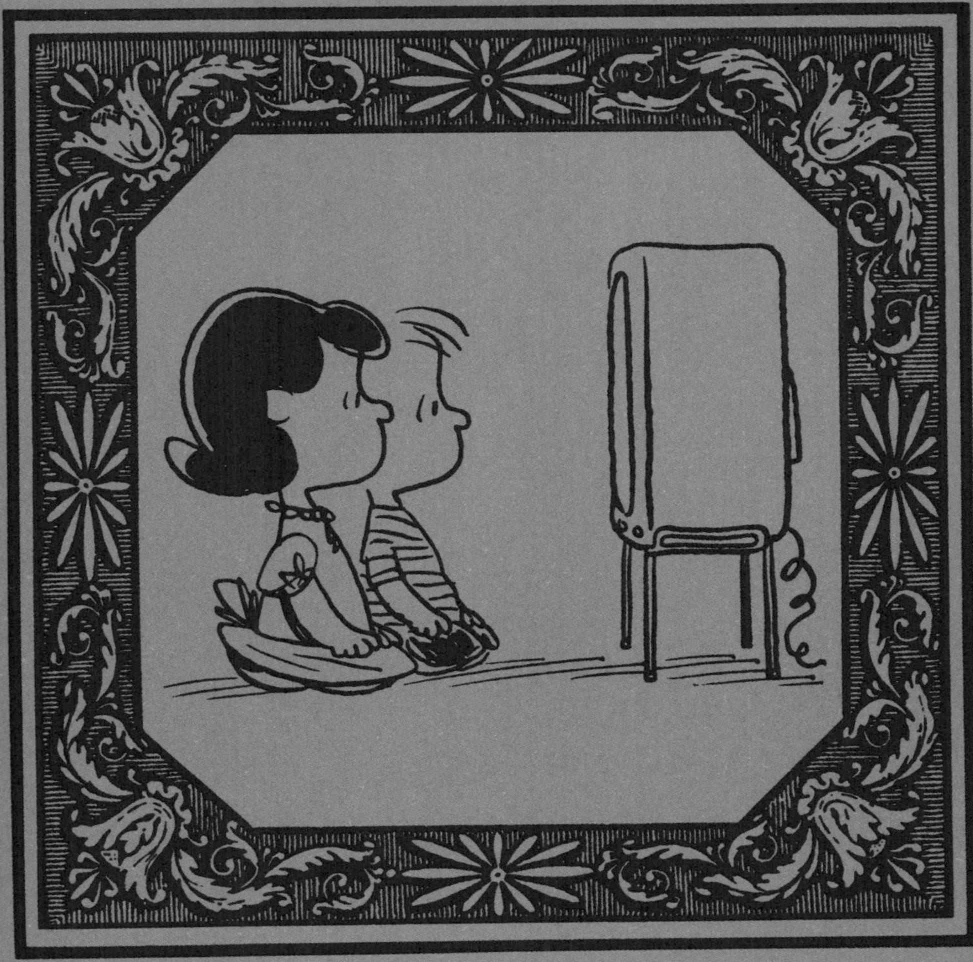

Christmas is
a time of waiting...
and waiting...
and waiting...
and waiting.

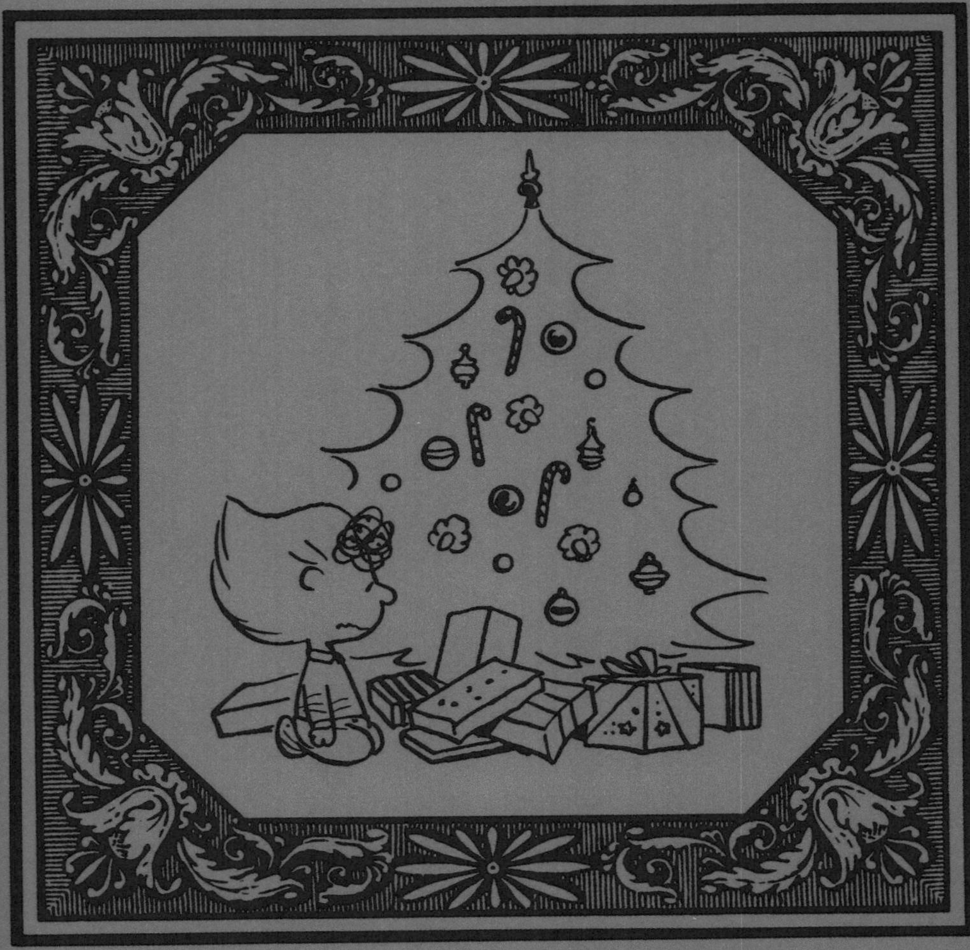

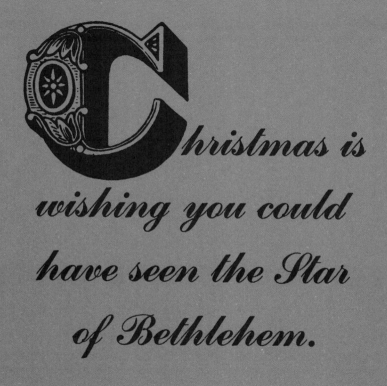

Christmas is wishing you could have seen the Star of Bethlehem.

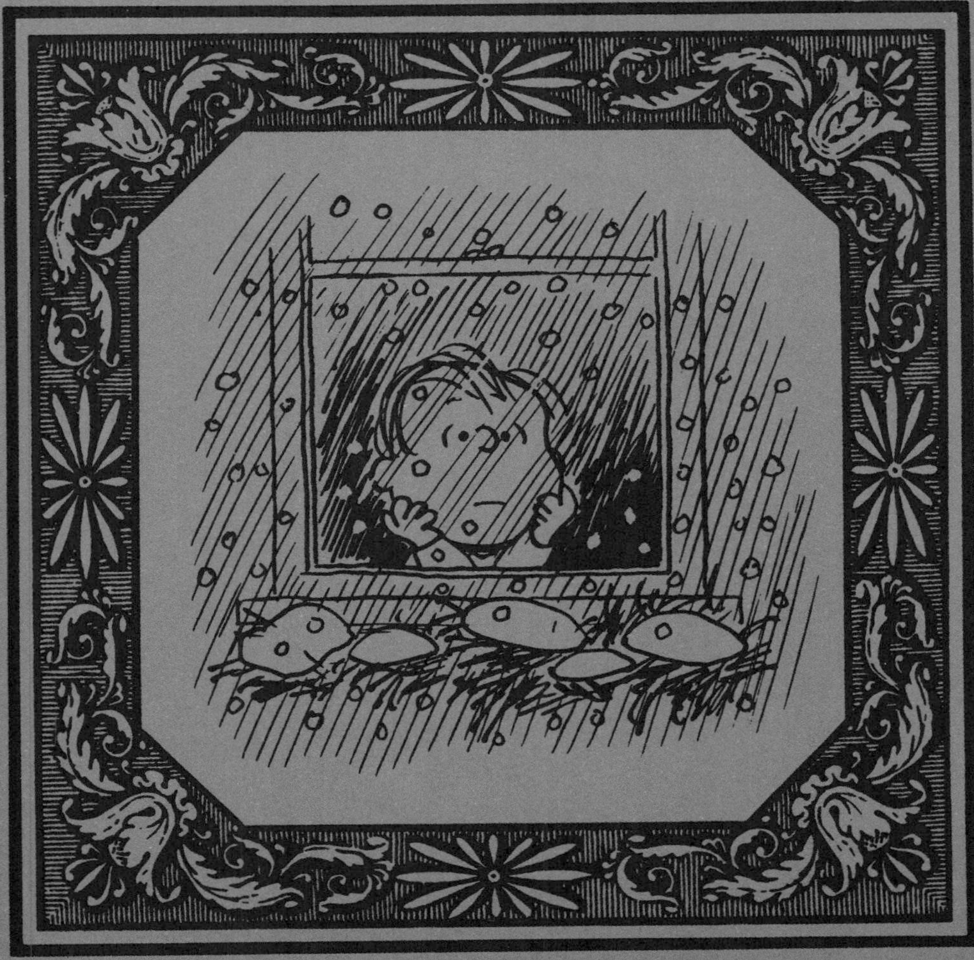

Christmas is
a time of hope...
a time of loving...
a time of joy.

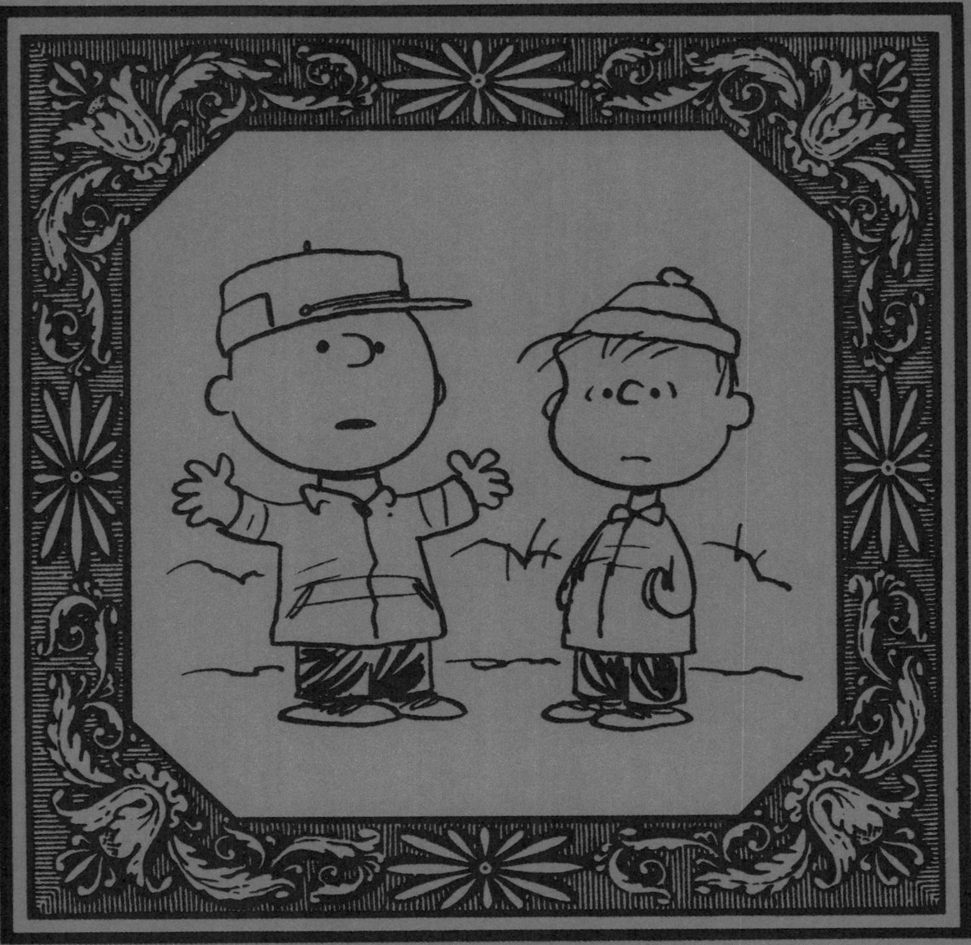

Christmas makes the rest of the year worthwhile.

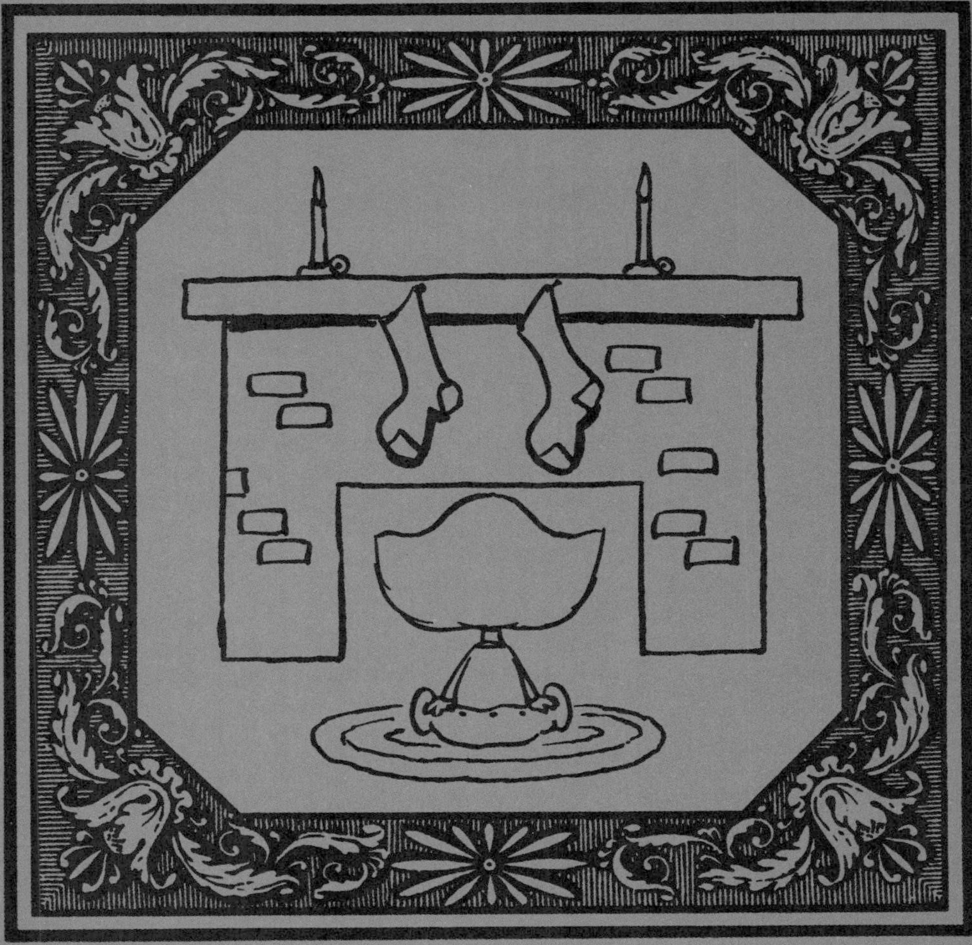

About Cider Mill Press Book Publishers

Good ideas ripen with time. From seed to harvest, Cider Mill Press strives to bring fine reading, information, and entertainment together between the covers of its creatively crafted books. Our Cider Mill bears fruit twice a year, publishing a new crop of titles each Spring and Fall.

Visit us on the web at
www.cidermillpress.com
or write to us at
12 Port Farm Road
Kennebunkport, Maine 04046

CIDER MILL PRESS
BOOK PUBLISHERS

Where Good Books are
Ready for Press